MY BEAUTIFUL OBSESSION

Chasing the Kerry Dream

Weeshie Fogarty, born in 1941, grew up on Lower New Street, Killarney. After thirty-eight years as a psychiatric nurse in St Finan's Hospital, Killarney, he became a sports broadcaster and analyst with Radio Kerry and writer for *The Kerryman*. He won several awards over the years: four McNamee Awards; the prestigious National PPI Radio Award for his programme, *Terrace Talk*, in 2008; and in 2010 he won the National PPI Radio Award as National Sports Broadcaster of the Year.

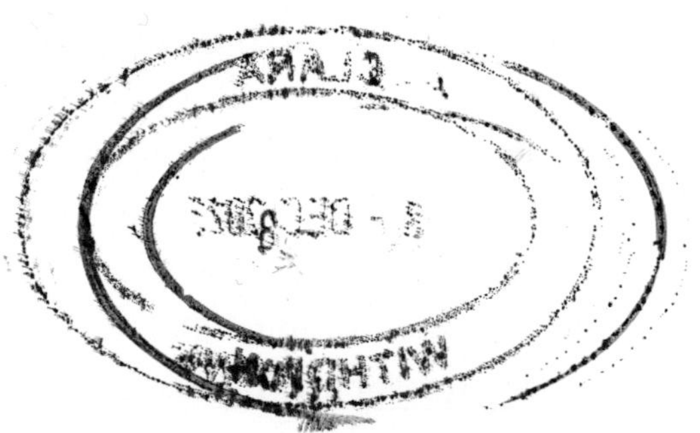

MY BEAUTIFUL OBSESSION

Chasing the Kerry Dream

WEESHIE FOGARTY

The Collins Press

First published in 2012 by
The Collins Press
West Link Park
Doughcloyne
Wilton
Cork

Fogarty, Weeshie.
My beautiful obsession : chasing the Kerry dream.
1. Fogarty, Weeshie. 2. Gaelic football players—Ireland—Killarney (Kerry) —Biography. 3. Kerry G.A.A. —Anecdotes.
4. Gaelic football referees—Ireland—Biography.
5. Sportscasters—Ireland—Biography. 6. Psychiatric nurses—Ireland—Biography.
I. Title
796.3'3'092-dc23

Paperback ISBN-13: 9781848891562
ePub ISBN: 9781848899827
mobi ISBN: 9781848899834

British Library Cataloguing in Publication Data

Typesetting by Patricia Hope, Dublin
Typeset in Sabon
Printed in Malta by Gutenberg Press Limited

CONTENTS

FOREWORD

The seeds for this book have been floating around in my head for a good number of years, but for one reason or another I have always shied away from beginning the task. I think I felt that no one would be the slightest bit interested in my story. However, when the realisation hit me that I was the last remaining brother of the Fogarty family, I became more inclined to put pen to paper. Indeed, at the time of writing, I have just passed the seventy-year mark in my life's journey. I have been involved in media work of some description for a long number of years and had one book published five years ago. I suppose this gave me the necessary confidence and experience to plough ahead and record my memories, and so I finally took the decision to sit down and begin. Still, it's all very well to make a start with writing memoirs: to have one's memories actually published is a horse of a different colour.

I have not set out to trace my career as a Kerry footballer in these pages, for the simple reason that, while I did have the privilege of playing for my county at Minor, Under-21 Junior and Senior level, I was never under any illusion that I was anything other than just another of the hundreds of young Kerrymen who played for their county but were that little bit short of the level necessary to become a Kerry 'great'. It is that massive influence – the history and traditions of

Kerry football and, for me, Kerry sport in general – that I have tried to portray on these pages, to give readers a glimpse of the all-consuming power and passion for sport in the county where I grew up.

Pride of place is very important and special to me. I was blessed in growing up on the side of the street in the town of Killarney, for me one of the most beautiful places God has created. Killarney has influenced my way of thinking all my life. It is a wonderful environment and, with its mountains and lakes and national park on our doorstep, it is easy to understand why tourists flock to our town from all over the world, year after year. The people of my town have had a big influence on my life and that of my family. The old Killarney stock are a special breed and, when Killarney was declared winner of the National Tidy Town Competition for the first time in 2011, it brought great pride and joy to all Killarney hearts. I was glad that I had contributed to this win in a tiny way by promoting the efforts of the people behind the scenes on my radio programmes. A truly amazing man, Father Michael Murphy, together with a remarkable lady, Evelyn Quill, were the leaders of a vast array of volunteers who brought the national title to 'Heaven's Reflex'. Our exemplary town council are forever improving, encouraging and trying new ideas as they strive for perfection. Well done to one and all. This sense of home, town and county, has been a constant throughout my life and that of my family. I am utterly convinced that if I had spent my life in another part of the country, or indeed this county, I would not be writing these words. Killarney is my special place.

My three brothers have all died of cancer and all three thought of Killarney in their last hours. I sat by my brother Jimmy's bed and, with a determined voice that could still be heard over the hum of the morphine pump, he told me, 'You know what, Weeshie, I wish I could fly out that window, fly over Killarney and see the mountains and lakes for the last

The Fogartys at my mother's eightieth birthday (l–r): Weeshie, Jimmy (RIP), Sheila, Dermie (RIP) and Geni (RIP).

time, but maybe my soul will travel back there when I die, I loved Killarney.' In 2010 my eldest brother, Dermie, died in Marymount Hospice in Cork City. As he sat looking out over the city on a sunny May day just weeks before his death he told me, 'I would love to get home for one more day, go out on the lake and enjoy a day's fishing.' Pride of place, pride of home and pride for their town, Killarney. Their words have helped me, their faces have flashed before me and their memories have strengthened me as I worked on this book.

I have attempted to pay tribute to Kerry sports, and football in particular. You will read a bit of history, events that shaped the careers of individuals, old memories that resurfaced as the work continued, names of long-forgotten friends and neighbours. I must repeat that it was not my intention just to tell my own, individual story, but also that of others who shaped my life as I grew up on the streets of Killarney, boy to man.

You will also read a little of my thirty-eight years working in St Finan's Hospital, Killarney, and in this I literally just scratch the surface. That was a different world completely, locked away from the outside, close to one thousand patients housed there in 1962 when I began. A cacophony of voices shouting, banging doors; faces, incidents, names, many sadly now forgotten forever. But for me it was a special time and shaped my life in a huge way. I dedicate this foreword to those lovely men with whom I sat and nursed during long, lonely nights as their lives ebbed away, men who were laid to rest with just a handful of people at their graveside and were remembered by no one. This is for them. It is little, but I have an overpowering need to mark their lives.

Finally, without the urging and encouragement of my family I would not have finished this work. They pushed me, cajoled me and emphasised that it was important for the family that I did it. Thanks to Joan (a patient wife, listening to sporting talk for decades), to Denise, Carol Ann, her husband Glen (ever interested in how the work was progressing), and to my son Kieran for all the times you sorted out my computer illiteracy problems and took charge of the photographs. And finally to Lucy and Eva, two angelic granddaughters: just to look into their faces inspired me. There were days when they sat on my lap, pushed buttons on the laptop, demanded paper to scribble on and insisted I do this, that or the other – anything but what I wanted to do. These are all the extra-special memories of a doting grandfather. I hope that you, too, will find something between these covers that you will enjoy.

Weeshie Fogarty,
Killarney, October 2012

Weeshie with his granddaughters Lucy and Eva.

Hussystown (near Cahir) in County Tipperary, the farm where my father was born and I spent many a childhood summer.

ACKNOWLEDGEMENTS

Now that the book is completed and before you, as always, there are a number of people who helped greatly in one way or another, even without being aware of their involvement. My sincere thanks to one and all, and especially to the following. The Collins Press for their support and encouragement. John Kelly of the Spa GAA club, Killarney, for his help and advice in my St Finan's chapters. Sylvester Hennessey, GAA correspondent with *Kerry's Eye*, always encouraging and helpful. Gabriel Fitzmaurice, renowned north Kerry author and poet, always generous with his poems and advice. Journalist Kieran McCarthy, for his help and encouragement. Kerry County Library and my local branch in Killarney; they were invaluable to my research. The O'Donoghue family of the Gleneagle Hotel, Killarney, and 93-year old Alex O'Donnell, from Monaree near Dingle, for his wonderful advice. Alex now lives in Dublin and is a true gentleman. Radio Kerry has played a huge part in my life over the last twenty years and has always encouraged and facilitated me in every way possible. *The Kerryman* newspaper, for which I have written a weekly column over a number of years; work for the paper has opened doors for me in the line of meeting and interviewing sports people. Alan Groarke from Moyvane, living in Colarado, who is the manager of my website, www.terracetalk.com; this massive site has helped me hugely in my research, so thank you, Alan. GAA historian Tim Slattery from Tralee, and Niall Flynn, author of the superb Kerry history *Thirty-six and Counting*; both great friends. Author of so many books, Colm Keane, who was always prompting me to write down my memories.

Without the generosity of my photographer friends many of the photographs reproduced here would have remained unpublished. Kerry is blessed with highly professional men and women in this regard. I have huge admiration for each and every one of them. Don McMonagle, Eamon Keogh, Michelle Cooper Galvin, John Reidy, and the Kennelly archives; the late Padraig Kennelly was one of my favourite people. There are numerous photographs included to which I cannot put a photographer's name and any omissions are entirely unintentional and regretted. The publishers will be happy to hear from copyright holders not acknowledged and undertake to rectify any errors or omissions in future editions, but people like Kevin Coleman, Valerie O'Sullivan, Dominic Walsh and John Stack have always been courteous and accommodating to me. My great friend Tommy Regan also provided photos from his own collection. Monsignor Liam Brosnan in San Antonio was, as always, very generous as he provided some priceless pictures from his massive collection. And finally, to Christy Riordan of CR Video and DVD Productions, Cahersiveen, his wife Geraldine, daughter Michelle and son Tony. Christy granted me full access to his vast collection of photographs and took many himself for this publication. A true friend and top professional at his work. We travelled the world together.

PROLOGUE

1946 and the heart of the secret

Through my column in *The Kerryman* newspaper I befriended a remarkable lady who has been an avid reader of the paper throughout her life; she became a nun in 1944. Some time ago she presented me with a letter her father had written to her in 1946. His is a remarkable story and a historic letter. In many ways it captures the real secret of Kerry and what football means to its people. Judge for yourself as you read Sister Vianney Buckley's own account of her life and how she received this precious letter:

> I will be brief in recounting some aspects of my life's story that began on December 6, 1925, as I reach my eighty-sixth year in 2011. I owe a deep debt of gratitude to God, my parents, my teachers, and to all whom I encountered on the journey of life, for it is true, as the poet wrote, 'I am a part of all that I have met.'
>
> I had a very happy childhood in spite of the many deprivations Ireland underwent in those years of the Great Depression, the Second World War, and

I have been a journalist with *The Kerryman* newspaper for a number of years and contribute a weekly sports column. Paddy Foley (RIP), John Barry and Eamon Horan (both retired) have been three of the paper's outstanding and highly-respected GAA journalists since the early 1930s. I am pictured here with Michael Brennan (Managing Director) *on the left* and Paul Brennan (Sports Editor) *on the right (courtesy Micheal Cooper Galvin).*

Ireland's struggle for Freedom and Independence. I was the sixth child in our family of six girls and one boy ('Deemie'), all born at home in Clounmacon, a townland three miles outside Listowel, County Kerry. I am certain that from the day I came into this world I shared in the passionate love for God and for Ireland which we inherited from Mom and Dad, a love and passion for God and Ireland that filled my Soul. My love for God led me to answer God's call to dedicate myself to Him in the Religious life. I entered

South Presentation Convent in Cork City [First Convent of the Presentation Congregation] in September 1944. It was a sacrifice for my Parents, made willingly by them in spite of the heartbreak it must have been. I remember seeing the tears, but I confess I did not understand till later that it must have been a deep heartbreak for them as they saw four of the girls leave home and enter Presentation Convents in Kerry, Cork, and Tipperary. Letters from Mom and Dad in those early years to me revealed by degrees what they sacrificed in Faith. However, I often recall a line Dad wrote to reveal the mingling of sorrow and joy: '. . . if I were any happier, I could not stand it.'

I shared in my father's love for music, dancing, singing and partying, and especially in his love for Gaelic Football and the Kerry Team. I kept his letter to me [written] in 1946 when, I believe, we played and defeated Roscommon. At the time I was in the Convent and we were not allowed to listen to the Radio (Wet and Dry Battery Days!) so I read and reread my Dad's report of the game: the players who played well, Paul Russell, Paddy Kennedy, Paddy 'Bawn' Brosnan etc., the neighbours who crowded our kitchen, while the younger generation had to listen outside the window. If my diminishing and ageing memory leads me astray here, ask Weeshie Fogarty who can give you every detail and prove me wrong or right. From a very young age we walked to Moyvane, to Ballylongford, etc., to cheer on Clounmacon, or North Kerry in their local games against their foes!! I remember once going to see Kerry play Offaly in Listowel – [a game I] relived [for my audience] when I travelled from Sacramento to the Irish Culture Centre in San Francisco – when

Kerry sadly lost the battle for 'Five-in-a-Row' to Offaly!

I volunteered to go to open a Catholic School in Sacramento with three other Presentation Sisters from South Pres. in August 1961 and have lived in USA for 50 years. And when the All-Ireland is played on the third Sunday of September every year, I am at Fiddlers Green in San Bruno, California, if I am not at Croke Park. That All-Ireland Football Game is played with as much passion as it is in Ireland and I have never since missed an All-Ireland if Kerry is in the 'Battle!', but I do not cry anymore if Kerry loses, because I know the Kingdom cannot be conquered for too long!

The vocation to become a Nun and join Presentation Order came from my early days in my home in Clounmacon, a home that was as Religious as any Convent – Family Rosary every night, morning and night prayers, shared prayer as we discussed what the Church said in English, etc., and strict observance of the Ten Commandments as we interpreted them. The second wonderful influence in my life as I began my High School Education in Listowel came from two Sisters entirely different in their teaching methods. Sister Louis, who taught Religion as well as Irish Literature and other subjects, was so gentle, trusting, and guileless, revealing the God of love to us as she read for us the Lives of the Saints. I recall a book she read called *Fabiola* [by Cardinal Nicholas Wiseman] that gave me my love and understanding of the Eucharist. I remember the life of St Pancratius. Sister Dympna on the other hand gave me a passion for life and living through the Literature classes as well as her own sense of freedom and joy. I learned so much from her, and loved Shakespeare, and the Romantic Poets, etc. We learn more from every person we encounter in life than from books and structured classes. But I am not to go any further in this 'brief' account of my life and living these past 86 years.

From Mom and Dad and family and friends I developed a passion for my God, my Country, and my Beautiful Kingdom of Kerry! As I near the end of my journey of life I want to thank also every person whom I encountered. God bless you all.

Sister Vianney Buckley
26 November 2011

And so to the letter that Sister Vianney's father wrote to her in America sixty-five long years ago, reproduced here exactly word for word. Study it, and I expect each reader will take their own message from what it contains. It is a fascinating look into the rural thinking of Kerry in 1946. It is poignant; a beautiful loving message from a father to his daughter. It also captures for me, yet again, just another one of the secrets of Kerry football and the passion it aroused back then, just as it does today. I thank Sister Vianney for giving permission to publish what is a very personal letter. It is doubtful if another such as this even exists:

Clounmacon, Listowel
Nov 27th Wed Night 1946

My Dearest Hanna, Sr Vianney,
Hoping you are very well as this letter leaves me at present, if I was any better I could not stand it. You seem very anxious about Kerry's victory and the long letter from all. I was over at Leahys last night and Peggy told me she would be writing to you for Christmas. We were playing two fiddles and she also

Tady Buckley of Clounmacon, Listowel, County Kerry, who wrote the very poignant and beautiful letter to his daughter, Sister Vianney, in America following the 1946 All-Ireland final when Kerry beat Roscommon.

sang a song; last winter I used join in on the song. Kitty and her boy is out. Kitty and Lizzy are at variance. I will try and answer all your questions, I would like to make you happy. Now about Kerry's victory. The Kerry halfbacks broke up the Roscommon half forwards, especially Bill Casey against Murray this great Roscommon forward. Joe Keohane Kerry's fullback was in great form also Danno Keeffe in goal; he brought off some wonderful saves. He is now the possessor of six All-Ireland medals. They are now top dogs in 16 All-Ireland wins beating Dublin by one. Gus Cremin, sub, came on near the finish and turned the scales with a long point, then came the goal, they drove man and ball back to the net. The closing minute of the game was most exciting; it was a case of blocking the ball at each side. Kerry had the better of staying power; they are noted to be great in the closing minutes. You can imagine the excitement of the onlookers, it was a record crowd and listeners. Now about the crowd at our radio, Margret Mullane and little girl and Bridgie. The Mullanes brought this cap with up Kerry printed on it. I put it on Paddy Ahern and every time Kerry would score I would lift the cap off Paddy's head. There was Mary Healy, Margaret Babe, Ann Doyle, John Joe Doyle (he played the sets for myself and Paddy Ahern), Monty Leahy, Stephen Enright, Danny O'Donnell, Pat Doyle and John Griffin. We gave tea to all. Glad to hear Peggy is in good form. The Leahys were at Galvins radio. The weather here is the same as in Cork. The Listowel races were put back owing to the harvest, all our crops are O. K. we sold a share of turf by the rail, we built a new poultry house, also wall to stall, I think I told you that news before. We had no letter from Mary for a while and we are feeling anxious about her, not so bad now since we got your letter. We had five sudden deaths in the parish last week, the Gospel last Sunday as you know was be prepared. Our Cannon Brennan is every Sunday talking about the state of the parish especially the new houses [on] O'Connells Ave. and Ballygolague; he is shocked. We put the clock on the kitchen wall to-day. I think I have told you all the news except we have two cats and other simple things and that you have no cause for grumbling as far as my letter is concerned. The presentation letter was in the short side, Kitty was in a hurry with the pen. The same word did for the three nuns. My taste for music, song and dance is only increasing, I suppose I must be only doting. Christmas is not far away now and we are hoping to meet you

in the near future and have a very pleasant day. I think I am imitating you with writing the four pages. You must excuse us for not writing more in the long days, we were too busy for the short days and you will be only plagued from reading them.
Cheerio, keep smiling,
Sure, I need not tell you I remain ever

Your loving Father

Brian O'Conchubhair, PhD Associate Professor, University of Notre Dame, summed up the importance of the document beautifully as follows:

> I sat down and read the letter last night and it struck me deeply in several different ways. It is a wonderful insight into a lost Ireland and a lost cultural and socio-economic enclave in rural Ireland. In a few lines it achieves more than an hour's work of film documentary while reaching the intensity and brevity of a short story. The use of language is startling, almost Heaneyesque at times, and the way it nonchalantly and casually captures the slow encroachment of modernity is breathtaking. But the controlled and unspoken emotional intensity is palpable in the letter and it speaks of a time before Skype, instant messaging and email, where letter writing was an art in maintaining and preserving emotional and familial bonds and preserving identity and heritage across time and distance. A truly wonderful letter. Thank you for allowing me to read it.
>
> Yours, Breen

1

I am hooked: Old Joe passes on the tradition

The youth of Kerry becomes immersed in the history and traditions of its county's glorious football story in so many different ways. Tales may be handed down from generation to generation through families all around the county. Becoming involved in a local club will have a huge bearing on one's outlook and football ambitions. Watching Kerry teams training and playing matches while young invariably leaves a lasting impression and will drive on many an ambitious youngster to wear the Kerry jersey at one grade or another. Likewise, watching Kerry play on the television is another way in which the great traditions of our county are handed down and can help imbue that passionate interest. The magnificent homecoming of victorious Kerry teams following a Croke Park triumph is a sure bet to spark off a driving ambition to be up there on the back of (in the old days) the lorry or (nowadays) the luxury bus, as the boys are paraded in splendid triumph through the streets of Killarney and Tralee. Then, of course, you have the cup visiting every single school in the county and this is probably the most

Joe Smith, who first introduced me to the wonders of Kerry football and was directly responsible for my joining the Killarney Legion GAA club.

effective way of all to ingrain a passion for the secrets of Kerry in the minds of our youth, both girls and boys.

My passion for the green and gold was fostered on the side of the street where I grew up in the 1940s and 1950s. Number 40 Lower New Street, Killarney, is now that superb restaurant called Chapter Forty. A recent visit there for a meal with friends caused all sorts of old, seemingly long-forgotten, memories to rise up once more, in particular a magical encounter one Christmas Eve in the early 1950s. That memory concerns a wonderful old gentleman who lived just four doors up the street from our home. It was he, Joe Smith, who first introduced me to the wonders of Kerry football and was directly responsible for my joining the Killarney Legion GAA club.

Until his death in 1953 at the age of eighty, Joe ran his butchering business with his lovely wife, Maggie, who was always dressed in a long black skirt and a shawl that was invariably wrapped around her head and shoulders. Now Joe's shop was so small that if you walked in you would nearly have to back out when you'd finished your business. As well as the meat, Maggie also sold sweets, jams, Brylcreem for the hair, bags of sugar, and so on, from behind her little counter. The premises were lit by gaslight and had flagstones

Lining out for a team photograph with my club for a Towns Cup match in March 1967. *Back row (l–r):* Connie O'Sullivan (RIP), Weeshie, Killian McCarthy, Seamus O'Neill, Geni Fogarty (RIP), Jim Broderick, Kieran O'Keeffe, Michael Culloty and Gerald O'Sullivan (Gerald played in the Polo Grounds, New York, in 1947, and has since passed away); *front row (l–r):* Tommy Regan, Johnny Healy, Brendan Lynch (RIP), Padraig O'Meara, Mikey Lyne, Adrian Culligan, Johnny Culloty and Mickey Culloty (RIP).

on the floor. The tiny kitchen was just inside the shop and a little yard at the back served as an abattoir for Joe. There was no back entrance so how did Joe get his cattle, sheep and pigs from the street into that little yard? He simply drove them through the shop and the kitchen and into the yard where he slaughtered them with a knife and bare hands. I recall vividly

A magnificent crowd shot during the 1950s in Fitzgerald Stadium, Killarney, at a Munster Senior Football Final between Kerry and Cork. Note the absence of colour, no flags, banners or county jerseys as we see today. The tiny old commentary box is in the background and it is from here I often saw Michael O'Hehir broadcast the finals. There are a number of spectators sitting high on the boundary wall of the terrace that is now called the Michael O'Connor Terrace in memory of a great Killarney Gael of the Dr Croke Club. Michael became chairman of the Munster Council in 1986 and it is generally accepted that only for his premature death in 1991 he would probably have become Kerry's first GAA president.

the day that a cow destined for slaughter went berserk as Joe was driving it through the kitchen. It was probably the smell of death from the yard that warned it of its forthcoming fate. The street was in an uproar as the sounds of crashing tables and chairs emanated from Joe's shop. Calm was eventually restored and the street returned to normality.

Joe was an ardent follower of the Legion GAA Club (the first supporter I ever met), and he would sit me down in front of his old black range and, in the flickering light of the gas lamp as Maggie stocked the range with turf and sticks, he would recall his days walking to Tralee – yes, walking – to see the Legion playing in the county championships of the 1940s. It was here that I first heard the names of those illustrious men in whose footsteps I walked when I later joined the club myself: the Lynes of Cleeney, the O'Sullivans of Ballycasheen, that wonderful little corner forward Timmy O'Leary who won three Minor All-Irelands in a row, the Coopers, John Joe Sheehan, Tom Spillane, father of the Templenoe brothers and many more. Kerry legends all.

Then one dark, wet winter's evening as I sat by his fireside listening to the stories and secrets of Kerry, Joe disappeared upstairs to his little bedroom and when he reappeared he had, clutched in his huge hands, an old, tattered book. It had lost its cover and was brown with age and it was very evident it had been thumbed through on countless occasions. He handed it to me saying, 'Little boy there is a present for you, read that and keep it safe.' Joe had presented me with one of the most priceless GAA books that had ever been printed up until that time. It was Paddy Foley's beautifully written and superb production published in 1945 and entitled *Kerry's Football Story*. It has proved to be a veritable treasury of football lore, a wonderful comprehensive chronicle of achievements and stories that continues to captivate and enthral right up to the present day. Paddy Foley was known to his *Kerryman* readers as 'P. F.'. He was that paper's GAA correspondent from the mid-1920s up until shortly before his death in 1965. His book covers Kerry's football story from the foundation of the Laune Rangers right up to and including 1944. His chapters on Kerry's first American tour in 1927 make for fascinating reading and his words have certainly contributed to my 'beautiful obsession' with Kerry football. It is a pity that the Kerry County Board has not taken it upon themselves, after all these years, to have *Kerry's Football Story* reprinted and made available to the present generation. That book is still, to this very day, one of my most prized possessions and has never left my home.

I will always remember Joe's wonderful artistic talent for creating giant Christmas candles. He would save up the sheep's fat each year and that, combined with the right home-brewed 'stiffeners' and his unique skill, brought to life these magnificent yellow, marble-like candles, almost five feet tall. I particularly remember a Christmas Eve around 1951 or 1952. My late mother pressed a penny into my hand and added, 'Run up to Maggie and get a box of matches to light the Christmas candle.' Joe met me at the door and said, 'Little boy, come out here a minute and help me.' My job was to hold the tip of the giant candle and Joe with his massive hands then twisted and pulled the candle from the metal mould that I learned had been in the family for over one hundred years – and another Joe Smith masterpiece had been created. It proved sadly to be his very last.

Joe suffered from very poor eyesight in his later years. Now, every Christmas when I ramble down Lower New Street, I can see clearly in my mind's eye that small, stooped man in half-belted jacket, knickerbocker trousers and dark, knee-length socks with the cap pulled well down over those forlorn and oft-times troublesome eyes. When he died my mother and her New Street friends laid him out in the tiny room over the little shop. Maggie joined him in death shortly after this. Two exemplary people who would not say 'boo' to a goose or harm a fly. Joe Smith introduced me to the secrets of Kerry football and ingrained in my mind the words 'Killarney Legion'. My club, the club for which I would later play and which I would serve in so many capacities. His rhyme to me on the street as I rushed to school remains fresh in my memory, 'Little boy, number one, hurry up the bell is gone.'

Even some of my closest friends are mildly surprised when I tell them that I come from a very strong farming background on my late father's side. He was born Richard Fogarty in a little townland called Hussystown, halfway between Cahir and Clonmel in County Tipperary. His mother had died very young and his father (my grandfather) had married a second time. My father and his sister, Eileen, were children of that first marriage.

Four O'Sullivan brothers, all now deceased, who lived in Brasby's Lane, High Street, Killarney, County Kerry, *(l–r)*: Billy, Mickey, Neilly and Mysie. They were staunch members of Killarney Legion Club and their mother washed and repaired the team jerseys. Another brother, Mattie, died in America in the 1960s. None of the boys married and there are no known relations. Their knowledge of Old Killarney was immense and I befriended them in my youth. The photograph was taken in the kitchen of their home in 1946.

Father would often tell me stories of how tough life was on that farm and openly admitted that my grandfather had worked them very hard. Up at the crack of dawn tending to the farm jobs, and he and his sister would only set off for school when the schoolyard bell could be heard ringing out across the fields. One of his daily tasks was to bring the milk to the creamery in Cahir, a distance of two miles. Finally, one bright day in September, he made the visit to that creamery for the last time. He had saved up a few shillings, the price of a train ticket to Dublin. He tied the horse and cart to a pole outside one of the local pubs, asked the landlord to pass a message out to Hussystown and shortly afterwards he boarded the train to Dublin and a new life. He joined the Gardaí and was later stationed in Bandon, Kanturk (where he met my mother) and Mallow, before arriving with his family of four boys and two girls in Killarney in 1941. But – of course – we always went back to Tipperary.

I have vivid memories of long, hot, hazy summer holidays spent on the farm at Hussystown with my brother Geni. Saving

In April 1937, my father *(left)* was on detective protection duty for Minister Boland *(centre)* outside the Central Hotel, Mallow, County Cork. He was stationed in Mallow before being transferred to Killarney in 1941. Prior to that, he had been in Kanturk and Bandon. He ran away from home in Tipperary to join the Gardaí.

the hay and bringing home the beautifully made cocks on the hay cart. Driving the horse and cart to the well where we would fill the churns with sparkling, ice-cold water. Growing and selling beet was a huge income for the farmers of the area and it demanded back-breaking hours of work, kneeling with canvas bags to protect the knees as each drill was carefully weeded. And then, after the day's work was done, sitting before the open fire and turning the bellows as the fire belched out smoke and flames while my grandmother, my grandfather's second wife, stirred the huge black pots filled with meal and other unknown ingredients to feed the yard animals.

My grandfather, who died at the age of eighty-two, was known as Jim 'Pope' Fogarty, and in his young days was a fairly noted footballer in the area. The Cahir club published their history in 2009 (M. Hussey & C. O'Flaherty, *Memories and Achievements: 124 years of the GAA in Cahir*) and my grandfather is included in a cover photograph of the 1986 Cahir Faugh-A-Ballagh football team who had won a tournament in the area. They were presented with a set of silver medals for the win and he kept it, as was the custom back then, on his waistcoat watch chain. I was always fascinated by this medal and he would tell me about how he had won it; when he died the medal was, to my great delight, left to the family with instructions that it was to be given to me. It is, to this day, one of my prized possessions and now a family heirloom.

I believe it must have been from my grandfather that I inherited my love and passion for Gaelic games. He would read the GAA match accounts from the local Tipperary weekly paper, *The Nationalist*, to Geni and I as we sat with him in front of his whitewashed, thatched farmhouse on those long summer evenings. Legendary hurling names of Tipperary seemed to excite, inspire and thrill him. John Doyle, Donie Nealon, Liam Devaney, Tony Reddan, Mick Byrne, Tony Wall and many more. One year, however, stands out head and shoulders above all others on those Hussystown holidays.

My grandfather had a beautiful little pony and trap, which he took tremendous pride in tacking up every Sunday. He would dress in his Sunday best, spick and span, bright and glossy, looking the real gent in the three-piece suit, including the mandatory waistcoat and dapper little hat that helped frame his strong-featured, moustachioed, weather-beaten face. It would be early mass in Cahir, then a couple of pints in his local pub, Samson's.

Then, one beautiful Sunday, all my dreams came together when he informed me that he was taking us to a football match in Clonmel. And so off we went accompanied by the beautiful, soothing clip-clop of the little pony along the road – a road that back then was all but devoid of motor vehicles. Memories of the game naturally are hazy, but it was the home side against Waterford in the Munster Championship and I recall my grandfather being as happy as Larry when Tipp won. A few names of that Tipperary side remain etched in the memory despite the passing of time: O'Dea, Tony Newport in goal, Liam Boland and Leo Dooley. It was the first inter-county game I had ever seen.

Years later I travelled back to Cahir to bury my grandfather. It was to be the first of many family funerals but I did not realise then that death would sit constantly on my shoulder, for I was to bury three brothers, my sister, mother, father and a beautiful young niece in succession.

My late mother, Kathleen Crowley, was born in Strand Street, Kanturk, where the family had a little sweet shop. Her father spent a number of years in Ballykinnler prison camp for his IRA beliefs and my mother would tell us (in graphic detail) stories of frightening raids conducted by the notorious Black and Tans on their home. Her mother lived to a great old age and often spent months with us in Killarney. I remember her as an avid reader on those visits; the *Cork Examiner* had to be delivered to her first thing every day and straight away she would turn to the death column saying, 'Let's see who gave up smoking yesterday.'

One of the guests at my parents' wedding in Kanturk was the legendary Dr Pat O'Callaghan, the only Irishman to win two Olympic gold medals. He was the champion hammer-thrower. My mother and her friends would cycle from Kanturk to Banteer on summer evenings to watch Dr Pat in action at the local sports meeting. She loved to speak of him and the excitement in the town when he returned with those gold medals. As a wedding present to my parents the good doctor gave them a beautiful mahogany mantel clock won at a sports meeting. Today it sits proudly in my living room chiming and ticking the hours away as it has done for over eighty years.

My father was only sixty-two when he died. His last few years were difficult and the memory of his suffering remains vivid to me. He first suffered a heart attack and then a very severe stroke, which paralysed his right side. This necessitated his early retirement as driver for the one and only Garda squad car at that time. He then developed prostate cancer, which was to take his life in the end. Eventually he became unable to climb the stairs at night and Geni and I would have to be home around 10.30 p.m. most evenings. Then, with the help of our mother, we would lift him in a chair up two flights of stairs and help settle him for the night. I was only twenty-one at the time and it is only now as an older man I realise how difficult those last years must have been for him. He bore his illness with great dignity and patience and his only mention to me of approaching death was one winter's evening as I sat by his bed reading the paper to him. Suddenly he suddenly said out of the blue, 'I don't mind dying, Weeshie, but I will miss you all so much.' He died two months later.

My mother passed away in 1999. Like most of her generation she was a woman of great faith and the rock of our family. Despite seeing her husband, daughter and niece

One of my favourite family photographs: me with my mother and father in 1953 outside our home at 40 New Street, Killarney. Today, it's a restaurant called Chapter Forty.

buried she always had the good word and imbued in all of us a deep belief and faith in our Catholic religion. Every week she would sit by her radio to listen to myself as I presented *Terrace Talk* on Radio Kerry. Then one July evening as I finished my programme, Fiona Stack (the station's exemplary general manager) was waiting for me. 'Your mother has been taken to hospital in Tralee,' she said, 'The family is waiting there for you.' When I got to Tralee General she was dead. She had sat, as usual, by her little radio to listen to the programme, her tray with her evening meal placed on her lap. Feeling unwell all of a sudden, she was able to call her daughter-in-law next door, but by the time the ambulance arrived she was already dead. It was for me the end of another era in my life.

In 2009, while attending a college game in Cahir for Radio Kerry, I rediscovered my grandfather's grave in the burial ground situated directly behind the church, which itself is just

I played at senior level for sixteen years with my club, Killarney Legion, and also helped them to win minor, junior and senior East Kerry Championships. This is a team photograph from 1969. *Back row (l–r):* Jim Broderick, Jim Fitzgibbon, Dan Moynihan, Pat Healy, Derry Kerrisk, Johnny Culloty, Lui Nolan, Tommy Regan, James Lucy and Seamus O'Neill; *front row (l–r):* Weeshie, Pat Lucey, Mickey Culloty, Mick O'Sullivan, Noel McCarthy, Mikey Lyne and Timmy Loone.

across the road from the football pitch. It was a poignant moment, my first visit to kneel at that graveside, and memories of those long gone, happy days on the farm in Tipperary came flooding back.

The most precious memory of all is following in the footsteps of our grandfather as he ploughed the fields, expertly guiding two beautiful working horses. He was a master at his trade and Geni and I trotted along behind him, marvelling and enthralled as the blade of the plough sliced through the rich, fertile soil. It was such a different world back then; yes indeed, blood is thicker than water. When I watch Tipperary playing in Croke Park or in Munster hurling finals, I can literally feel the Tipperary blood coursing through my veins.

2

From the stars of the 1940s to defeat and despair in the early 1950s

As 1948 dawned, it was obvious to the knowledgeable Kerry follower that many of the legendary men who had brought such honour and glory to the county since the 1930s (including the great 'three-in-a-row' years of 1939, 1940 and 1941 and the contested All-Ireland finals of 1944, 1946 and 1947) were coming to the end of their illustrious careers. This great era of Kerry football had run parallel with the emergence in the county of the all-conquering Dingle team, which won six glorious Kerry County Championships in 1938, 1940, 1941, 1943, 1944 and 1948. These west Kerry men had played a huge part in the Kerry story of that time, but by 1948 household names such as Paddy 'Bawn' Brosnan, Bill Dillon, Bill Casey, Tom 'Gegga' O'Connor and Batt Garvey had already retired or were entering the autumn of their honour-laden careers.

Although it definitely did not look that way when Kerry hammered Clare, 6-6 to 1-8, in the first round of the Munster Championship in Ballylongford on 10 July at the start of the 1948 campaign. Many of the old stalwarts were still there:

Superb action shot of Denny Lyne (Kerry) on the ball in the 1946 All-Ireland final against Roscommon. Kerry won following a replay. John Joe Nerney and J. J. Fallon are the two Roscommon men in picture while Paddy 'Bawn' Brosnan (Kerry) watches on. Denny Lyne was a member of the legendary Killarney football family known as 'The Lynes of Cleeney' from just outside Killarney town. A member of my own club Killarney Legion, Denny had two brothers who also won All-Ireland senior medals, Jackie (1946 and 1953) and Mickey (1937 and 1941). Another brother Teddy won a Junior All-Ireland medal with Kerry in 1941. Jackie trained Kerry to win the 1969 and 1970 All-Ireland titles. Denny captained Kerry in the 1947 All-Ireland defeat by Cavan in the Polo Grounds, New York. Maura, a sister of the Lynes, was the mother of the renowned Spillane brothers of Templenoe, Pat, Tom and Mick. 'An ounce of blood is worth a ton of feeding.'

Danno Keeffe, Denny and Jackie Lyne, Bill Casey, Eddie Dowling, Gus Cremin, Batt Garvey and Dan Kavanagh. Gerald O'Sullivan (a sub in the New York Polo Grounds defeat of 1947) scored two goals against Clare, while a young twenty-year-old named Donie Murphy from Muckross in Killarney made his debut at corner back when Paddy 'Bawn', the Dingle fisherman, failed to reach port due to stormy weather. Both Gerald and Donie were from my own Killarney Legion club and I would later play with both men in club and county colours.

In 2004 I was honoured for my service to the GAA by the North Kerry Football Board and here, the legendary Kerry footballer and exemplary gentleman Eddie Dowling (RIP) makes the presentation. On the left is Der O'Connor, chairman of the Board. Eddie, one of my boyhood heroes, played with Kerry at midfield in the historic 1947 All-Ireland final in the Polo Grounds, New York, when Cavan were the winners. He was badly concussed in the first half and had to be replaced. It is generally accepted that his injury probably cost Kerry that final as Eddie was in magnificent form. He played with Kerry from 1944 to 1954, making nineteen Championship and ten League appearances and winning five Munster Championship medals but sadly he never won a Senior All-Ireland medal. Eddie's club, Ballydonoghue, had some fantastic players such as his brother Denis 'Black' Dowling, Mike Finucane, Gus Cremin, Ger D. O'Connor, Robert Bunyan and Liam Flaherty who have all graced the greens of Croke Park. Indeed, two players have captained Kerry on All-Ireland final day: Ger D. O'Connor in 1964, when the Seniors lost to Galway, and Robert Bunyan, when the Minors won the title in 1975.

The late Donie Murphy who played for Kerry in the 1953 All-Ireland win over Armagh. A superb defender, Donie was outstanding in the 1955 Munster final win over Cork but tragically he would never play for Kerry again. Following that Munster win Donie was diagnosed with tuberculosis, spent twelve months in hospital and missed out as Kerry beat Dublin in 1955. Donie was a clubmate of mine and I played in goal behind him numerous times as he lined out at fullback. From Muckross, Killarney, he is buried in County Mayo where he resided.

The Munster final played in Killarney attracted a crowd in excess of 40,000. The ball was thrown in to begin the game by Monsignor Hugh O'Flaherty, who is better known for his exploits in Rome during the Second World War when he defied the entire German espionage service and saved the lives of hundreds of refugees. A Killarney man, his name was commemorated in the town by the road named for him in 2008. A film of his life was also shot, with Gregory Peck playing the part of the Monsignor. Kerry retained that 1948 Munster title, defeating old rivals Cork 2-9 to 2-6. An early second-half goal from Gegga O'Connor was decisive. The team did not train for the match. Many had played in the county championship the previous Sunday, when Dingle beat Killarney. Paddy 'Bawn' had travelled eight hours in a fishing boat from Galway to Dingle on the Saturday to play with his home town and had not docked until midnight on the Saturday.

A meeting with Mayo awaited Kerry in the All-Ireland semi-final and the Connacht men literally trounced the Kingdom, 0-13 to 0-3. It was the county's worst defeat since Dublin had been victorious in the semi-final of 1934 in Tralee, 3-8 to 0-6. The side had not trained for the game and had scored just one point from play during the entire hour. Full back for Mayo that day was the legendary Paddy Prendergast. Paddy later came to work and live in Tralee. I often had the pleasure of chatting with him and he would speak highly of his teammates, such as Sean Flanagan, Eamon Mongey, Paddy Carney, Joe Gilvarry and Tom Langan. Mayo lost to Cavan in the final but went on to become champions in 1950 and 1951. The Kerry team in 1948 was: Danno Keeffe, Denny Lyne, Joe Keohane (captain), Paddy 'Bawn' Brosnan, Eddie Dowling, Jackie Lyne, Eamon O'Connor, Gus Cremin, Tom Spillane, Gerald O'Sullivan, Bruddy O'Donnell, Batt Garvey, Dan Kavanagh, Martin McCarthy and Teddy O'Connor. The subs were: Teddy O'Sullivan, Gegga O'Connor, Derry Burke, Frank O'Keeffe, Brendie Kelleher, Donie Murphy and Brian

O'Sullivan (Castlemaine). Bill Casey was injured and missed the game.

The last year of the 1940s proved to be a disaster for Kerry and it was now clear that all the old stars were well and truly dimmed. The county was in transition and new faces were apparent on the day that Kerry travelled to Ennis to take on Clare on their home turf in the first round of the Munster Championship. The home side created a national sensation when they defeated the Kingdom, 3-8 to 1-7. Mick Finucane and Jas Murphy, who both played, were unanimous in their view that it was complete lack of preparation, old legs and the unavailability of some players that contributed to their downfall under the very warm conditions of the day. It was the first time Clare had beaten Kerry in the championship (it would not happen again until 1992) and the first time that Kerry had ever lost an opening round. That defeated side lined out as follows: Paddy Dennehy, Denny Lyne, Jas Murphy, Tom Spillane, Teddy O'Connor, Mick Finucane, Bill Casey, John Joe Sheehan, Eddie Dowling, Tom Moriarty, Jim Brosnan, Gerald O'Sullivan, Batt Garvey, Tom Ash and Willie O'Donnell. The subs were: Denis Baily, Tom Spillane, Tim Healy, Michael Lynch and Bruddy O'Donnell. Jackie Lyne and Paddy 'Bawn' Brosnan were absent through injury.

The Kerry Juniors made amends for the Senior loss, as they defeated Lancashire in the All-Ireland final, 2-14 to 0-6. Down were defeated in the Home final, 3-11 to 3-5. The team was: Liam Fitzgerald, John O'Connor, Tadgh Flynn, Denis Dowling, Michael Lynch, Paddy Batt Shannahan, Michael McElligott, Sean Murphy, John Dowling, Padraig Murphy, Phil McCarthy, Tom Long (captain), John C. Cooper, Mixi Palmer and James Kennedy.

It was defeat, however, for the Kerry Minors in the All-Ireland final, as Armagh were victorious 1-7 to 1-5. On the team were: Johnny Foley, Jerome O'Shea, Paddy Coughlan,

Mick Galway, Michael Kerins, Pluggy Moriarty, John Costello, Sean Murphy, Dinny Falvey, Paddy Coleman, Pa O'Donnell, Paudie Sheehy, Brendan Galvin, Colm Kennelly and Bobby Miller.

With Kerry still trying to come to terms with the shock defeat to Clare the previous year, the same county travelled to Tralee in June 1950 for the opening round of the Munster Championship and a late point gave Kerry a very fortunate reprieve, enabling it to escape the indignity of a second successive defeat by the Banner County. It finished 2-3 to 1-6. Kerry, however, made no mistake in the replay in Ennis, winning 5-6 to 2-4. Three men from the town of Killarney goaled that day: the O'Sullivan brothers of the Killarney Legion, Gerald and Teddy, and Dr Crokes' Teddy O'Connor all raised green flags. The Munster final in July attracted an attendance of 25,000 to the Cork Athletic Grounds where they witnessed a thrilling contest. Cork led at the short whistle, 1-5 to 0-3, but two great goals within a minute of each other by Dan Kavanagh turned the tables in Kerry's favour and they regained the title on the score 2-5 to 1-5.

Kerry trained under Dr Eamonn O'Sullivan and it was the very first time that the Kingdom had actually come together and trained for a semi-final. Amazingly, the committee that selected the team consisted of thirteen selectors representing all districts in the county. Louth proved the masters in the semi-final, 1-7 to 0-8, and probably the deciding moment was a brilliant save by Louth's legendary goalkeeper Sean Thornton, when he dived at the feet of Batt Garvey to prevent what seemed like a certain goal. The county was still undergoing transition and some of the heroes of 1946 continued to answer their county's call. On that day back in 1950 Louth had outstanding players in Hubert Reynolds, with Jack Regan remarkable at midfield, Stephen White, Paddy McArdel and Sean Boyle. Trailing by a point and with minutes to go, Kerry did have an opportunity to level the game amid high drama, as P. F. wrote in *The Kerryman* the following Thursday: 'A free for Kerry 35 yards out from the Louth goal. A point down, there is a huddle between the Kerry players. Teddy O'Sullivan is entrusted with the kick. He walks up to the ball in a hush where even the sea gulls wheeling and diving overhead seem to stifle their cries. Teddy's kick falls short and Kerry are out.' The Kerry team was: Liam Fitzgerald, Jas Murphy, Paddy 'Bawn' Brosnan, Donie Murphy, Mick Finucane, Jackie Lyne, Teddy O'Connor, Jim Brosnan, Eddie Dowling, Teddy O'Sullivan (0-1), Mixi Palmer (0-1), Paddy Godley, Dan Kavanagh, Phil McCarthy (0-1) and Batt Garvey (0-4) The subs were: Paddy Batt Shannahan, Gerald O'Sullivan (0-1), Bruddy O'Donnell, Tim Healy and Michael O'Connor (Rathmore). Others who played in or trained for that campaign: Tom Dowling (goals), Dermot Hannifin, John Joe Sheehan, Paddy Murphy (Castlegregory), D. J. McMahon (John Mitchels), Tom Spillane, Tom Long, Sean O'Connor (Knocknagoshel) and Ger Pierce (John Mitchels). Teddy O'Sullivan was top scorer for the year with 2-6.

There was joy for the county, however, when the Minor footballers captured their sixth provincial title in a row and went on to defeat Antrim in the semi-final, 2-9 to 0-1, and Wexford in the All-Ireland final, 3-6 to 1-4. The team was: Donal 'Marcus' O'Neill, Mick Galway, Mick Brosnan, John Collins, Tommy Murphy, Paddy O'Donnell, Joe Kerins, Sean Murphy, Paudie Sheehy, Bobby Miller, Colm Kennelly, Connie Riordan, Brendan Galvin, Tommy Lawler and Pa Fitzgerald. The subs were Mick O'Driscoll, Kevin Barry, Dan McAuliffe, Tony Gaughan, Sean Walsh, Mick Kerins, Liam Sheehan and Tom Keane.

At the county convention of 1951 the selection committee was reduced from thirteen to ten. The chairman told the meeting that picking a Kerry team was 'like being present at

Three O'Sullivan brothers with the Sam Maguire Cup, *(l–r):* James (RIP), Eddie (RIP) and Robert, at the launch of my book on their father Dr Eamonn O'Sullivan, the legendary Kerry footballer trainer. Sadly, a fourth brother, Anthony, died shortly after my interview with him for the book.

a county council meeting'. However, this slight change did not bring All-Ireland winning joy to the county as 1951 began. Waterford at home were easily overcome in the opening round of the Munster Championship, 5-6 to 1-1. Colm Kennelly played at full forward, scoring a goal, while Sean O'Connor of Castleisland at wing forward scored two goals. Tom Ash and Frank O'Keeffe were the other goalscorers. Neilly Duggan (Cork) and Paddy 'Bawn' were the stars of the Munster final played in Killarney, as Kerry retained their title, 1-6 to 0-4. A late goal from midfielder Dermot Hannifin, who had moved into full forward, sealed the victory. Young

Paudie Sheehy, son of the legendary John Joe who had captained Kerry to All-Ireland glory in 1926 and 1930, appeared on the scene and made his debut in the second half. His brothers, Niall, Brian and Seán Óg, would also wear the green and gold with great distinction during the following years.

An emerging Mayo team awaited Kerry in the All-Ireland semi-final. The star of a side sprinkled with stars was Sean Flanagan. A superb corner back, he was one of the finest fielders of the ball ever to have graced Croke Park and he was the driving force as that Mayo team won two All-Ireland titles (1950 and 1951) and two league crowns (1949 and 1954). However, in this 1951 semi-final, Mayo were four points down against Kerry as the match entered injury time. Paddy 'Bawn' was having a blinder at full back. Tom Langan was switched in on him. From a Kerry kick-out, Eamon Mongey out-fielded John Joe Sheehan, centred the ball and Langan, lurking on the verge of the square, flicked the ball to the net while well off the ground. Paddy Irwin pointed for Mayo from far out and the full-time whistle went immediately after this. Mayo had snatched a draw (1-5 all). Pat Godley had been the Kerry goalscorer.

Jas Murphy lined out at corner back that day and when I spoke to him many years later he was under no illusion as to what had transpired in those closing minutes. 'We sat back on our lead; our preparations were very poor for the game and they finished very strong. I still regret that day and I firmly believe with our Croke Park record in All-Ireland finals we would have beaten Meath in the final.' Then he remarked on the team's preparations. 'Kerry teams were very badly prepared for big games around that period and I clearly remember that the duals between Jackie Lyne and Padraig Carney were the highlight of those two matches.'

Sean Murphy arrived on the big stage that day and the doctor from Camp in west Kerry would go on to become one of the all-time greats of Gaelic football. Three weeks later the sides returned to Croke Park to settle their differences in a semi-final replay and, before a crowd of 53,345, two goals from Mayo corner forward Mick Flanagan saw the Connacht champions advance to the final, 2-4 to 1-5. Kerry fought to the bitter end. Bruddy O'Donnell set up Eddie Dowling and the Ballydonoghue man blasted the ball to the net. However time ran out and the Kingdom had lost a semi-final replay for the first time in thirty-two years. On the Kerry team were: Liam Fitzgerald, Jas Murphy, Paddy 'Bawn' Brosnan, Donie Murphy, Sean Murphy, Jackie Lyne, Mixi Palmer, John Joe Sheehan, Dermot Hannifin, Paddy Godley, Eddie Dowling (1-1), Jim Brosnan, Tom Ash (0-1), Gerald O'Sullivan (0-1) and Paudie Sheehy. The subs were: Sean O'Connor (played in the drawn game), Teddy O'Connor (on), John Dowling (on), Tim Healy (on), Dermot Lawler (St Brendan's), Bruddy O'Donnell (0-2), Mick Finucane, Frank O'Keeffe and Gearoid Byrne (Foxrock Geraldines).

It was the last Croke Park appearance for a number of the legendary Kerry players who had served their county with great distinction. Paddy 'Bawn' had played for Kerry from 1938 to 1952, scoring 2-6 in 40 appearances, while Frank O'Keeffe, Gus Cremin, Eddie Dowling, Teddy O'Connor and Bruddy O'Donnell all bid farewell to the stadium they had graced since the early 1940s.

In June 1951 the Kerry Minor hurlers were beaten in the Gaelic Grounds in Limerick in the Munster Championship by the home side, 1-7 to 2-0. This game marked the arrival on the inter-county scene of a fourteen-year-old youngster named Johnny Culloty. He gave a brilliant performance between the posts and Paddy Foley of *The Kerryman* wrote of him: 'The game was best remembered for the superb display of Kerry's diminutive young goalkeeper Culloty, who saved his side from a heavy defeat. After the final whistle Limerick's legendary hurler Mick Mackey approached the youngster and shook his hand in appreciation of his brilliant display of goalkeeping.' Culloty would go on to win five Senior All-Ireland football medals with Kerry and to serve his club and county in various capacities during the following sixty years. That Kerry Minor hurling side of 1951 was: Johnny Culloty, Denis Hegarty, James McCarthy, Liam Murphy, John Carroll, Derry Kennelly, Pat Joe Brosnan, Kevin Barry, J. J. O'Sullivan, Michael Looney, Raymond Vaughan, Paddy O'Shea, Brendan Bourke, Eddie Barry and Willie O'Leary. The subs were: Pat Hennessey, Paul O'Mahoney, J. J. Brosnan, Liam Brosnan, Mick Fleming, Eddie Murphy and Patrick O'Donoghue. The Kerry Minor footballers, just like the Seniors, drew in the All-Ireland semi-final with Armagh but lost the replay 2-3 to 0-7.

There was to be further heartbreak for the suffering Kerry supporters the following year, 1952. An unconvincing 0-14 to 1-7 win over Waterford did nothing to dispel the fears that another barren season lay ahead. The Munster final played in the Cork Athletic Grounds was a disaster for the Kerry side, now showing lots of changes as the old guard bowed out. Cork won 1-11 to 0-2, as Kerry scored just one point in each half. If not for goalkeeper Marcus O'Neill and Paddy 'Bawn' Brosnan playing his final championship match for his county, the score against would have been much greater. The winners had stars in Denis Bernard, Eamon Young, Donie Donovan, 'Toots' Kelleher and Paddy Harrington, whose son Padraig would later emerge as one of the world's great golfers, winning the British Open Championship in 2007 and 2008 and the PGA Championship in 2008.

The Kerry team was: Donal 'Marcus' O'Neill, Jas Murphy, Paddy 'Bawn' Brosnan, Gerald O'Sullivan, Sean Murphy, Jackie Lyne, Mixi Palmer, Dermot Hannifin, Brendan O'Shea, Paudie Sheehy, John Joe Sheehan, Tadghie Lyne, Jim Brosnan, Sean Kelly and Tom Ash. The subs were: Teddy O'Connor, Colm Kennelly, Eddie Dowling, Brendan Galvin, Paddy Godley, Jer Spillane, Jerome O'Shea, Paddy Murphy (Foxrock

Geraldines), Tim Healy, John O'Connor and Bobby Miller. Jackie Lyne was now the only remaining playing link with the sides of 1946 and the defeated New York Polo Grounds men. The names of Teddy O'Connor, Eddie Dowling and Tim Healy had appeared on the match programme for the very last time.

The big surprise of the year was the defeat of the Kerry Minor footballers in Tralee by Clare, 3-4 to 2-5, while the Junior footballers were defeated in a replay by Tipperary in the Munster final, 0-8 to 0-6.

3

The glorious Jubilee All-Ireland victory over Armagh in 1953

September 1953. The date remains forever etched on my memory. It was my very first personal experience of the mystery, magic and greatness – and the secrets – of Kerry football. In faraway Dublin (far away, that is, for a twelve-year-old Killarney youngster still wearing short pants) Kerry were playing Armagh in the Jubilee All-Ireland football final.

It was one of those beautiful Sunday afternoons in September that we relish at the end of a glorious, long, hot summer. McNeill's little shop, which combined a pub and grocery section, was just five doors down the street from where we lived. The owners, William McNeill and his wife Alice, were a quiet, unassuming couple but James had in his possession something special that, on this particular afternoon, attracted a huge crowd of neighbours to his premises. He had one of the very few radios on the street. Not only that, but he was also the only agent in the town of Killarney for the biggest selling radio brand on the market, Bush radios.

He was a man well ahead of his time and, in his little workshop at the rear of the house, he was capable of repairing whatever radio was brought to him from far and wide. He also boasted the very first sales slogan that I had ever seen, for posted over the shopfront in big, bold lettering were the words, 'It's a wise bird that settles on a Bush'. That September afternoon a great crowd of neighbours (and some from farther afield) had gathered to hear Michael O'Hehir's broadcast from Croke Park. The radio had been placed on the sweet counter in the shop and people were seated on the counter itself and on the stairs above. They had even spilled out on to the street and it was here that I was seated – on the kerb of Lower New Street. The wonderfully distinct, dulcet tones of Michael O'Hehir were plain to be heard as the hushed followers literally hung on his every word.

Directly across the street was the Garda barracks where my father was stationed and the man on duty that day, Guard McDonald, had thrown off his tunic, discarded his peaked cap, and joined us on that side of the street. It was an era when cars were as scarce as hen's teeth and the words 'heavy traffic' had yet to enter our vocabulary. New Street was deserted. The game had ebbed and flowed. Armagh had begun their year unfancied and unsung. Now, with just six minutes remaining, they stood on the brink of history. Just one point behind, they were presented with a golden opportunity to defeat mighty Kerry and become the first team to bring the Sam Maguire Cup across the border. Years later, in my position as Radio Kerry sports reporter, I talked to Kerry's goalkeeper from that memorable day. Johnny Foley was a member of the Kerins O'Rahillys club in Tralee and his recall of the incident that occurred in those pulsating closing minutes was still crystal clear.

'A high ball dropped into the square just in front of me; I failed to collect it at the first attempt and when it landed on the ground it gave a slight hop and I gathered it at the second attempt. There was a definite hop on the ball,' he emphasised forcefully. However, referee Peter McDermott of Meath saw it completely differently and adjudged that Foley had picked the ball straight off the ground, which was then illegal. Nowadays it is permissible for the goalkeeper to do just that inside the small square. Peter McDermott then consulted with his two umpires, Billy Goodison and Peter O'Reilly. They confirmed what the referee had suspected. It was a penalty for Armagh. Silence fell on the huge crowd gathered around that little radio. You could hear the proverbial pin drop as Bill McCorry, who had never failed with a penalty kick on the big occasion, stepped forward to take the kick.

'It's wide, McCorry has blazed the ball wide of the posts.' O'Hehir's words brought a huge roar of relief from the New Street supporters. I have heard thousands of Kerry supporters cheering their Kerry football heroes since that day long ago, but I swear that massive cheer was the greatest I have ever heard. Armagh were stunned. Kerry went on and points from my own Killarney Legion club men, Jackie Lyne and John Joe Sheehan, sealed a memorable Kerry win, 0-13 to 0-6.

Jas Murphy from the Kerins O'Rahillys club in Tralee accepted the Sam Maguire Cup that day in 1953. It was a hugely significant success for the Kingdom. Kerry had failed to win the title since 1946 when the legendary Paddy Kennedy had captained them to victory over Roscommon following a replay. So from that day until 1953 had been Kerry's longest spell without a win since the Sam Maguire Cup was first contested in 1928.

The captaincy has frequently caused huge controversy in Kerry and the occasion of this spectacular win was no exception. The man who leads Kerry is determined by the team that wins the previous year's county championship and the player who assumes the mantle would not always be assured of his starting place on the first fifteen. In 1946, for example, four separate men led the team in the pre-match parades. Shannon Rangers had won the county championship in 1945 and two of their stalwarts, Gus Cremin and Eddie Dowling, had captained the team during its march to Croke Park. Injury and loss of form saw both men lose their place. Bill Casey was also captain for one of the matches. Following the drawn final against Roscommon, Gus Cremin, who had been captain for that match, was dropped for the replay and Paddy Kennedy was handed the honour of leading Kerry to victory.

Many years later I visited Gus at his home in Ballydonoghue. Now into his eighties it was very evident that losing captaincy for that 1946 replay had been painful and he pulled no punches. 'I blame Dr Eamonn O'Sullivan, the trainer, as being responsible for me losing my place for the replay. I was just a hard-working farmer and he always favoured the student or the man with the white-collar work. However, I did come on in the replay and scored the point that was responsible for defeating Roscommon.' (Renowned GAA scribe Eamon Mongey wrote in a national paper that the point Gus scored was '. . . the most perfect and valuable point ever scored in Croke Park'.) Gus continued, 'I came straight home from Dublin and the following morning I was out in the fields saving my crops. I avoided all the celebrations and to this day I am still deeply hurt due to the way I was treated. The officers of the Kerry County Board never came to me and the following year, 1947, I missed a trip to the Polo Grounds final in New York, as I broke my leg in the North Kerry League final. I played my last game for Kerry in 1948 when we lost heavily to Mayo in the All-Ireland semi-final.'

Once again, as Jas Murphy marched up the steps of the Hogan stand to accept the trophy in 1953, controversy raged around the captain's appointment. Paudie Sheehy had been captain for the semi-final win over Louth. His father, the legendary John Joe, was a selector that year and when the team was being chosen in the Park Place Hotel, Killarney, where the panel were staying, John Joe Sheehy announced that he would leave the meeting when Paudie's position came up for discussion. What transpired was to cause a sensation in the county. Paudie was dropped from the starting fifteen and the position of captain for the final was now vacant.

Fifty-five years later I visited Jas Murphy in his home in Cork where we recalled that momentous day of his sporting life. He was, at the time of my visit, the oldest surviving winning Kerry captain alive. Jas, a retired garda, takes up the story. 'The first I heard of the captaincy was on the Thursday before the match. A friend rang me from Tralee and said that the John Mitchels club, who had the nomination of the captaincy, was honouring me with the appointment. I was very sorry for Paudie and it made it more difficult for me because we were great friends and travelled to matches and training together. I felt that there were others on the team more deserving of the honour than myself. But Tralee would not let the honour leave the town. Johnny Foley was the other Kerins O'Rahillys player on the team and it could have gone to him just as easily. Nevertheless I look back on that day with great memories.'

The tradition in Kerry is that the captain is always the first man to alight from the train with the cup when the victors return to the Kingdom. I had always been slightly puzzled when studying a magnificent photograph of Jackie Lyne being shouldered high by a massed crowd of jubilant supporters on the platform of Killarney railway station that year of 1953. No sign of Jas, where was he? All those years later in his comfortable home in Cork he cleared up the mystery. 'Would you believe that I missed the train on which the team returned to Kerry? I had met friends at the Garda Club in Dublin and lost track of time. However, I caught a later train and met up with the lads in Tralee where I was shouldered through the town with the cup. One of my lasting memories of that All-Ireland victory is a card I received from Jakes McDonald, a great John Mitchels man. He wrote, 'Congrats, Jas, on bringing home the jug.'

Over 86,000 spectators attended that final, which marked the Golden Jubilee Year of the county's first All-

Ireland success. It was later estimated another 8,000 forced their way in through the gates after the start of the match. Listening to the commentary on that old Bush radio on the side of Lower New Street, Killarney, was one of the most magical things I have ever experienced. The Kerry players were gods soaring high into the skies over Croke Park. Dublin was, for me, a million miles away and I whispered a little prayer to myself that some day I might play in Croke Park and wear the green and gold of Kerry. My ambition from that day on was just to play in Croke Park – not to win an All-Ireland, just to *play* there. My dreams would eventually come true.

For Jas Murphy, the man who had led Kerry to their seventeenth All-Ireland Senior title in 1953, there would be great heartbreak the following year. When I spoke to him in 2009 about his career, he was still visibly upset over the shocking treatment he had received from the Kerry County Board and selectors. He played just one more championship match for Kerry when they defeated Waterford 3-10 to 1-4 in the first round of the 1954 Munster Championship. He was never again contacted by the county board and was never offered an explanation as to why his services had been dispensed with. 'I was playing the best football of my life at the time,' he told me. 'I was dropped from the panel and I felt deeply hurt and gave up even going to see Kerry playing. My late wife, Mary, was very upset also and to this day I have never heard from any one in authority as to why I was totally ignored.'

I have seen numerous instances of very hurtful wrongs inflicted on Kerry footballers down through the years. In some instances it is a case of what club do you come from, or did your father or brothers play with Kerry, or have you a friend on the selectors committee? Jas Murphy, like many others, was badly wronged. A dignified gentleman, such as himself, certainly did not deserve to be totally ignored following the great win in 1953. He remains the only Kerry captain to have his services dispensed with the year after leading his county to All-Ireland glory.

The issue of the Kerry captaincy would continue to surface at various intervals through the succeeding years and I myself was involved in one of those controversies. The year was 1984. I was a member of the Killarney committee that had steered our town to a historic Kerry Senior County Championship win in 1983. That Killarney team was comprised of players from Dr Crokes and Killarney Legion clubs. When Kerry took the field against Tipperary in Tralee in the first round of the Munster Championship in 1984, Diarmuid O'Donoghue of the Legion was the only player from the Killarney winning side to gain a place on the first fifteen. He captained Kerry to a 0-23 to 0-6 victory, and also got on the scoreboard. When the team was announced for the Munster final in Fitzgerald Stadium against Cork, Diarmuid had been dropped from the starting fifteen. It was a cruel blow for the young man and it was felt by many in the town at the time that at least he should have been afforded the honour of leading the side out for the final in front of his own supporters.

However, as far as Mick O'Dwyer and his fellow selectors were concerned, sympathy did not enter the equation and the Killarney committee was instructed to meet and nominate a player to succeed O'Donoghue as captain. We met at the Park Place Hotel in Killarney, then the spiritual home of Kerry football. It has since been completely demolished. Donie Sheehan, Jackie Looney, Johnny Culloty and others came to a unanimous decision. I proposed that Ambrose O'Donovan of the Gneeveguilla club be nominated to lead Kerry. It was quickly seconded and the wholehearted and all-action Ambrose went on to lead Kerry to a glorious centenary All-Ireland victory, defeating Cork, Galway and then Dublin in

Here I am in goal for Kerry in San Francisco in March 1970 as we toured the world following our 1969 All-Ireland victory. A memorable experience, we visited Amsterdam, Bahrain, Bancock, New Delhi, Auckland, Melbourne, Wagga Wagga, Perth, Fiji Islands, Hawaii, San Francisco, Chicago and New York. The memories will linger forever.

the final. No man deserved the honour more than the man from Sliabh Luachra, and one of my lasting memories of that victory involved the homecoming that followed. The team were paraded past thousands of fans lining the streets of Killarney and on the back of the lorry, when the speeches were completed, the bold O'Donovan brought roars of approval from the Kerry supporters as he gave a passionate rendering of that beautiful ballad, 'Sweet Forget-me-not'.

Those triumphant homecomings following All-Ireland victories are an integral part of what may be the secret of Kerry. Thousands of watching youngsters are imbued with a deep desire to emulate their conquering heroes and many the Kerry youngster falls into a beautiful deep sleep following those memorable evenings. His dreams are of Croke Park, All-Ireland medals, green and gold jerseys and arriving home to a Kerry where bonfires are blazing and that wonderful gleaming silver goblet that is the Sam Maguire Cup, symbol of all that is great and good in Kerry football, is carried triumphantly aloft.

4

1955: The sweetest of them all

Only two years later, in 1955, came another never-to-be-forgotten year. It was the year that I attended my very first All-Ireland final. I travelled to Dublin with some of my boyhood friends, including cousins Con O'Mara and Con Clifford, both of whom later wore the famous Kerry green and gold. Indeed, Con O'Mara holds the unique record of captaining Killarney to their one and only Kerry Senior hurling county championship victory in 1969. Sadly, both men died at a young age; a cruel blow to their wives and families.

Earlier in the year Kerry had had a convincing 3-7 to 0-4 win over Waterford in the opening Munster Championship round, a game played in Listowel, with Tom Costello helping himself to 2-2, while Bobby Buckley bagged a goal. Kerry used no substitutes that day. Then, in July, I watched the green and gold in action in a Munster final for the first time in my life, as Kerry beat Cork in sweltering conditions in Killarney, 0-14 to 2-6. Forty-five-thousand supporters crammed into Fitzgerald Stadium, Killarney, on that memorable day. The terrace was black with people packed together like sardines in a tin. There was no mention of health and safety, and not a safety barrier to be seen. Even the boundary wall separating the grounds from the local mental hospital served as a vantage point; it was from here, perched on high, that I viewed the game. My lasting memories of that day are of some superb long-range points lofted over by Kerry's wing forwards, Paudie Sheehy and Tadghie Lyne.

One Kerry star, however, would forever have bittersweet memories of that 1955 Munster final. When the Kerry team togged out for the game under the direction of renowned trainer, Dr Eamonn O'Sullivan, little did their brilliant full back Donie Murphy realise that he was pulling on the Kerry jersey for the very last time. Donie, a member of my own Killarney Legion GAA club and one of my boyhood heroes, had won a Minor All-Ireland medal with Kerry in 1946, after beating Dublin 3-7 to 2-3. In later years Donie told me about that Minor victory, as we sat in his home in Castlebar where he later settled down. 'We did no training for the final,' he recalled, 'and I was on Kevin Heffernan and I held him to a point. I can still hear the Kerry followers in the long stand singing as the final whistle sounded, "Roll out the barrel, we have the Blues on the run, roll out the barrel, we'll have a barrel of fun."'

Two years later, in July 1948, Donie made his championship debut against Clare when Kerry had an easy win in Ballybunion. He went on to capture his only Celtic Cross in 1953 when Kerry defeated Armagh in that wonderful and dramatic final. He would continue to be first choice for one of the full back line positions until 1955 when illness ended that brilliant career. Donie wonders, looking back, if a bout of pleurisy he developed following a club game in Dublin in 1951 (which necessitated six weeks in Jervis Street Hospital) left a legacy that would later force his retirement.

After the 1955 Munster Championship win over Cork Donie began to feel unwell and a visit to his doctor, Jim

McCarthy (an All-Ireland hurler with Limerick), followed by a series of X-rays, confirmed his worst fears. He had developed tuberculosis, far more serious in those days than now. He would undergo an operation and spend seventeen months in hospital. While he lay in his hospital bed, Kerry marched on to win the All-Ireland and the team visited him with the cup. Ironically, during the same 1955 match that saw his career come to a premature end, one of his clubmates and great friends, Johnny Culloty, made his debut, since he was brought on as a sub. But for 25-year-old Donie Murphy from South Hill, Muckross, Killarney, those months of 1955 were a shattering experience. Nevertheless, his marvellous attitude to life came shining through and he told me, all those years later, 'It could be far worse, Weeshie. Thank God for that one All-Ireland medal. It's many the great player that has none.'

Donie's story has a rather happy postscript, in which I was personally involved. Four years later in 1959, when I was eighteen, I was selected for Killarney Legion in goal when we faced a star-studded South Kerry side in Con Keating Park, Cahersiveen. They had won the Kerry County Championship in 1955 and 1956, and names such as Donal O'Neill, Mick O'Dwyer, Mick O'Connell, Ned Fitzgerald (father of Maurice) and Jerome O'Shea – all legends of the game – were on the opposing side that Sunday afternoon. For me it was, and still remains, a particularly special day in my football life. Donie Murphy made a comeback at the end of his long road to recovery. He had answered the call for the Legion and lined out at full back where he was marking his old friend and former clubmate, Gerald O'Sullivan, one of the New York Polo Grounds All-Ireland heroes. So there I was, standing behind this powerful, huge man (6 foot 4 inches, carrying 12 stone 7 pounds), as he fielded and cleared every ball that dropped from the clouds in our square. We lost the battle but on that game alone the big man from Muckross left a lasting

I captained Killarney Technical to County Championship victory in 1959 following my three years in St Brendan's College. *Back row (l–r):* Pa Mannix, Johnny Healy, Donal 'Sox' Lynch, Dan Herlihy, Matt Leahy and Michael Greaney; *middle row (l–r):* Sean Russell, Dermot Doyle, James King, Kevin Coleman, Gerald Cullinane, Florry O'Donoghue, Sylvester O'Grady and John Joe Bambury; *front row (l–r):* Sean 'Nip' O'Connor, Barry Horgan, Weeshie, Mickey Cronin, Paudie Doolan and Jerry O'Leary.

impression on me. As the full-time whistle sounded, Jerome O'Shea and Gerald O'Sullivan approached Donie Murphy and, in a beautiful gesture, threw their arms around him and whispered a few encouraging words in his ear. It was his last game in Kerry. He later took up employment in Wicklow and played with their Juniors. He also became chairman of the

Na Gael Club there. We would not meet again until 2009, thirty-three long years later.

Back to the shining year of 1955. On Sunday 11 September, before a record attendance of 71,504, Kerry met Cavan for a Croke Park semi-final replay. On the same day at the very same venue, Dublin took on Mayo, also in a replay. Three weeks before Kerry had been extremely fortunate to draw with Cavan. It was during that Cavan game that Tadghie Lyne scored the goal he remembered as probably not the greatest, but certainly the most important he had ever scored for Kerry.

Tadghie recalled that magic moment for me during the only interview he has ever given, shortly before his death: 'Peter O'Donoghue of Cavan was a deadly kicker of points. He had Cavan ahead with five minutes left and they were all over us. Then, in a rare breakaway, Johnny Culloty [playing his first Senior game in Croke Park] crossed a high ball, I got my fist to it and it landed in the net. We were now two points ahead against the run of play. They finished very strong and Keys scored for them to draw the match.' The game finished 2-10 to 1-13. Mick Murphy raised the second green flag that day for the Kingdom.

Tadhgie then told me about the replay that took place three weeks later. 'We were flying for that game. Dr Eamonn was bringing us on nicely and very few fancied us that year because Meath had hammered us the year before.' Roles were reversed in that replay as the two Killarney men combined to goal at the Railway End in Croke Park. Tadghie centred and Culloty rose high in the Cavan goalmouth to fist the ball to the net. John Joe Sheehan and Mick Murphy, with a brace, were the other goalscorers for the winners that day. Kerry were through to the final, winning 4-7 to 0-5, where Dublin awaited following a one-point win over Mayo.

The huge build-up to that match in September 1955 when Dublin were squaring up to face Kerry was, in my opinion, the

All-Ireland winning Kerry captains Johnny Culloty (1969), *on the left* and Donie O'Sullivan (1970), *on the right*, with 'Small Jer' O'Leary *(centre)*. O'Leary was a Killarney Dr Crokes man who played a huge part in Kerry GAA affairs in the 1920s and 1930s and was involved in the purchasing of Jones Road, now Croke Park. He lived on Main Street in Killarney and often talked to us about great games and players – I would listen in fascination to this marvellous historian. He died in 1974.

first time the Irish public had witnessed the kind of hype and media attention that have become commonplace today. We had no television back then and Michael O'Hehir was the king of the GAA airways. His contribution to the growth of the GAA was massive, just as Michael Ó Muircheartaigh's is today.

It was a lovely touch by Croke Park to name the superb media centre there in O'Hehir's name following his death. Both men, whom I have had the privilege of knowing, are irreplaceable and their commentaries on games were always compulsive listening. The press also had some wonderful scribes during this period and their writings certainly left a great legacy of this and other finals: men such as Mick Dunne, Pádraig Puirséal, John D. Hickey, Pato (Paddy) Mehigan, Paddy Downey, and the one and only Seán Óg Ó Ceallacháin, whose Sunday RTÉ radio programme, *Gaelic Sports Results*, is the longest running sports show in the world of radio. (I was fortunate to interview Seán Óg in Croke Park in 2009 in a fascinating hour-long record of his exemplary life and times.) And, of course, *The Kerryman* newspaper covered the build-up and homecoming superbly.

Perhaps it was because it was my first All-Ireland final, but never again during the following decades would I experience a magic such as I felt that day in Dublin with my dear departed friends. I will never forget savouring the atmosphere in the capital as, completely overawed, we strolled up and down O'Connell Street on the morning before the match, meeting friends and mixing with the massive crowds milling outside the Gresham Hotel. And how can I forget the white horse ridden by a young Dublin supporter dressed in the blue of the city, as he trotted down O'Connell Street and led hundreds of chanting and dancing Dublin fans, thus adding to the magic of the day?

The morning was bright and clear. The early arrivals on the ghost trains from the peninsulas of Kerry had helped to fill the city and the churches were packed for Sunday morning mass. Following a breakfast of rashers, eggs and black pudding, it was off to Croke Park. We were at the stadium for 11 a.m.; the sideline accommodation was quickly occupied and the gates were closed at 11.30 a.m. The Kerry people were first to take up the best vantage points. Supporters had even climbed onto the roofs of the stands, yet there were few, if any, incidents. Others gained entrance by climbing a ladder at the Railway End. Many years later when I befriended Renault supremo and author of *Penny Apples*, Bill Cullen, he informed me that he had been the youth charging Kerry supporters to gain entry via the ladder. Believe it or not, a great friend of mine, the late Sylvester O'Donoghue (his father was one of Killarney's last blacksmiths) told me that as he was nearing the top of that ladder he froze with fear when he looked down at the drop to the ground. However, when he tried to go back the way he had come, he was also charged for the return journey! When I questioned Bill Cullen, he denied this, saying, 'Never would I take unfair advantage of a Kerryman!'

I will never forget my astonishment at my first view of that pitch – the sheer size of it and the stunning green of the grass. I had never seen such beauty before and from that single moment, as a fourteen-year-old boy, I swore that someday I would play on that magnificent green sward. As we watched Dublin beat Tipperary in the Minor final, the vast streams of people entering the grounds increased in volume and, by the time that the Minor game was over, the stands and terraces were filled to overflowing. I maintain that this was the very first time Dublin supporters claimed the Railway End as their own; it was a virtual sea of blue and white, though not as colourful as it has been in recent years with the fashion for supporters' jerseys and flags.

It was truly a memorable final, with Kerry up against a so-called 'unbeatable' Dublin machine that included Danno Mahoney, Mick Moylan, Dessie 'Snichie' Ferguson, Nicky Maher, Ollie Freeney and Kevin Heffernan (who would, in later years, go on to become an outstanding trainer of Dublin's winning All-Ireland teams). The hour of the match was dramatic and tense in the extreme; supporters from both sides were emotionally involved in the theatre unfolding before them to an extent that I have never again witnessed.

During the last five minutes of play the tension was so fraught and seemingly physical that you imagined you could reach down to the pitch and touch it.

Dublin were six points behind as Ollie Freeney stepped up to hammer a 14-yard free to the Kerry net. Now there were just those three points in the difference. And then Jerome O'Shea wrote himself into Kerry folklore with two soaring catches under his own crossbar. Every year since then an inch has been added to the height of those catches that saved the Kingdom. Ned Roche, Mixi Palmer, Tom Moriarty, John Cronin – the giant of a man from Milltown where the world bodhrán festival is now held – and Sean Murphy were magnificent, as they constantly repulsed the waves of Dublin attacks that pounded the Kerry rearguard in those closing minutes. It is during times like this that the secret of Kerry is handed down to all of those fortunate enough to be present. Kerry won that final, 0-12 to 1-6.

There were many changes to the Kerry teams during the five games it took to win that All-Ireland, including, of course, the replay against Cavan. The final line-out was as follows: Garry O'Mahoney, Jerome O'Shea, Ned Roche, Mixi Palmer, Sean Murphy, John Cronin, Tom Moriarty, John Dowling (captain, 0-1), Dinny O'Shea, Paudie Sheehy (0-1), Tom Costello, Tadghie Lyne (0-6), Johnny Culloty, Mick Murphy (0-1) and Jim Brosnan (0-2). The subs were John Joe Sheehan (0-1, on for Tom Moriarty who was injured after ten minutes), Bobby Buckley, Gerald O'Sullivan, Colm Kennelly and Dan McAuliffe. Other players who helped in that campaign, both as players and panel members, but did not receive All-Ireland medals were: Ned Fitzgerald, Donal 'Marcus' O'Neill, Donie Murphy, Tom Spillane, Dermot Dillon and Pop Fitzgerald.

There are a multitude of great stories – some true and some unfounded – surrounding that memorable win. Dr Jim Brosnan scored two priceless points in the second half and it was the one and only championship game he played for his county that year. He was studying in New York and had only arrived home the Wednesday before the final. It was a lucky day for Kerry that he made it, because his strong, powerful, bustling style completely upset the Dublin defence. Jim Brosnan was the man who began the highly successful Kerry county leagues while chairman of the board. His father was the legendary Con Brosnan who captained Kerry to All-Ireland victory in 1931 and who trained the all-conquering three-in-a-row sides of 1939, 1940 and 1941. I spent a captivating hour one Sunday morning at his home in Dingle in 2008. The previous evening Páidí Ó Sé had honoured the retired doctor, handing him an Irish Hall of Fame award in conjunction with Páidí's renowned football weekend back in Ventry, an event where teams from all over the country gather for a joyful two days of football and fun.

Ned Roche was the towering full back for Kerry that day in September 1955 – and the man who curbed the genius of Kevin Heffernan. One evening some years ago, on my way home from a Kerry Under-21 win in the Gaelic Grounds, Limerick, I stopped off at Eddie Walsh's pub in Knocknagoshel, in north Kerry. Eddie's son Eamon and family had organised an evening of celebration to honour Eddie and Ned, both All-Ireland winners and both from the village. The place was packed and the stories were flying. It was one of those unforgettable Kerry evenings where football is the one and only topic. The late Garry McMahon, perched precariously on a tall bar stool, brought down the house with his superb rendering of Kerry's 1955 All-Ireland victory song, written by his father Brian. I cornered Ned Roche late into the night and asked the question that had bothered me and thousands of Kerry people for decades. 'So what were the instructions Dr Eamonn O'Sullivan gave you that day before you left the dressing room to face Kevin Heffernan?' I enquired. Ned paused for a while, studied me closely before speaking, and then replied, 'I will never divulge what the

Doctor said to me that day and I will bring those instructions to my grave.' His answer was short and sweet, but in many ways it just added to the mystique of that day which is continuously spoken of when great games are discussed. Ned joined the army in 1949 and played with Tipperary while stationed there, as did his brother Denis. He declared for his native county in 1953 and played full back in the win over Armagh. And yes, he did bring that secret to his grave.

It was also a memorable day for Kerry captain John Dowling, one of the most wholehearted and committed footballers that ever donned the green and gold. No man deserved the honour more than the Kerins O'Rahillys midfield colossus, especially following the despair of captaining the team to its dismal loss against Meath the previous year. John was a larger than life figure and football was a passion with him. I befriended him following his retirement from the game and he was a wonderful conversationalist. He told me a little about that year of 1955; in the same season he had opened his own shoe shop in Tralee and was unable to attend the daily training sessions in Killarney, although continuing to be ever-present each evening. 'I was in great shape.' he said. 'My clubmate Dinny O'Shea and myself did reasonably at midfield, and scoring a point from over 50 yards out was one of my greatest memories.' I had heard stories of John leading out the team for the game, only to discover that there was no team behind him. So was it true? 'Yes, that did happen. When I ran out into that wall of sound I looked back to the lads but I was out on the pitch all on my own as the rest of the team were held up in the old timber dressing rooms, as a door had locked or something,' John Dowling recalled. 'A friend of mine, John Savage, was sitting on the sideline so I went over to him and sat on the grass alongside him and we chatted for a few minutes about home until the rest of the lads appeared.'

The homecoming of that 1955 Kerry side was one of the most celebrated ever. Bonfires blazed along the Kerry hills and in Rathmore, Killarney and Tralee, as the bangers on the railway lines signalled the return of John Dowling and the Sam Maguire Cup. It was not only on the field of play, however, that John Dowling demonstrated his magnificent fighting abilities and utter bravery against all the odds. At the age of fifty he was diagnosed with a form of cancer that would necessitate many days of treatment and spells in hospital during the following eighteen years.

During those years his pride in six daughters and their exploits at basketball while representing their county and country gave him immense comfort and happiness. I would meet John regularly all over the country as he followed basketball and all football competitions, especially his club and all the Kerry schools. And he would launch into wonderful lengthy talks about the young players in Kerins O'Rahillys, the Kerry team and the styles of football being played. Daughter Bernice has wonderful memories of their dad and his bravery and continued football obsession during his final years. 'He would have to go into hospital at various times for rest and treatment but this never stopped him from going to see Kerins O'Rahillys and Kerry playing,' she recalled. 'On a number of occasions when he was refused permission to leave hospital for the day he would wait for the opportunity and when the coast was clear he was off and the nurses would be frantic looking for him. He was a wonderful father and we were, and of course still are, so proud of him. And to this day we are always introduced as John Dowling's daughters.'

Jerome O'Shea confessed to me during one interview that this 1955 win was one of the most significant in the history of the county. He himself became the first Cahersiveen man to play in a final and win a medal. He had been a sub in 1953. He made a very relevant point in relation to the enormity of the victory. 'What would have happened if we had lost? Remember we had been beaten the previous year by

Meath and the following three years we suffered crushing defeats to Cork, Waterford and Derry. Would Kerry football have recovered without the impetuous of that glorious defeat of Dublin?' Again, here, we wonder at the beauty and secret of Kerry football.

5

1956: I see my first defeat of a Kerry team

It is February 1991 and I am waking up in a haze of confusion and pain without the slightest idea where I am. I am just after leaving the recovery room in the Bons Secours Hospital, Cork city, and have been returned to my four-bed ward where I was prepared for a hip replacement operation, hours before. Years of savage training, pounding roads and playing basketball on poor surfaces while wearing completely unsuitable footwear, had left me with a seriously arthritic hip. There were only two options: to have a hip replacement or to put up with the excruciating pain of arthritis day after day. Thankfully the operation was a complete success; so successful, in fact, that five years later the second hip would receive the same treatment.

And so I am coming round from the heavy anaesthetic when suddenly, out of the fog in my head, I hear a voice asking, 'So you're Weeshie Fogarty from Kerry, the nurse tells me, and you're stuck in the football down there?' Slowly opening my eyes and beginning to recover my senses, I peer at the man in the bed alongside me. He is sitting up, wearing

This is the first Kerry team I ever saw losing. This side drew with Cork in 1956 and lost the subsequent replay in Killarney. *Back row (l–r):* John Cronin, Tim 'Tiger' Lyons, Mick O'Connell, John Dowling, Tom Moriarty, Ned Roche, Sean Murphy and Tadghie Lyne; *front row (l–r):* Colm Kennelly, Tom Long, Donal 'Marcus' O'Neill, Jerome O'Shea, Paudie Sheehy, Dan McAuliffe and Jim Brosnan. This game will be remembered for the championship debuts of Mick O'Connell and Tom Long, two of Kerry's greatest ever player.

glasses, and reading the *Cork Examiner*. 'Nice to meet you,' he adds. 'My name is Niall Fitzgerald and I'm from Cork.'

Immediately alarm bells begin to ring in my confused brain. I feel that I recognise this person from somewhere and, gathering my thoughts, I reply, 'Are you Niall Fitzgerald, the Cork footballer?' He answers with a little chuckle, 'That's me.' And now I ask the question that set the alarm off in the first place: 'Don't tell me you're the same Niall Fitzgerald that kicked the winning point against Kerry in that replayed Munster final in Killarney in 1956?' 'That's me,' he says, 'the very man.' Here I was, thirty-five years after the event, talking to the very person who had caused one of my major boyhood traumas – the first time in my life that I ever saw a Kerry team defeated on the field of play. The very man who had scored the point that knocked the Kingdom out of the 1956 championship.

Niall and I became great friends during our stay in the Bons. He was also recovering from a hip replacement operation and we talked and discussed Kerry and Cork football long into the night, after the lights of the ward had long been dimmed. I celebrated my fiftieth birthday during that period in hospital. One night myself, Niall and the other two men who shared the ward polished off a bottle of brandy; the sing-song that ensued was quickly silenced when

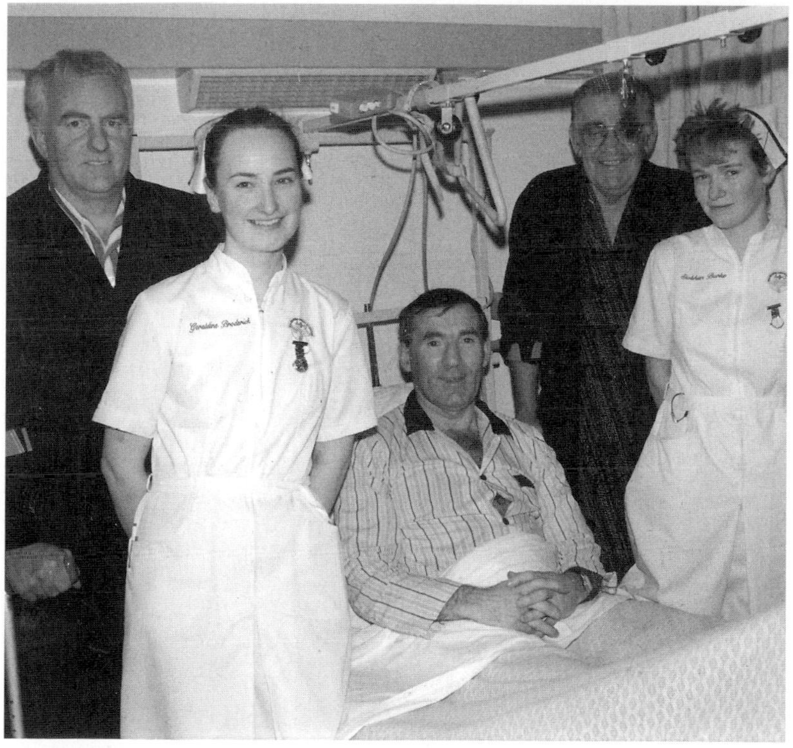

In February 1991, while I was in the Bons Secours Hospital, Cork, for a hip replacement operation, I befriended Niall Fitzgerald, the Corkman who scored the winning point against Kerry during the Munster final replay of 1956 in Killarney, *(l–r):* Johnny McNamara (Blarney), Nurse Geraldine Broderick (Kerry), Weeshie, Niall Fitzgerald, Nurse Siobhan Burke (Kerry). That was the very first time I saw Kerry lose a championship match (*courtesy Tommy Regan*).

the night matron burst in the door, declaring us a disgrace to Cork. I enjoyed that . . . no mention of Kerry!

I was just sixteen years of age in 1956 and my father shipped myself and brother Geni off to the luxurious Parknasilla Hotel just outside Sneem where he had arranged summer work for us both. It was fairly tough going and only the best was expected from you in this five-star luxury retreat, which later became the holiday destination of An Taoiseach Bertie Ahern. I was assigned to the silver pantry where my boss was a Louth man by the name of Harry Levans. It was a small room, but one of the busiest centres of the hotel. Here, morning and evening following breakfast and silver-service dinner, I spent hours washing and shining the silver-plated cutlery, tea and coffee pots, sugar bowls, salt and pepper shakers and anything else that Harry considered to contain even the tiniest morsel of silver. He inspected everything before close of business, and woe to me if there was even a slight blemish on his beloved ware.

It was a great learning process but football was always somewhere in the background. There was a small, very sloping field near the hotel where the staff would spend hours of their time off catching and kicking in all kinds of weather. We even had one lad, a goalkeeper and hall porter, who boasted that he had played League of Ireland soccer for Transport, then in Division 1. Nearby Sneem had a team in the Murphy Cup and, even though I was small and light, I togged out and played corner forward under an assumed name (Paddy Downey) whenever they were short.

Back home in Killarney the Monastery school were playing in a summer league in east Kerry and my late, great friend Michael 'Hawker' O'Grady would write to me and let me know when the games were on: usually a Thursday evening in Fitzgerald Stadium. His were the very first letters I ever received. I would then think up some lame excuse to get off work for the evening and transport back to Killarney would be provided by the van man delivering the *Evening Echo* around the Ring of Kerry. I would spend the night at home and the following morning it was up at the crack of dawn to get the mail van back to Parknasilla. Even then football came first, the job second. Then it was July 1956 and the word came through: Kerry and Cork had drawn in the Munster final in the Cork Athletic Grounds, 2-2 to 0-8. I had tried all in my power to get off and go to the match but my father had put his foot down. Money at that time was as scarce as hens' teeth, so I was condemned to work and my first expedition outside the county had to be put on hold. But *The Kerryman* newspaper was eagerly awaited the following week. After walking the few miles into Sneem's only paper shop, the newspaper was scanned (as is still my habit today) back to front, starting with the sports page. The sports reporter P. F. pulled no punches. Kerry had played abysmally and, for the first time in their history, had failed to register even one point in the opening half, going back to the dressing room 0-6 to 0-0 in arrears.

'Marcus' O'Neill had replaced Garry O'Mahoney in goal from the first-round win over Tipperary (3-7 to 3-2) and John Cronin, who had been centre back in the 1955 win over Dublin, was now lining out at full forward. In the second half O'Neill played a blinder against Cork, bringing off a series of magnificent saves to deny the rampant home side. Dinny O'Shea scored a goal but, with seconds remaining, Cork were still ahead 0-8 to 1-2. Then Jim Brosnan gained possession around the halfway line and set off on a blistering solo run, beating a series of tackles and, from 30 yards out, he unleashed a bullet of a ground shot. Before Paddy Tyers in the Cork goal could move, the ball had rebounded from the stanchion supporting the net back out the field. It was a sensational goal and as dramatic an ending to a Munster final as was ever seen. Cork would travel to Killarney two weeks later for the replay and I would be there.

Mick O'Connell has vivid memories of that dramatic drawn game:

> That final was the first of what might be termed my 'big' games. As a midfield assistant to the well-established John Dowling, we were up against Eric Ryan and Sean Moore. This pair was the mainstay of Cork's National League win earlier that year. Moore was also a well-known athlete and a short time afterwards had his career prematurely ended due to a road accident. The first high ball that came in my direction I jumped for and fielded beautifully, I thought. But before planting myself on the ground to complete the job I was flattened. Not by any of the Corkmen, mind you, only the mighty strong Dowling himself. That collision took the wind completely out of my sails and my game was subdued thereafter. Cork were on top everywhere but could not translate this into scores. Jim Brosnan's late goal saved us and also saved my bacon because just prior to it the selectors were discussing my replacement. Anyway I was granted a reprieve and was selected for the replay in Killarney in a new position, right half forward.

I was determined to be at the replay come hell or high water, and applied for and was granted a day off work. A series of thumbed lifts had me outside Fitzgerald Stadium in good time. It was a special occasion for a number of reasons. Tom Collins, a great servant of Kerry hurling and football, entered the GAA record books that day when he participated in three Munster finals. First he helped Kerry defeat Waterford in the Junior football final, 4-10 to 1-4. Then he was outstanding as the Kerry Junior hurlers beat Waterford 6-7 to 0-3, and finally he was introduced as a sub during the second of the Senior finals. A remarkable achievement by one man all in the one afternoon. I also have vivid memories of Mick O'Dwyer playing in his bare feet for the Junior footballers; he had made his inter-county debut against Tipperary in Thurles at centre forward some weeks previously. It was my first time seeing O'Dwyer in a Kerry jersey. He will probably be remembered mostly as one of the greatest GAA managers of all time, but for me Mick was first and foremost one of the best players ever to don a Kerry jersey. In a Senior championship football career that lasted from 1957 to 1973, excluding league and challenge games, he made forty appearances and scored 6 goals and 130 points. I had the privilege of playing with him and against him.

The terrace was black with supporters as Cork and Kerry battled it out in the thrilling replay. John Cronin's goal kept Kerry in touch and, entering the closing second, the sides were deadlocked at 1-7 each; it appeared we were heading for extra time. I was situated high on the boundary wall at the entrance goal and I had the perfect view of the drama that unfolded in those closing seconds. The man at the centre of that final dramatic passage of play was Niall Fitzgerald. Years later, when I met him in the hospital, he explained to me exactly what had happened that day. 'I ran on to a pass in the middle of the field and I just took off in a solo run towards the goal. A number of Kerry defenders came in with tackles but I kept the head down and kept going. I must have been about 25 yards out from the goal and I just had a go for a point and it sailed over. And let me tell you, Weeshie, I have got more mileage out of the point over the years, and every time I tell the story I kick the point from farther out.'

The full-time whistle went immediately and Cork were through to the All-Ireland semi-final on the score 1-8 to 1-7. I had seen Kerry beaten for the first time in my life. Cork stars included Johnny Creedon, Dan Murray, Eric Ryan, Tom Furlong and full back 'Big' Donal O'Sullivan; Cork went on to lose to Galway in the final, 2-13 to 3-7. The Kerry team was: Donal 'Marcus' O'Neill, Jerome O'Shea, Ned Roche, Tim 'Tiger' Lyons, Sean Murphy, Tom Long, Colm Kennelly, John Dowling, Dinny O'Shea, Mick O'Connell, Bobby Buckley, Tadghie Lyne, Jim Brosnan, John Cronin and Paudie Sheehy. The subs were: Tom Moriarty (on), Tom Collins (on), Mick Murphy (on), Dan McAuliffe, Sean Lovett, Tom Costello, Gerald O'Sullivan and Tim Barrett. The Kerry selectors that year were: Jackie Lyne, John Joe Sheehy, Fr Curtin, Johnny Walsh and Bob Stack.

Kerry full forward Tom Long (Number 14) in action against Cork in the Munster final in Fitzgerald Stadium, Killarney, in 1963. Mick O'Dwyer is the other Kerry player in picture and Kerry won the final, 1-18 to 3-7. Note the massive crowd on the terrace and the spectators sitting high up on the boundary wall. Health and safety was unheard of and I never recall an accident occurring. Tom Long, a retired teacher, lives in Killarney and I did a lengthy interview with him about his life and times that won a McNamee GAA National Award in 2005.

6

Ronnie Delany and Timmy O'Leary: stars in the firmament

It all began for me with a simple phone call one evening some years ago. Paudie O'Shea was on the line. 'Weeshie, any chance you could attend the launch of my football tournament in the Burlington in two weeks' time?' I had always found the Kerry great a very easy man to deal with, both as a player and as trainer of the Kerry team, and he never failed to stand for an interview – to refuse him a turn would be out of the question. And then he added, 'You might get some great interviews on the night and one man who will be there is Ronnie Delany.' I must admit my heart skipped a beat when the name Ronnie Delany was mentioned in the same breath as the possibility that I might even meet him. Straight away Paudie got his reply, 'Count me in, I will be in the Burlington for your launch.'

And so it came about. The foyer of the Burlington was packed with celebrities on the night of the launch and there in the middle of the crowd was the unmistakable figure of my boyhood hero, Ronnie Delany. Tall, slight of build, impeccably dressed in a light blue suit, shirt and tie, the hair now greying;

but there was a unique freshness about him, typical of a great athlete who had not abused the body with the demon drink and junk food. Seeing him in the flesh for the first time, my mind raced back to the early morning of 1 December 1956.

It was a completely different world back then: an era of mass emigration and frugal living. Television was unknown and the great sporting events of the world (and, indeed, those at home) came to us courtesy of our radios – that is when we were lucky enough to get coverage at all. We had an old Bush radio perched at head height in the kitchen of our home at 40 New Street, Killarney, and it was on that radio that my brother Geni and I listened to Ronnie Delany achieve what is accepted as Ireland's greatest ever sporting victory. That crackling race commentary from the Melbourne Olympics on the other side of the world will forever remain one of my fondest sporting memories. Absolutely unforgettable the closing moments of that race, as the English commentator's voice rose to fever pitch and two little boys in a small Killarney kitchen began to jump for joy. It was the first time in our lives that we had heard of an Irish person winning a world event.

'And it's Delany, Delany of Ireland is going to win the gold, Richtzenhain of Germany will be second, John Landy of Australia will take the bronze and finishing fourth out of the medals is our own Ian Boyd of Great Britain.' And then the commentator told his listening public something quite extraordinary. 'And Delany is kneeling down on the track just past the finishing line, he is blessing himself as the other runners crowd around him offering their congratulations to the Irishman and new Olympic champion, Ronnie Delany.' Even in his greatest moment Delany offered his thanks in prayer.

Now I approached him in the Burlington and excused myself for interrupting, as he was in conversation. His response to my approach was to say how glad he was to meet someone from Radio Kerry sports. (I have always found that when you mention the words 'Kerry sports' to any personality it opens up many doors.) Ronnie Delany is the supreme gentleman and, despite the fact that he must be inundated with requests for interviews, he immediately replied that he would be delighted to talk to me. Nevertheless he did add, 'We better do it now, because I will be leaving immediately after the launch takes place.'

I sought out a quiet corner and there, in his low, gentle voice, he brought me back to that memorable day in Melbourne when he wrote himself into history's sporting pages. Delany had been studying at Villanova University in America at the time and some Irish Olympic officials perceived the 'collegiate champion' as a type of professional sportsman who was effectively being paid for running in America. Remember this was 1956, everything was utterly different, and even the fact that he had taken up the scholarship at all was frowned upon by many of the old guard in Ireland. When it came to deciding who would represent Ireland in Melbourne, Ronnie was selected by just one vote. However, he told me that if the vote had been split he was confident that Lord Killanin, President of the International Olympic Committee, would have made the final decision and given him the go ahead. Nevertheless all this is now pure speculation. The rest is history.

People continued to crowd around us in our supposedly quiet corner of the Burlington, all just wanting a chance to meet this icon of Irish sport, and it was an effort to steer the conversation back to 1956. He asked after the legendary Caseys of Sneem, that well-known rowing family with whom he was great friends, reminding me also that he had unveiled a bronze statue in the village some years previously to Steve Casey, the world wrestling champion. He spoke about our great runners, Tom O'Riordan of north Kerry and Jerry Kiernan of Listowel, and was particularly interested in the progress of Gillian O'Sullivan, Kerry's first lady Olympian. Gillian was, at the time, the world race-walking record holder. He explained how Paudie O'Shea and he had become great friends and told me that he visited Kerry on a fairly regular basis. He then proceeded to talk all about the great Kerry footballers – and he really knew his GAA history.

Three of the seven legendary Casey brothers from Sneem, County Kerry, *(l–r):* Jim, Tom and Steve. Wrestlers, oarsmen and boxers, their story is one of the most amazing I have ever come across. I was privileged to meet and interview Paddy, the last of the boys, before he died in February 1992, aged ninety-two. Steve retired as undefeated World Wrestling Champion. Christy Riordan (CR Videos) and I travelled to Houston, Texas, USA, in 2008 to meet Jim's wife and she gave us access to the entire family history collection including a priceless interview with Jim, Steve, Paddy, Dan and Jack; old newsreel and video of the boys in action and being interviewed; a large selection of superb black-and-white photographs (which included this one reproduced here) and newspaper articles from the *Boston Globe* and *The New York Times* together with various magazine articles tracing the amazing careers of the seven boys. Myrtle also presented us with a copy of a rare book of the family history. Unfortunately, this book was never published and we were given written permission to reproduce this history some time in the future.

(L–r): Jim, Tom and Steve Casey

I had always heard that Ronnie had never set out to break records, so I put this to him and he told me:

> I was very fortunate to come under the tutelage of the great coach Jumbo Elliott and he improved my style of running greatly. I always had a strict 'run-to-win' attitude. Record-chasing was not my game, which did not go down too well with the American fans; I even hated and detested time trials in training. About a year before the games I really felt I could become an Olympian and six months before the race I ran a four-minute mile in California. I was only the sixth man ever to break the barrier and the youngest ever. I knew then in my heart that I could win a gold medal.

And what about the greatest day of his sporting life? What were his memories? They were crystal clear:

> The day I had lived for dawned bright and warm; it was difficult to remain calm but I tried as best I could. I resigned myself quietly to the will of God and prayed not so much for victory but the grace to run up to my capabilities. I took up the outside position at the start of the race, I was very comfortable because no one was making a break at that early stage and the whole field was bunched together in about 10 yards. At about the 300-yard mark Hewson was taking over the lead from Lincoln. I moved outside and we were in the back straight, so I was losing no ground on the outside. I moved up slowly, still feeling very good; Landy was slightly ahead of me and he was really moving. I got him pretty easy and that put me in fourth position, about 180 yards to go. Then I put the boot down, as we say, and I found that I was surging to the front with very little difficulty. Then I hit the front with 50 yards to go to the tape. I realised that I had the race won; I remember breaking out in a big smile and when I went through the tape I was so delighted I threw my arms in the air. I never felt so happy in all my life.

I asked him about kneeling on the track. 'Yes, Weeshie, I did kneel down and thank God for what I had achieved. It was later I discovered that some commentators had said that I had collapsed with exhaustion; that was not true.'

It was fascinating, indeed riveting, for me to hear this unassuming legend with the quiet voice recall with such great clarity those momentous events of 1956. Listening to him brought back memories of my youth and the excitement this man had generated for the whole country. And when I put it to him that he had lifted the spirits of everyone back home in Ireland with his gold medal win, he replied, 'Yes, that becomes more and more obvious to me as I continue to meet people like yourself who grew up in the mass emigration days of the 1950s; for many my victory was the highlight of their lives at the time.'

And then the interview came to an abrupt end. Without any warning the Artane Boys' Band struck up a welcoming salvo for the Taoiseach, Bertie Ahern, who had just arrived in the hotel, and when the thirty-five members of that renowned band begin playing in a confined space you do not attempt to best them by continuing an interview. We shook hands, I thanked Ronnie Delany for his time, and he disappeared into the milling crowd. I counted myself one lucky individual; Paudie O'Shea's launch had certainly been my lucky day.

Ronnie Delany's 1956 victory had been Ireland's first Olympic gold medal on the track since Bob Tisdall had claimed his own gold in the 400-metre hurdles in 1932. Ronnie retired from athletics following a magnificent career in 1962, at the age of twenty-seven, and returned to live in Dublin where he was later honoured with the freedom of that city in the company of Bob Geldof. (Ronnie was born in Arklow.)

On Kerry's around the world trip in March 1970, following the All-Ireland win of 1969, we played a game in the same Melbourne Stadium that had witnessed Delany's great victory fourteen years previously. I made sure I arrived at the venue well before match time, sought out the caretaker, and he showed me the very home straight that had seen Ronnie's historic finish.

I raced up the stretch and felt the joy of those precious memories of our old Bush radio and that kitchen in New Street, Killarney, flooding joyfully back as the oxygen pumped through my lungs. And I remembered the characteristically simple but beautiful advice that Delany had passed on for younger runners in the course of our interview: 'Seek the guidance of a good coach, train regularly, set high aims. The sky is the limit, don't allow yourself to be rushed and seek to master the art of feeling relaxed when running.'

Little did I think when I took up employment in the Kerry Mineral Water factory on the Muckross Road, Killarney, early in 1960 that I would befriend the man who had scored two goals for Kerry in the dramatic replay of the 1937 All-Ireland final when the Kingdom overcame Cavan.

On my first Friday I went to the factory office to collect my weekly wages in a little brown envelope, following a week delivering drink to the hotels and public houses around Kerry. I was the assistant on the lorry, helping driver Mike Kiely, a great character and GAA enthusiast. My pay packet was handed to me by a dark-skinned man of only about 5 feet 6 inches in height, impeccably dressed in a Persil-white shirt and tie and a sharp, dark navy, double-breasted suit. No words were passed between us, but for some reason or another I was greatly impressed by this individual. The pay packet, by the way, was handed to my mother that evening and she returned a few bob to me for the week. That was the way it was in our family: we gave our pay to our mother for the upkeep of the entire family.

The following Monday, as we faced our delivery lorry for north Kerry, I mentioned my meeting to Mike and immediately he responded, 'That is my good friend the great Kerry footballer Timmy O'Leary, one of the greatest small men ever to wear the green and gold of the Kingdom.' I quickly became friends with Timmy and the fact that he was a member of my own club, Killarney Legion, made it very easy for me to engage in conversation with this unassuming and, indeed, very private person. Slow to discuss his career, his was a reticence born out of shyness and a feeling that he had not done enough to be talking about. A trait, I should add, that is common to most Kerry greats.

Many years later, while researching the history of my club for a book entitled *A Legion Of Memories* (which went on to win a McNamee award as best club history in 1979), I had the privilege and good fortune to sit with Timmy O'Leary again and hear his own account of his life and times. His was a short but magnificent football career, largely forgotten and untold in a county where football legends appear on the horizon decade after decade. Four All-Ireland Minor appearances in a row and three wins in 1931, 1932 and 1933 marked the debut of his glittering career. In 1933 he had the distinction of captaining the winning Minor side. That same team became the first to receive All-Ireland medals, a new innovation at the time.

Timmy O'Leary *(right)* with Johnny Walsh *(centre)* and Danno Keeffe *(left)*. I became friends with Timmy, an All-Ireland medal winner in 1937 and 1939 and a member of my own club, when we worked in the Kerry Mineral Water factory, Killarney, in the early 1960s. He was only 5 foot 6 inches in height but that didn't stop him from being a brilliant scoring forward who scored 4-1 in one league game for Kerry.

Timmy grew up in the town of Killarney. Mangerton View is situated just off Lewis Road and just a good drop kick from Fitzgerald Stadium. Football was his life and he had as a next-door neighbour one of the greatest Kerry footballers of all, Paul Russell. Paul had won six All-Ireland Senior medals, his first in 1923 when only eighteen years of age and, amazingly, lining out for his county for the first time. He was a student at St Brendan's College at the time, and it is said that the great Dick Fitzgerald had to get special permission from the college to release the student for the final.

Russell had a huge influence on the young O'Leary, as Timmy recalled for me in that interview a year before his death. 'Paul was finishing up at about the time I was beginning to play,' he told me. 'He spent a lot of time training us and we picked up so many skills from him, kicking around the terrace in front of our houses and also in the cricket field.' The cricket field was situated on the Muckross Road, Killarney, and the River Flesk ran beside it. In the early 1920s and 1930s all local and inter-county games were played there. As a youngster Timmy admitted to being a bit overawed at times by the great Russell, who later went on to train winning Kerry sides with his friend Dr Eamonn O'Sullivan.

Football was the only sport in the town as Timmy was growing up and he was surrounded by legends, as he explained to me. 'I knew the great Dick Fitzgerald and remember him kicking around in the cricket field and indeed it was he who advised me to move from the wing forward position to the corner.' Timmy went to school in the local Presentation Monastery and here he really began to blossom. 'I captained the Mon to win the Dunloe Cup, which included all the Kerry colleges. This has never been achieved since and a young teacher, Brother Avaloin, was the man responsible for that historic win.

Recalling his first All-Ireland final in 1937, he spoke of his teammate the great Purty Landers and his words to

Timmy as he ran on to the field at Croke Park: 'It's just another match, Tim, and when you get the first ball you will think that you are back in Killarney with all your young friends.' Then Timmy added, 'How right he was – and I was fortunate to score two goals in that game.' Timmy played again in 1938 when Galway were the winners 2-4 to 0-7 following a draw in the first game. He captured his second Celtic Cross the following year as a sub when Meath were defeated 2-5 to 2-3. Sadly, ill health was beginning to blight his wonderful goalscoring skills.

He travelled to America in 1939 with the Kerry team, but was unable to play due to that illness, and he told me of his great joy when they visited Michigan and he was reunited with his cousins Liam and 'Congo' O'Leary and his sister, uncles and aunts. 'Only for football I would never have travelled and met my family I loved so much.' He was one of the Legion's greatest ever players and one of their top goalscoring forwards of all time. He also played in an All-Ireland Junior final in 1934 and in a league game against Offaly in 1937 when, at the height of his powers, he scored four goals from play.

Timmy O'Leary is seldom mentioned in the great pantheon of Kerry footballers, nevertheless his record and goalscoring abilities can stand with many of his Kerry peers. When he answered that final whistle in 1978, a massive crowd attended his funeral and two of Kerry's greatest sons, Joe Keohane and Jackie Lyne, led the guard of honour as he was brought to his final resting place. I feel greatly privileged to have known this superb footballer and it is he and many like him whose legacy continue to inspire generations of young Kerry footballers. He was a wonderful footballer but above all I will forever remember Timmy O'Leary as a true gentleman.

7

Down dazzle the Kindom in 1960 and 1961

Despite the bitter disappointment of defeat by Cork in the Munster Minor final of 1959, my fascination and obsession with Kerry football continued to grow. Kerry, captained by Mick O'Connell, faced Galway in that year's All-Ireland final and, together with some boyhood friends, I secured tickets from our club and headed for Dublin on the legendary ghost train, which left Killarney at midnight on the Saturday night. The station was a heaving mass of humanity. Many of the Kerry supporters present were in high spirits, having spent the previous few hours in the local pubs. Teddy O'Connor's, the Park Place Hotel and Jack C. O'Shea's in High Street, Charlie Foley's in New Street, Christy McSweeney's, Jimmy O'Brien's, Murphy's and the Arbutus Hotel in College Street were all big GAA gathering houses.

No flags, jerseys, banners to be seen back then. The only Kerry colours available were the green and gold paper caps and maybe a two-penny badge sold by Killarney town bell man, Pats Coffey. It was a common sight following a rainy day to see supporters whose faces were streaked with the

In 1958, I was in Croke Park to see Derry beat Kerry in the All-Ireland semi-final. Mick O'Connell *(left)* and Jim McKeever, Derry, *(right)*, two of the game's greatest ever midfielders, opposed each other for the first time that day. Over fifty years later, I was greatly privileged and a little overawed as they sat before me as my guests on *Terrace Talk* on Radio Kerry. It was a memorable programme broadcast from Caitin's Pub in Kells, Cahersiveen. *(courtesy CR Videos & DVD Productions)*

Kerry colours as the dye from those paper hats ran down their necks and faces. Practically all the men were dressed in their Sunday suits, shirts and ties. Jeans were not yet in vogue and tracksuit tops and the various items of Kerry GAA attire were a fashion to come in another generation. The trains were usually packed. Each carriage would seat about ten people and I have vivid memories of seeing youngsters sound asleep on the baggage racks overhead. As the old steam engine huffed and puffed out of the station, the pack of cards would be produced, somebody's overcoat spread across the knees of the occupants to act as a table, and a game of Thirty-one would begin. All kinds of sandwiches packed in shoe boxes would appear as the miles sped by. Big lumps of pig's head and crubeens were highly popular, especially after the few pints of porter. I recall big Cidona bottles that were passed around and contained beautiful, dark, draught Guinness. The sound of music as a box player warmed up would lift the spirits and by the time the train had left Mallow mighty sing-songs were to be heard all along the corridor.

Towns and villages flashed by in the pitch darkness as the men and women from all corners of Kerry discussed the big match. Just as today, all the great players of days gone by would be recalled with huge reverence. Great games, memorable scores, and tales of previous journeys helped shorten the trip. Hours into the journey heads would begin to nod and loud snoring would reverberate around the carriages as everyone attempted to find the most comfortable position – not an easy task. And of course the train would stop, for one reason or another, at every station along the way. Finally, around 6 a.m., Heuston station would be reached. First stop was some church along the Liffey for mass, where many a supporter could be seen fast asleep, and then a big breakfast in the first café found open for business.

That day of 1959 we were queuing outside Croke Park among massive crowds for 12 p.m. Dublin beat Cavan in the Minor final and little did I realise as I watched this curtain raiser that fifty years later I would become friendly with the corner forward on that losing Cavan team. Kevin McCormack was, I recall, a lovely nippy corner forward that day and caused the Dublin defence plenty of worry. And now, please fast forward to my home town of Killarney and the summer of 2011. I fall into conversation with a street musician sitting on the sidewalk outside Reidy's century-old pub in Main Street. He is playing a variety of musical instruments, dressed in a vivid red jumpsuit and sporting a long, flowing, snow-white beard. He recognises my voice from my Radio Kerry sports programmes and football quickly becomes the main topic of conversation. I subsequently learn that he is the same Kevin McCormack who I had seen play in Croke Park all those years ago. He had fallen into hard times, taken to the road, and was now one of the few remaining true street musicians. We have since become great friends and when the summer ends in Killarney Kevin heads for Spain or some other sunny clime where he can entertain and make a few pounds. A true gentleman, his life story can always kick-start a fascinating conversation.

Kerry had an easy win in the Senior final that day, defeating Galway 3-7 to 1-4. Around 86,000 supporters were in attendance and Mick O'Dwyer, one of the greatest players I have seen, won his first All-Ireland medal. The story of Captain Mick O'Connell and the 'forgotten cup' is still told to this day. Mick had suffered a knee injury during the game as he contested a high ball with Frank Evers. He was substituted and Moss O'Connell, who later joined the priesthood, replaced him. As tradition had it then, following the presentation of the Sam Maguire Mick was shouldered across Croke Park by a huge mass of jubilant supporters. Between shaking hands, slaps on the back, shouting and cheering, the cup was lost from his grasp and disappeared quickly into the crowd. Attending receptions was not a habit of the legendary O'Connell. He changed quickly and, still limping from the badly injured knee, headed for Heuston station and began the long journey home to Valentia Island minus the trophy.

Many hours later in pitch darkness O'Connell rowed his little punt back to his island home and was already well wrapped up in his bed while the celebrations were still in full swing in Dublin. The Sam Maguire Cup had never been brought to south Kerry by a captain from that area, and it seemed as O'Connell was not be the man to change this.

However, the following Wednesday as Mick lay in bed resting his injury, he heard the sound of a band playing and approaching the house. Paddy Murphy had laid on a special late ferry to the island, so that members of the Kerry team who had found the cup could bring it out from the mainland. The Laune Pipers' Band from Killorglin led the parade and the lorry bearing the group of players and the cup. Mick himself then made an appearance at an upstairs window. Mick O'Dwyer, the vice-captain, made a short speech and the celebrations continued long into the night with a dance in the local hall. So the cup had eventually found its way to the home of the greatest midfielder of them all.

Little did we think, following that victory over Galway, that dramatic events awaited this particular team in the years ahead. Down were about to change the whole landscape of the GAA.

Croke Park, 26 September 1960. I was seated high up at the back of the second deck in the old Hogan stand. I was about to witness one of the most momentous games in the history of the GAA. Down seeking their first All-Ireland title would be in opposition to the aristocrats of Gaelic football, Kerry.

The background to the game was simple: the Sam Maguire Cup had never crossed the border into the six counties. Could Down end decades of failure by all the other Northern counties? Sitting next to me on that memorable day was the late Mickey O'Leary, my Killarney Legion clubmate. Both of us had got our tickets from the club treasurer, Pat O'Meara, who was also treasurer of the county board. Mickey had been one of the founder members of our club in 1929 and his knowledge of football was as good as any one I had ever met. His brother Timmy O'Leary had won three All-Ireland Minor medals with Kerry in 1931, 1932 and 1933 and had had the distinction of being captain on one of those occasions; he had also won two Senior medals with the Kingdom. One of

Mickey's sons Jimmy, now resident in Killarney, was a handy club footballer, and in fact earlier in that year of 1960 had captained the Kerry Minor basketball team to All-Ireland victory, defeating Dublin in the final.

The atmosphere in the stadium that day was simply electric, more so than anything I have experienced since. Most followers knew in their heart and soul that there was something special about this side from the North. They had won their first Ulster title the previous year, beating Cavan 2-16 to 0-7, but had failed to beat Galway in the All-Ireland semi-final. Now they were back stronger and cockier than the previous year. So what is the real story behind the amazing rise to glory of the men in red and black? Well, in my opinion it can all be traced to one man, Maurice Hayes, now a senator.

In 2010 Maurice was in Dingle to honour the great Dr Jim Brosnan, and I took the opportunity to chat with him and to draw out of him the secret of that great Down side. I was successful, but only to a degree. Nevertheless it was a fascinating conversation and gave me a wonderful insight into one of the most historic games ever played in the Association. Hayes was, and still is, a bit of a visionary. Back then, in his capacity as the Down county secretary, he persuaded delegates at the 1959 convention to change the system of team selectors and they agreed to the formation of a selection committee that was completely different to anything the county had seen before.

Brian Denvir, Barney Carr and Hayes were appointed as selectors and during their initial meeting after convention they agreed that Carr would become the team manager and Danny Flynn would train the side. It was the first time, to my knowledge, that the word 'manager' had been used in Gaelic football. They were then given a two-year period to 'justify' themselves. Successes beyond even their wildest dreams were to unfold during those years. Then came another master stroke when the leagues and championships in the county were reorganised; some players from very weak clubs were given permission to join the stronger clubs, thus ensuring them competition at a far higher level and intensity.

Hayes then set about guaranteeing that his players would meet some top-class opposition such as Kerry, Galway, Dublin and other stronger counties. I remember well when they played at the opening of the Frank Sheehy pitch, Listowel; Kerry won well. I travelled that day by train – unfortunately you can no longer take the train to Listowel, as this service, sadly, has been long since discontinued. They played a Whit Sunday tournament in Killarney and also set Wembley, the home of English soccer, alight when they beat a battle-hardened Galway side, 3-9 to 4-4. Patsy O'Hagan had two goals, Sean O'Neill another and Paddy Doherty scored seven superb points. Now Hayes knew that his county was ready for the championship battles ahead.

The first danger signals began flashing for us down here in Kerry when Down edged us out in the League semi-final that same year, 2-10 to 2-8. It was a great Kerry team's first defeat in any competition for over twelve months. I left Croke Park that day knowing well that a new force in Gaelic football had arrived on the scene. But as we watched Down sprinting onto Croke Park for the final in September, little did the crowd realise that all was far from well in the Kerry camp.

I can now state, all these years later, that the Kingdom's very poor preparation gifted Down the Sam Maguire in 1960. Training here was a disaster. The legendary Dr Eamonn O'Sullivan, who had led Kerry to seven previous titles, had decided to opt out. Years later one of Kerry's greatest players Tom Long explained to me what had occurred:

> Eamonn was just the trainer and not a selector and once the All-Ireland would be over he would simply be forgotten about. There were very few perks going for players back then, unlike today. Eamonn was

> never even considered for a trip to the States or even England or anywhere in thanks. It wasn't right. A group of us living in Dublin met and discussed this. We made a complaint to the Kerry County Board and I think Eamonn agreed with our actions.

So Tom Long and a few others refused to train with the team in support of Eamonn and instead went about preparing themselves as they wished. All-Ireland medal winners Gerald O'Sullivan and Johnny Walsh came in at the last minute to organise things, but there was never a full muster at training. Believe it or not, there was no collective training of any kind for that final. Eventually Gerald and Johnny fixed up the differences with Tom and his 'strike' was over. 'We of course were badly beaten by Down and Eamonn was badly missed,' Tom concluded. So was this the first ever strike in Gaelic football? Probably so.

Another factor that definitely hindered Kerry on the day of the final came to light during the pre-match parade when John Dowling appeared, clearly limping. He was later substituted during the course of the game by Jack Dowling, which necessitated numerous changes in the team. Sitting in his van one cold, wet February day watching Tralee CBS play St Flannan's in a Corn Uí Mhuirí game in Macroom, that 1960 Down final came up in the conversation and John revealed to me exactly what had happened on the eve the final:

> Some newspaper had posed the question, was the Kerry full forward line slower than the Kerry full back line? So I was nominated to represent the full forward line in a race to decide the argument and Jerome O'Shea would be the full back line representative. To race each other was a bad decision and had very serious repercussions for the team. We were

> staying in Malahide. Our 50-metre dash around the lawn saw us cross the roadway, our legs became entangled, and I went down heavily on the tarmacadam and badly lacerated my left leg, tearing my togs in the process. There was much debate as to whether I should play or not. Our bagman, Gaffney Duggan, was literally picking tiny little stones out of the cuts and grazes from my leg and ribs. I was greatly restricted and had to be taken off. I was devastated.

In my opinion it is an indisputable fact that few of Kerry's players were fit enough for Down that day. I had played in a Probables v. Possibles game the previous Monday in Fitzgerald Stadium just to make up the numbers and I can say, with hand on heart, that the renowned Kerry player I was marking was away off the pace.

Take all this and stir in Kerry's over-confidence. A number of players have since told me that they fully expected to win that September day, as the team had swept all before it in 1959; many even thought that Down would freeze like rabbits in the headlights when they took the field for the final. And so, on the day, a record attendance for a final at Croke Park saw Down triumphant, 2-10 to 0-8. The new force had arrived.

My great friend Johnny Culloty was in goal for Kerry that day and the Legion man, one of the game's greatest ever players, was to concede a goal that he was never allowed to forget during the following decades. In an interview I conducted with Johnny for a DVD called *Secrets of Kerry: A Captain's Story* in 2010, he recalled the events of that momentous day. 'Kevin Mussen took a sideline kick; McCartan got possession well out the field and sent a high, lobbing ball in towards the goal at the Hill 16 end. I had the ball well covered, it was dropping under the crossbar, and as I reached up to field it I took my eye off the ball having a quick glance as to whom I would kick it to.' His decision to take his eye off the ball would literally change the course of football history as he continued to explain. 'In a split second the ball had slipped through my hands and was in the back of the net. Shortly afterwards I was on my honeymoon with my new wife, Joan; we decided to go to a film in Dublin and the very first thing that came on screen in the old English Pathé newsreel was that goal.'

Down became inspired following this score. Paddy Doherty was brought down in the square by the late Tim 'Tiger' Lyons and the Down man blasted the ball to the net. In those few telling minutes the destination of the Sam Maguire Cup was decided. It was to cross the border for the very first time. It meant a lot of things to a lot of people. My late father-in-law, Jack Slattery, a staunch republican and an avid Kerry follower who had spent terms in jail for his beliefs, always told me that it was the one and only time in his life he was happy to see the green and gold defeated.

But Down did have a bit of luck that day; indeed, I vividly recall Paudie Sheehy missing a great goaling chance before Down scored their two goals. If Paudie's effort had gone in, I firmly believe Kerry would have won. The northern side had some magnificent players: Paddy Doherty, Sean O'Neill and the great all-action bustling, centre forward Jim McCartan. This Down team changed the face of Kerry football. Never again would we see the traditional 'catch and kick', which had laid the foundations and tradition of the Kingdom. Their style had to change. Down had shown them the arrival of a new era and during the following decades Kerry adapted, as only Kerry can, to the more open, short passing style.

Dr Eamonn was back to train the team as the two counties met again in the semi-final of 1961. Sadly, once again the Northerners proved too good on a 1-12 to 0-9 score. They went on to win their second title, defeating Offaly in a superb game in which James McCartan scored a memorable goal at the Railway End.

As was then the tradition, a Probables v. Possibles match was held on the Monday preceding the semi-final in 1961 and I played in it, just as I had done in 1960. I was playing good club football at the time and was picked for the Possibles to play at wing forward. Young and flying fit, I found it no problem to win plenty of ball and range across the field from wing to wing. However, I had a rude awaking at half-time when Dr Eamonn called me aside and warned me in no uncertain manner that if I did not remain in what he termed 'my sector of the field' I would be soon substituted. I was shattered and, when tied down to 'my sector', my opposite number easily got the better of me.

Now here is a wonderful example of just how far Kerry football had fallen behind the times. Dr Eamonn's philosophy had been highly successful until this point. His strict mantra had been that each player had his own section of the field to control. When the ball entered that section it should be a simple man-to-man contest. Down had their homework well done for those historic matches against the Kingdom and they ran Kerry all over the wide open expanses of Croke Park. Those were defining games and in 1963, 1964 and 1965 Galway hammered home the message that the old style 'catch and kick' was well and truly a thing of the past. The Westerns, playing fast-flowing football, beat Kerry in two finals and a semi-final. Down have beaten Kerry each time the counties have met in championship football. As late as 2010 Kerry's outstanding manager Jack O'Connor saw his superb side also go under to the Northern men in the semi-final of that year.

Dr Eamonn O'Sullivan retired following the 1964 defeat. He had given his county magnificent service. His tenure covered five decades. Although he was not in charge every year, he was always available when the occasion demanded him. He trained eight All-Ireland winning teams and still remains the only person to have been involved in inter-county training for that incredible time span. These were very bleak years for Kerry football. However, for me a cherished All-Ireland Junior football medal was just around the corner and I was to win my place on the team as goalkeeper in the most unusual way imaginable.

8

Dan 'Bally' Keating: memories of a century of Kerry football

Kerry's oldest citizen, 105-year-old Dan Keating, was laid to rest on 2 October 2007. St Carthage's Church, about two miles from the village of Castlemaine, was packed to overflowing as the parish priest, Father Luke Roche, celebrated the funeral mass. The local choir sang beautifully and Maura Begley played some hauntingly beautiful tunes as the eight gifts symbolising Dan's long and fruitful life were brought to the altar. This exemplary son of Kerry was afforded, and rightly so, the full trappings of a republican funeral. The rich, slanting autumn sun lit up Killtallagh cemetery as his Tricolour-draped coffin was lowered into the grave. A lone piper played 'Amazing Grace'; we heard stirring orations recalling Dan's more than ninety years of service to the All-Ireland Republic of 1916 and the first All-Ireland Dáil.

There was respectful silence as Kerry's queen of song, Peggy Sweeney, sang one of Dan's favorite songs, 'Shannagolden'. Following the burial, old friends and comrades were slow to depart the graveside, lingering to recall stories of Dan's amazing life. While his republican beliefs were the

A Republican guard of honour for David Fleming (RIP), a former player from Killarney Legion Club, who died in 1971. David was jailed in Crumlin Road Prison for his republican activities and spent seventy days on hunger strike. Included in this picture, which was taken at High Street, Killarney, County Kerry, are *right of hearse (from back):* Pat O'Meara, Mickey Culloty, Maurice Casey, Darby Moynihan, Michael O'Grady, Donie O'Leary, Pa Doyle and Jack Slattery; *left of hearse (from back):* Redmond O'Sullivan, Mickey O'Leary, Jack O'Shea and Connie Horgan. Sadly, all these great Killarney men are now dead.

main topic of the day, his deep love for Kerry football and its footballers was also acknowledged. It was through this facet of Dan's life that I befriended him years ago and, in a series of recorded, priceless interviews and general conversations, he related to me stories of great games and legendary players, offering lavish praise for the men who had kept the flame of

Kerry's rich football heritage alive through our country's troubled times.

For me, personally, Dan Keating was a man with whom you would spend a few hours and come away the richer in mind and spirit. I once asked him what was the secret of his long life and he replied unhesitatingly, 'A good bowl of porridge in the morning, a brisk daily walk, a true faith and abstain from eating from 7 o'clock [at night] before you go to the bed.' What particularly amazed me about this exemplary Kerryman was his ability to peer back through the mists of time and recall people and events in a way that would shame people much younger. Mention the name of any Kerry footballer since the early 1920s and he would describe for you in precise detail the strength, weakness and personality of that particular player. I firmly believe he had a photographic memory, so precise was his recollection.

His republicanism has been well documented, but my conversations with him centred mainly on Kerry football and All-Ireland finals. He had attended every All-Ireland final since 1919. In all 150, between football and hurling. He was the only man alive that had seen every Kerry footballer from Dick Fitzgerald to Maurice Fitzgerald. Indeed it was fitting that Maurice's father, Ned, was present for Dan's funeral, accompanied by the legendary Mick O'Connell. Dan would have smiled quietly to himself to have seen two Kerry captains from the 1950s there to pay their respects at the graveside. So how good was Mick O'Connell? Was he the best midfielder Dan had seen during his long life?

> Mick O'Connell was a marvellous footballer. He was all skill. He had everything going for him. But you can never say who the best was. He was up there with the best of them. Kerry has been blessed with great midfielders. Paddy Kennedy was something special. A very talented footballer, but very prone to

> injuries.In the old days we had 'Airplane' Shea, Bob Stack and Con Brosnan. Then along came Ambrose O'Donovan, Sean Walsh, Jack O'Shea, Darragh Ó Sé. No, you could never say who the better was. It would be unfair to single out one that was better than the other.

Wise words indeed.

Dan played a bit of football with Ballymacelligott and, while he never played in Croke Park with those famous Kerry footballers of the time, he fought alongside and against them. His republican activities saw him spend nineteen months in internment, between Portlaoise and the Curragh camp. It was here that he became friends with some of Kerry's greatest footballing legends. Great friendships and great teams were formed in the huts in those jails, he recalled. Men like Joe Barrett, Purty Landers and John Joe Sheehy came together and remained life-long companions. He was unequivocal in his view that the men in those huts had built the greatest football team that was ever seen: the four-in-row Kerry team of 1929 to 1932. The then current Kerry team, he told me, 'wouldn't keep the ball kicked out to them'.

Dan's memories of names and events always astounded; he once spoke to me of the games played in 1924 between the ex-internees and the Kerry team who had beaten Tipperary in that year's Munster final. He was insistent that those games had played a huge part in the regrowth of Kerry football following those troubled times. 'This should never be forgotten,' he emphasised. The ex-internees threw out a challenge to that winning Kerry team. Once again names of past comrades and great footballers he admired came easily to Dan's mind. On the Kerry side you had Dee O'Connor, Con Brosnan, Jack Sheehy, Tom Ryle, Mick Graham and Tom Mahoney. The ex-internees boasted names such as Jerry (Pluggy) Moriarty, Joe Barrett, Jackie Ryan, Bill O'Gorman,

Johnny O'Riordan and Johnny Tagney. Kerry won the game, but in a second clash the result went to the ex-internees.

In all my football discussions with Dan I always had the strong feeling that John Joe Sheehy was his best friend and his favourite footballer. 'Sheehy was a great footballer, no doubt,' he recalled. 'He began his career around 1918; he was very young at the time and was the mainstay of his club. He spent three years on the run and when he came back he continued to play great football. He had one failing, he was too unselfish. If there was one fellow, one of the forwards not scoring or doing badly, he'd go out of his way to get that fellow into the game. He was an awful man that way. Oh yes, he was a great team man.' Dan told me that when he retired after spending more than fifty years as a barman in the Comet on the Swords Road (a 'short walk' from Croke Park, in his words) he returned to Kerry. John Joe would collect him a few times a week and they would traverse the county together. He continued:

> While they were on opposite sides, Con Brosnan and Sheehy put all their differences aside for Kerry football. Kerry and Clare met in the Munster final in Limerick in 1924. John Joe Sheehy was still on the run. Brosnan, an officer in the Free State army, guaranteed safe passage to Sheehy if he played in the final. Sheehy was not interfered with, he played the game and straight after the final whistle he disappeared into the surrounding countryside. And I firmly believe from that moment on the bridge was built.

I had begun research for my book on Dr Eamonn O'Sullivan (*A Man Before His Time*) during a spell when I was interviewing Dan, so I asked about Eamonn's influence on the teams in the 1920s.

'He was one of the best ever, based in Killarney, he was a great man for getting the players physically fit. He told me one time that if the skills were in the players then fitness was the next greatest thing. He was always there when Kerry were in trouble; they would get him to train the side. Oh yes, he had a great record as a trainer and should never be forgotten. He had great respect from the players. If the players respect you then it's half the battle.'

Kerry had won the All-Irelands in 1924 and 1926, so I wondered what had happened in 1927 and 1928 before Kerry won that historic four-in-a-row? Once again names and dates came tripping from the tongue without a moment's hesitation. In many ways it seemed unreal; as he spoke, he rolled back the decades and it was as if these historic events had occurred only yesterday.

> After 1926 Kerry suffered greatly through emigration. First of all, that wonderful Cahersiveen footballer Johnny Murphy died – I think he got meningitis and died very quickly. Phil O'Sullivan, our captain from 1924, went to America, the poor man died there and is buried there. Gal Slattery also went to America so did Paddy Clifford, there was no work for them here.
>
> Paul Russell went to Dublin and declared for them. He was a great wing back and he loved to go forward. He was always bulling for a few points and one particular day in a semi-final in the 1930s Dublin had them on the rack. They were leading by a goal and Russell let fly a drop kick from about 60 yards. Now it skidded off the ground and into the net, a draw. Kerry destroyed them in Tralee.
>
> Bill Landers and Mossie Galvin also emigrated. Half the team went to America. Kerry were badly wronged in 1925 and declared illegal. Kildare won in 1927 and 1928. Kerry were building and then we saw

> that great four-in-a-row side. They were trained by a Tralee man, Sean McCarthy; he was great friends with Sheehy and he played a huge part in bringing the players together. No one else would train the side at the time. He was from Blennerville and said he would do it for one year, and then he won the four in a row.

What astounded me most of all in my discussions with Dan was the fact that he could describe, say, Paul Russell from 1924 with the very same accuracy as he used when I questioned him about Pat Spillane, or any of today's players. The comments from Dan that I've given here are only a fraction of the jewels I heard from him during our interviews and conversations.

People travelled from far and wide to record his memories, mainly about his republican involvements. At least we have saved some of his fondest reminiscences about the secret of Kerry. May the sod of his beloved native Kerry rest lightly on this exemplary man. He touched many lives during his 105 years but for me his greatest attribute was the manner in which he could associate and relate to the very young and the not so old on equal terms. I was fortunate to have known him.

9

St Finan's Hospital: from custodial to community-based care

On the first day of March 1962 a whole new chapter of my life began. At 7.30 a.m. that morning I walked through the doors of St Finan's Hospital. It felt as if I was walking back into the last century. At the age of twenty-one I had come to take up employment as a student psychiatric nurse in what is still the largest building in Kerry. I would spend the next thirty-eight years of my life within those old Victorian walls and experience a life among psychiatric patients that was in stark contrast to life anywhere else in this county. And let me add straightaway that it was, for me, a rich and fulfilling life's work. In spite of the harshness of that early regime, I would enter the same profession if I had the choice again today.

The building had previously been known as the Killarney District Lunatic Asylum, which was later changed to the Mental Hospital; today it is simply called St Finan's Hospital. It has stood sentinel over the town of Killarney since it first opened its doors to the mentally ill of the county in 1852, and many the changes it has seen since that day when renowned architect Sir Thomas Deane first turned the key.

It was built by those who had been working on the erection of Pugin's Cathedral in Killarney, a project temporarily suspended due to the Great Famine, and its location was chosen in 1847 for its therapeutic value by a Mr John Radhill and a Dr Francis White, a Board of Works official and inspector of hospitals respectively. In September 1852, three months prior to its official opening, two British journalists from the *Daily News* and *The Builder* visited the new hospital. The *Daily News* journalist, a well-known social commentator and theorist, Harriet Martineau, mentioned the contrast between the elegance of this new 'palace' and the appalling state of the peasantry around Killarney. On 23 September she reported: 'We could not credit the information when told that it was a mental hospital. Looking from it to the pigsties on the outskirts of the town where human families were huddled like swine, we could not but feel that to build such an establishment in such a place was like giving a splendid waistcoat to a man without a shirt.'

The great Pugin himself, the architect who designed St Mary's Cathedral, reported in *The Builder* that the hospital was 'beautifully placed and very picturesque and effective'. When it finally opened its doors on 30 December 1852, it could accommodate 135 patients and initially there were more beds than patients. Martineau suggested that this could be rectified if the patients were financially rewarded for occupying the beds. When the commission delegated to the inspection of hospitals visited the Killarney Hospital in September 1855, their report was critical of the 'too decorative character of the façade' and the fact that too much accommodation had been provided for the wants of the district. The commission also proposed that to rectify the 100 unfilled beds the admission of paying patients should be considered.

Between 1852 and 1900 the hospital was managed by a board of governors nominated by the Lord Lieutenant of

Ireland, which included two bishops of Kerry (Dr Mangan and Dr Higgins) and the Earl of Kenmare. The first resident medical superintendent appointed to manage the hospital in 1862 was a Dr Lawlor, and he remained in charge until 1872. He was followed by Drs Murphy and Woods, and then Drs Lawrence and Edward Griffin. The last Dr Griffin officiated until 1933 when his son-in-law, the renowned Dr Eamonn O'Sullivan, took over and presided in that role until his retirement in 1962.

In contrast to the present day when the Health Services Executive has full responsibility for health services in general, in those early years funding for all health services came from the local ratepayers of the county and, as this was a period of severe economic depression, finance was always a problem. This is well described in the official history of thc hospital, as follows:

> The mental hospital was erected during the era of British Rule in Ireland and at the time of the erection of an institution for the treatment of the mentally ill, it was regarded as a hugely significant development. The reality, however, was quite different, as both patients and staff endured sub-standard conditions. Typhoid fever and TB were rampant and a number of patients died each month from various other diseases. Nurses, who were then trained under the Royal Medico Psychological Association (RMPA), worked 60 hours per week with little reward. The committee of management ruled with an iron fist and regularly sanctioned cuts in salaries and pensions, froze recruitment and significantly reduced patients' allowances and dietary rations.

However, there was one silver lining to emerge suddenly from this depressing outlook: a woman by the name of Albina

Broderick, a member of the visiting committee of the hospital. She abandoned her British aristocratic background and became a champion of the under-privileged and oppressed. During her tenure on the visiting committee, Albina Broderick (herself a fully qualified nurse) made a number of submissions to the committee in charge, suggesting improvements based on her own observations in European hospitals. An extract from one of her submissions reads as follows:

> Changes can only be accomplished gradually. But if we are determined that they should be made, the impossible will become possible. We shall meet only the same difficulties which have been met and conquered in Scotland, America and in England. Finance is a deeply serious consideration but is it possible that any of our taxpayers will grudge a farthing or even a halfpenny in the pound if they receive in return the happy assurance that it is expended in increasing the good nursing and the comfort of those whom they love and that cannot care for themselves? I wish to acknowledge the patience and kindness of the two doctors and staff in giving me the necessary facts.

Around the year 1920, on Albina Broderick's recommendation, the name of the hospital was changed from the Killarney District Lunatic Asylum to the Killarney Mental Hospital, which I have no doubt was an effort to reduce the stigma attached to such institutions. Some years ago in my work with Radio Kerry I developed a passionate interest in the life of this fascinating lady and took it on myself to visit Castlecove in south Kerry where she ended her days. There I interviewed numerous people who had actually worked with her.

She was the daughter of Viscount Midleton of County Cork, who also owned a large estate in Surrey. When visiting

Ireland she joined the republican movement and became actively involved in the War of Independence and Civil War. She was also a member of Cumann na mBan and Conradh na Gaeilge. When the armed struggle abated she qualified as a nurse and settled in Castlecove where she set up a cooperative movement and built a hospital. The ruins of this hospital complex can still be visited to this day. She subsequently opened a shop in Killarney called The Republican Bureau and was actively involved in a campaign to boycott British goods.

Gobnait Ní Brudair died in poverty on 16 January 1955 and I have often visited her grave just inside the wall in the Protestant cemetery at Sneem when travelling around there to games. In 1968 I was present to hear John Joe Sheehy deliver an oration at the unveiling of a simple plaque in her memory, which bears the following description: 'Erected In Loving memory of Gobnait Ní Brudair. Died January 16th 1955. Eternal Rest To Her Noble Soul. She Was Loyal Until Death. Erected by the Committee for Republican Soldiers in South Kerry.'

The problems of staff shortages and lack of finance continued throughout the 1930s. When the hospital committee eventually recommended the appointment of an extra medical officer in 1941, the members of the Kerry Farmers Union protested vehemently that the ratepayers could not afford the extra expenditure involved. However, in 1934 Dr Eamonn O'Sullivan made a successful submission to the Irish Hospital Sweepstakes to fund much-needed improvements at the hospital. With that financial aid the hospital was able to add an occupational therapy department, dental and general surgery, tradesman's shop and recreation room for staff, as well as extra furniture and decorations, a telephone and laundry equipment. The only treatments of note at the hospital during this period were the extensive use of ECT (electroconvulsive, formerly electroshock, therapy) in the treatment of depression and the use of occupational therapy.

This last was personally developed by Dr O'Sullivan, who was also responsible for compiling a very good publication on the subject of its curative effects (*Textbook of Occupational Therapy*, 1955). He believed so strongly in the benefits of OT that he involved his patients and staff in the construction of the new Fitzgerald Stadium, adjacent to the hospital, during the 1930s. The labour provided by the hospital caused a great deal of controversy at the time, but Dr O'Sullivan insisted on its therapeutic value and it certainly reduced construction costs considerably. This massive contribution was recognised in 2001 when a limestone slab was erected on the press box at the stadium, in thanks to the staff and patients who had worked so hard.

The mid-1950s saw the winds of change blowing through the corridors of the now renamed St Finan's Hospital, bringing with them modern medications and a greater appreciation for psychiatry as a medical speciality. With these changes came improved training for psychiatric nurses. Modern treatments gradually impacted on patient numbers, causing a gradual reduction from an average of a thousand residents at any one time during the early 1960s to the mere fifty or sixty patients who were still housed there by 2011. The average length of residential stays was also much reduced, as the emphasis shifted from custodial to community-based psychiatry. Out-patient clinics now became operational in all the larger towns such as Killarney, Tralee, Listowel, Kenmare and Cahersiveen, with the result that patients who were referred to those out-patient clinics rarely required admission to the hospital. If admission became necessary, it was usually on a short-stay basis. Other notable developments were day-care facilities, which enabled patients to return home at night, and low- and high-support hostels, which facilitated the transfer of many long-stay patients from St Finan's into the community where they were supervised by out-patient nursing and medical staff.

The 1950s also marked an era of improvements for the hospital staff, with several social and sporting organisations being founded for the large numbers of staff employed at St Finan's. Dr Eamonn O'Sullivan and Dr Jack O'Connor, both of whom were sports-orientated, were involved in the founding of the St Finan's Gaelic Football team in 1956, which won the inter-hospital competition for the Connolly Cup on several occasions. At that time the hospital rowing crews and basketball team also enjoyed much local and inter-hospital league success, while the golf society proved a suitable recreation for those retired from the more active sports. Drama was also popular and the hospital was a regular competitor in *Tops of the Town.*

Growing up in the Killarney of the 1940s and 1950s the hospital was, for us youngsters, a strictly forbidden place and I have vivid memories of hearing neighbours chatting to my mother warning that a patient had 'escaped from the mental'. The phrase always terrified me. However, the term 'escaped' was used incorrectly, as I discovered during my years working there. Many the patient simply left the hospital when the opportunity arose, wanting to return to the bosom and love of their family. Although there were certainly also those who left without permission, having been 'signed in' in the first place by unloving relatives anxious to have sole possession of land or home. Thankfully all that has now changed and safety measures are in place to see that only the seriously ill are hospitalised.

It was during my time at the Kerry Mineral Water factory that I saw positions for student nurses at the mental hospital advertised and I decided to apply. Following a written examination I was called for interview, which was held in the boardroom of the hospital. It was the very first time I had entered the building. The interview board consisted of the resident medical superintendent, the legendary Kerry football trainer Dr Eamonn O'Sullivan, and two more assistants. The interview seemed to have gone well and, as I got up to leave, the good doctor threw me one more question. 'If you were successful and offered a position here on the nursing staff would you sign up and play football with the hospital team?'

I knew the question was heavily loaded. A 'yes' would mean that I would leave my own club, Killarney Legion, for whom I had great love and respect, and a 'no' response might compromise my chances of securing a permanent job. I had a little bit of a profile as a footballer, having played Kerry Minor three years previously, and I was currently on the Kerry Under-21 team that was contesting the Munster Championship in that grade for the very first time. This was 1962. There was, of course, going to be only one answer and that was 'yes'. It eventually transpired that I transferred from my club to St Finan's and actually had the unenviable task of playing against the Legion in East Kerry Championship games during the following years. I later transferred back when the hospital team broke up; nevertheless, some of my Legion teammates and friends still remind me of my 'treachery' to this day.

Basketball also played a huge part in the life of the hospital staff and even before I began work in there I was invited to travel with their team to Clonmel where the All-Ireland psychiatric championship for the Antigen Cup was contested. I played under an assumed name, Paddy Roberts (also a staff member), and was warned not to get into conversation with any of the opposition as my illegality might be discovered. I kept my mouth shut during all four matches; we won the All-Ireland and, indeed, I think it no great boast to say that one holds an All-Ireland medal won under false pretences.

When I began work in St Finan's, it had its own school of nursing and to qualify as a psychiatric nurse I was required to attend many weekly medical and nursing lectures conducted by senior medical and nursing staff. Having achieved the required number of mandatory lectures, I was then allowed to sit for my preliminary examination after one year. Two more years of preparation followed before my final exam. This consisted of an oral, written and practical session. It demanded a lot of studying and failure to pass would set you back financially and otherwise. I qualified as a psychiatric

Clearing my lines for Killarney Legion against Dr Crokes in the 1960 East Kerry Senior Championship Final in Fitzgerald Stadium, Killarney. Dr Crokes won the game. *(L–r)*: Jimmy Redpath (RIP), Lui Nolan, Eamon O'Donoghue (partly hidden, RIP), Paddy 'Bomber' O'Shea, Gerald O'Sullivan (RIP), Jackie Looney, Weeshie and Timmy Horgan (RIP).

nurse in 1965, after successfully passing my preliminary and final state examinations. Our tutor at the time was a Killorglin man, Tadgh O'Reilly, who had been one of the stars of the Kerry basketball team that won the very first Senior title in that sport for Kerry in 1957.

My first full day at work was a daunting experience. Donning a brand new white coat, I reported to the head nurse at 7.45 a.m., whereupon I was given a large pass key designed to open all the wards on the male side of the hospital. I was then assigned to a ward at the very top of the building. Ward 5 consisted of a long corridor, a day room where the patients were served their meals, a series of small side rooms where disturbed patients would sleep, and a large dormitory capable of sleeping about forty patients. The one great redeeming feature of Ward 5 was the spectacular view from its windows: a magnificent panorama of Killarney's towering mountains and spectacular lakes.

During the following years I would work in all the various wards at one time or another, but those first years working in Ward 5 were the most memorable. Spring, summer, autumn and winter came and went and that magnificent vista changed on a daily basis. And then there was the Fitzgerald Stadium football pitch situated immediately in the shadow of the massive hospital walls. I particularly liked a window that offered a superb view of the vast playing area and it was many the evening when I worked late shift (then referred to as 'on guard', subsequently changed to 'late duty') that I looked down on Kerry teams training for the big matches. Sunday afternoons also gave staff the opportunity to view the games being played far below us from this window on high.

The number of wards in St Finan's fluctuated during my time there, as patient numbers waxed and waned with the decades. Each ward housed patients suffering from different forms of mental illness. I was at one time or another assigned to each one and quickly became accustomed to the daily routines, treatments and medicines that each person required. Working in a mental hospital, particularly in the 1960s and 1970s, could well be described as attending a 'university of life'. When I look back I see that it was an amazing experience, but it is not easy to relate accurately the events surrounding the admission and treatment of a person suffering from mental illness at that period.

Nevertheless, I would like to give as vivid a picture as possible. The following account from a patient with whom I became acquainted during my work at Tralee out-patients clinic was included in the wonderful hospital history, *St Finan's Hospital, Killarney: A Medical, Social and Sporting History 1852–2002*. I was a member of a committee assigned the task of producing this mammoth book, which was dedicated to 'all those patients who passed through the hospital over the past one hundred and fifty years, and in particular to those who, by nature of their illness, resided here during the greater part of their lives'. Retired nurse John Kelly was the driving force behind this remarkable history, and a young man from Kilcummin just outside Killarney, Dermot Dwyer, devoted months of his life to editing the publication. So I believe the following true-life narrative by this man (of whom I now have no trace) tells the story far better than my own words could:

> I was working on the farm in the month of June 1950 when I became restless and had this terrible urge to pray. I left work and went to the village church to do the Stations of the Cross, and three hours later, my mother found me on my knees outside the church. I went home but could not concentrate and continued to pray to all the pictures and even to the animals. Naturally, my parents became concerned and next day, the local doctor called to see me, and after chatting for some time he explained that he had received a number of reports about my bizarre behaviour and suggested that I should go to the mental hospital for some treatment.
>
> At first I refused but, on inquiring from my parents the reason for my hospitalisation, they

informed me that the doctor felt I was suffering from 'religious mania', and needed the advice of a specialist for treatment. After some persuasion, I agreed to travel with them in the taxi which arrived half an hour later. On my arrival at the front gate, the man at the lodge gate inquired about our business, then opened the gate and allowed us through.

After a brief chat with the hall porter, I was taken to the admission ward by two nurses wearing white coats. A bath was arranged and I was then put to bed in the admission dormitory and examined by the doctor, who advised the nurse to give me a special injection every six hours to help me settle down and sleep. I was allowed remain in bed for a further day but my urge to pray was still with me and I received a further few injections of this white liquid. I think that it was called sodium amatol. After a further day in bed, I was allowed out to the ward day-room for meals. Quite frankly, I felt rather frightened in a large ward full of men, some of whom, like me, were rather disturbed.

On the Wednesday, the doctor called me to his office and informed me that, in his opinion, I was suffering from a disorder that required a course of special treatment called electroconvulsive therapy. He assured me that this treatment had been a successful treatment for this illness. He explained the procedure and informed me that I may experience some memory loss for a brief period. After a course of six treatments, I was again interviewed by the same medical officer who informed me that, despite the fact I had improved, he would recommend that I remain in hospital for a further period of a month. During the next few weeks, I occupied myself with little tasks such as polishing the floors and helping with the preparation of the meals.

The afternoons were spent in the large Airing Court where patients played football and occasionally joined staff members for a game of handball. During the evenings we played cards and listened to programmes such as *Take the Floor* on the ward radio.

After a further two weeks, I was transferred to Ward 3 and informed that if my condition remained stable, I would shortly be considered for discharge. While I found Ward 3 to be less intimidating than the admission ward, I disliked having my meals in the large dining hall with 1,000 other patients as occasionally some tended to 'get a bit out of hand'. While in Ward 3 I was introduced to a large printing machine which was used to print all the office stationery for the hospital, and the charge nurse who was a friendly man, taught me some of the skills of the printing trade. Three weeks later, the charge nurse asked me to be ready for an interview with the doctor the following day, the same doctor who had admitted me. He informed me he was happy that I had made a reasonably good recovery from a condition known as Dementia Praecox, which had a tendency to re-occur, and he advised that should I feel unwell again, to immediately arrange for re-admission before the condition deteriorated.

A year later, I again felt unwell and the symptoms were somewhat similar, but on this occasion, I refused to accept medical advice and eventually the doctor requested that my parents sign a certification order. The treatment was somewhat similar: a further course of injections to settle me and a course of electro-convulsive treatment. However, on this occasion, I remained quite unwell over a period of months and, when I did eventually show some improvement, I was advised to go to the large occupational workshop where a number of patients were involved in various occupations, such as basket-making, weaving and making mattresses for the wards.

After a total period of six months in hospital, I was again discharged home but on this occasion I found it difficult to concentrate on my farm work and was inclined to spend much of my time in bed. Over the next four years, I was spending more time in hospital each year and was becoming increasingly dependent on the security it provided. Towards the end of 1956, I was interviewed by the doctor for a period of over thirty minutes during which time he informed me of a new form of medication which had come on the market, known as Stelazine, and which could be a useful treatment for my condition.

I agreed to commence on this form of treatment, but again unfortunately, I developed severe side effects such as tremors and stiffness of my limbs, and at one stage, I intimated that I wished to discontinue the treatment as the side effects were too crippling. Luckily the doctor prescribed a white tablet which, after a few days, cleared up those terrible side effects. I was again discharged home and came back to the hospital occasionally to have my medication reviewed and, while I was feeling improved, I still found it difficult to concentrate and was spending some time in bed. My medication was frequently changed to include such treatments as Orap and Largactil and I did subsequently show much improvement. Eventually the consultant, whom I attend regularly at the outpatient clinic in Tralee, advised me about a new injection which had come on the market to treat the condition from which I suffered and was now known as schizophrenia.

I commenced on a small dosage of this new

injection named Modecate, and a nurse called to my house to administer this treatment every two weeks. Gradually I continued to feel a new sense of improvement over the next year and the injection was then spaced to monthly intervals. My quality of life has improved dramatically in recent years and I have discovered a new-found interest in life. I continue to attend the out-patient clinic on a regular basis and thankfully have avoided admission to the psychiatric hospital since I commenced on this treatment so many years ago. Possibly the only real disadvantage is that relapse is a real possibility if the medication is discontinued, but in reality, it is a small price to pay for a much better quality of life.

10

1969: Living my All-Ireland dream

For seven years Kerry had been attempting to win a twenty-first historic All-Ireland championship. Defeats by Galway (1964 and 1965) and Down (1968) had stopped the county coming of age. Three galling setbacks when hopes had been sky high. But now, on 29 September 1969 before a crowd of 67,228 (the lowest since 1952 when Kerry had their day defeating Offaly in that year's final, 0-10 to 0-7), I was there on the substitute bench achieving a life's sporting ambition to tog out for Kerry in an All-Ireland Senior football final. Yes, I was just the reserve goalkeeper and by no means a player of note, but for me that one year of 1969 was very special and I cherish my brief experience as a Kerry Senior footballer.

While I had played championship football for the county Minor, Under-21 and Junior teams, in my own mind I considered myself just an average footballer and not possessing any great natural ability. I had worked hard all my sporting life, trained rigorously winter and summer, and was also greatly helped by playing months of winter basketball, never drinking or smoking. So when the call came to join the panel for the

I lined out at wing forward on this Kerry side for a charity match against Cork in Mallow in 1962. The teams drew with 1-10 each. *Back row (l–r):* Lui Nolan, Liam Scully, Timmy O'Sullivan, Tim 'Tiger' Lyons, Tom Burk, Tim Sheehan, Pa Kerins and Weeshie; *front row (l–r):* Unknown, Mickey Walsh, Alan Conway, Mick O'Connell, Seamus Murphy, Dave Geaney and Pat Ahern.

Here I am punching clear in the All-Ireland Junior Home final against Mayo in 1967 in Tipperary Town. Teammate Gerry McCarthy (Gneeveguilla) watches on as Mayo's Willie McGee goes to ground. We won 1-10 to 1-3 and went on to beat London (away) in the final, 3-8 to 0-7. McGee had scored four goals against Kerry in the Under-21 final the previous week. His achievement went unmatched until Billy O'Sullivan (Kerry) scored four goals in the 1990 Under-21 final.

championship, I was over the moon. Of course it helped greatly that my Killarney Legion clubmate Jackie Lyne was the team trainer and Johnny Culloty team captain.

That year was special for another reason: it saw my marriage to my wife, Joan. In fact the day we returned from our honeymoon, which we had spent driving around Ireland in my late friend Jimmy Murphy's Morris Minor, was the day I got the call. No sooner had we the honeymoon bags in the front door of our new house in O'Sullivan's Place, Killarney, just a stone's throw from Fitzgerald Stadium, when the knock on the door came. It was my neighbour Johnny Culloty informing me that I had better get my football gear ready as I was to be in Tralee later that evening where I would join the Kerry panel. It was the best wedding present of all. As Joan said, 'Somebody up there likes you.'

I quickly sensed the mood in the Kerry set up. The previous year's defeat by Down in the 1968 final had hurt badly and Jackie Lyne, the new trainer, was determined to win that 1969 championship. Lyne was just finding his feet, but it only took that one defeat to teach him everything he needed to know about his players. He would put his first twelve months in charge to good use.

One man who would play a massive part in the 1969 win had the most dramatic introduction ever to a Kerry football team. Din Joe Crowley later recalled his debut. 'It was Whit Sunday 1968 in Killarney and I was there with my father to watch the game against Dublin. As the opening game drew to a close, an announcement came over the tannoy system: "If Din Joe Crowley from Rathmore is in the stadium will he please go the Kerry dressing room?" I then met Jackie Lyne for the very first time. I had my gear in the boot of the car and I finished up playing on the forty. It was the beginning of my career.'

Training with Kerry was an amazing experience. Mick O'Connell, Mick O'Dwyer, Seamus Murphy, the O'Donoghue brothers, Paudie and Eamon, Liam Higgins, Tom Prendergast

I found myself in a unique position in Caitin's Pub, Cahersiveen, at the launch of *Secrets of Kerry – A Captain's Story*, when I was flanked by Kerry's oldest (surviving) and youngest winning Kerry captains: Jas Murphy (1953) and Darren O'Sullivan (2010). *(courtesy CR Video and DVD Production)*

Previously unpublished photograph of the Kerry goalkeepers who won All-Ireland medals since 1953. They were my special guests on my Radio Kerry *Terrace Talk* programme in 2009, *(l–r)*: Johnny Foley (1953), Garry O'Mahoney (1955), Johnny Culloty (1959, 1962, 1969 and 1970 – he also has the distinction of winning a medal as corner forward in 1955), Charlie Nelligan (1978–1981 and 1984–1986), Declan O'Keeffe (1997 and 2000), Peter O'Leary (1997 and 2000) and Diarmuid Murphy (2004, 2006, 2007 and 2009). Paudie O'Mahoney (1975, 1978–1981) was missing and, sadly, Garry O'Mahoney has since died. *(courtesy Seanie Kelly)*

At the launch of *Secrets of Kerry – A Captain's Story* in the Gleneagle Hotel, Killarney, *(l–r)*: Gus Cremin, John Lyne, Sean Kennedy and Weeshie. Gus Cremin scored the crucial point for Kerry in the 1946 All-Ireland replay against Roscommon. He was captain for the drawn game and then was sensationally dropped for the replay. Sean Kennedy, Paddy's son, holds his father's 1947 Polo Grounds jersey. John Lyne attended the launch especially to meet Gus Cremin, his childhood hero.

Here I am, in my element in 2010 in Kells Bay Gardens on the Ring of Kerry, interviewing my boyhood hero Ronnie Delany, who won a gold medal at the Melbourne Olympics in 1956. My brother Geni and I listened to his race on an old Bush radio in our kitchen in New Street, Killarney – there was no TV back then. *(courtesy CR Video and DVD Production)*

In 2011, I attended the launch of *Secrets of Kerry – A Captain's Story*, a four-hour DVD documentary about Kerry's winning captains, in Dublin. Christy Riordan *(right)* from CR Video and DVD Production in Cahersiveen and I had worked on this project for three years. Other launches took us to New York and London. Included here are Kerry legends Maurice Fitzgerald *(second from left)* and Donie O'Sullivan *(second from right)*.

Here, my family poses at the launch of my book, *Dr Eamonn O'Sullivan – A Man Before His Time*. The legendary Kerry trainer guided Kerry to eight All-Ireland wins and I worked under him at St Finan's Hospital, Killarney, *(l–r)*: Carol Ann, Denise, Joan, Weeshie and Kieran.

I became great friends with Dan Keating (RIP). Here he is at 104 years of age, casting his last vote. A remarkable man, he was a fountain of history and knowledge. *(courtesy MacMonagle, Killarney)*

One of the three Killarney Under-21 teams I trained to win Kerry county championships in the 1970s. *Back row (l–r):* Tadge Fleming (selector), Denis O'Donoghue, Josie O'Donoghue, Denis Courtney, Diarmuid O'Donoghue, John Casey, Justin Kidney (secretary), James Cronin, Tom Hill, Donal O'Meara (treasurer), Patrick O'Donoghue, Tommy 'Bracker' Regan (selector), Richard O'Brien, John Lyne and James O'Donoghue (chairman); *middle row (l–r):* Donie Sheehan (selector), Con Carroll, Tommy O'Shea, Johnny O'Donoghue (captain), Harry O'Neill, Sean Brosnan, Michael Lyne, Weeshie and John Galvin (selector); *front row (l–r):* Denis Lyne, John O'Leary, Thomas Lyne, Colm Galvin and Brendan Keogh.

Sitting in the Sam Maguire Cup is a great Kerry tradition. My nieces and nephews took the opportunity to pose when I had the cup following our 1969 All-Ireland victory, *(l–r):* Katherine, Gerald *(in the cup),* Sheila and Richard.

I interviewed Lyla Kennedy in Dublin for the DVD *Secrets of Kerry*. Lyla is the wife of the legendary Paddy Kennedy, captain of the Kerry team that won the 1946 All-Ireland. Here, I am holding the jersey that Paddy wore in the final in the Polo Grounds, New York, in 1947. On her right hand, Lyla wears a bracelet of Paddy's minor and senior All-Ireland medals. Following this interview, I visited Paddy's grave in Dublin. *(courtesy CR Video and DVD Production)*

Outside St Finan's Psychiatric Hospital in Killarney. When I began my nursing life here in 1962, there were close to one thousand patients (male and female) housed together with a staff of hundreds. It was a town on its own in many ways.

In 2008 I was honoured to interview three Olympic oarsmen from Killarney as they prepared for the Beijing Olympic Games – meeting Olympians from my hometown is one of my greatest sporting memories and I wonder if it will ever happen again, *(l–r):* Cathal Moynihan, Sean Casey, Paul Griffin and Weeshie.

(courtesy Eamon Keogh, MacMonagle, Killarney)

Joan and I are included in this jubilant Radio Kerry staff group as we celebrate in Kilkenny, following the station's selection as Best Local Station in Ireland 2007. We were also honoured with two PPI awards for Drama and Station Imaging. *Back row (l–r):* Brian Hurley, Terry Dunne, John Herlihy, Jason O'Connor, Deirdre Walsh, Weeshie, Joan, Muireann Ni Loinsigh and Francis Fitzgibbons (behind Weeshie); *middle row (l–r):* Mary O'Halloran, Sharon O'Mahoney, Elaine Kinsella (with PPI award), Alan Finn (with PPI award), Marie Sweeney, Eileen Moynihan, Sinead Prendergast, Sean Hurley and Mary Mullins; *front row (l–r):* Martin Howard, Treasa Murphy (News Editor), Michael Grant, Paul Byrne (Chief Executive, holding the trophy), Fiona Stack (General Manager and Program Controller), Melanie O'Sullivan (Events, Marketing & Promotions) and Claire Mulcahy.

In 1997, Muckross Rowing Club named a racing boat in honour of my niece, Karen, *(l–r):* Anne Fogarty, Clare Fogarty, James Mulligan, Geni Fogarty, Maureen Fogarty, Ulick Daly, Susan Fogarty and Margaret Cooper. *(courtesy MacMonagle, Killarney)*

In 2007, I interviewed Hollywood screen legend, Maureen O'Hara, for my *In Conversation with . . .* programme on Radio Kerry. She was one of my boyhood screen idols from the 1950s and 1960s. A great friend, Noel Harrington of Sneem, arranged the meeting with this fascinating personality. Maureen and I even exchanged books!

Renowned Manchester United goalkeeper Harry Gregg *(right)* was my special guest on *Terrace Talk* in 2003. He held listeners spellbound as he described, in vivid detail, the story of the 1958 Munich Air Disaster and his experience as a survivor of the crash. *(courtesy MacMonagle, Killarney)*

Broadcasting a South Kerry Championship final between Valentia and Sneem with Liam Higgins *(left)* from Waterville in 2000 (Valentia beat Sneem). All the divisional finals in Kerry are broadcast live and attract a massive listenership. They are the basis of all that is great and historic in Kerry football.

I spent a number of years tracing the history of Eamon Fitzgerald, who won two All-Ireland medals with Kerry (in 1937 and 1939) and was an Olympian in Los Angeles in 1932. In 2004, my efforts paid off when a group of supporters rededicated his grave in Deansgrane Cemetery, Dublin, *(l–r):* Sean Walsh (Kerry GAA County Board Chairman), Michael Heerey (Irish Athletics), Pat Hickey (Irish Olympic Council), Ronnie Delany (1956 Olympic gold medal winner), Dan Keating (who attended Eamon's funeral in 1958) and Eugene O'Sullivan (Chairman Dublin/Kerry Association).

The headstone on Eamon Fitzgerald's grave.

I am pictured with Mick O'Connell *(centre)*, arguably the greatest Gaelic football player ever, and Liam O'Connor *(right)*, one of the world's best accordion players – he entered the Guinness Book of Records in 2008 for his amazing musical talents. This was taken at the launch of *Dr Eamonn O'Sullivan – A Man Before His Time*, my book on the life of Dr Eamonn O'Sullivan who trained Kerry to win eight All-Irelands.

'Iron Man' Mick Murphy waves to the cyclists as the Rás Tailteann passes his house in south Kerry in 2008 on the fiftieth anniversary of his remarkable Rás win.
(courtesy CR Video and DVD Production)

Jackie Lyne trained the 1969 and 1970 All-Ireland winning Kerry teams.

– and here was I lining up with these greats of Kerry football, sprinting and racing around the field, playing backs and forwards and listening to the advice of Jackie Lyne. It was a completely different world of training from that of today. Lyne had trained under Dr Eamonn O'Sullivan in the course of his long playing career, which ended in 1954 when he was dropped for the final against Meath (a game Kerry lost). When he became a trainer himself, he continued on with Eamonn's style of training, using many of the doctor's successful All-Ireland methods. However he also introduced his own variations.

That year of 1969 Kerry also won the National League and it proved to be the foundation of the later All-Ireland victory. Kerry played ten games in that league, winning eight and drawing two. Jackie Lyne and his selectors used twenty-seven players as they continued in their quest to settle on the best fifteen. As Kerry scored 16-118 in their march to league victory, Mick O'Connell finished up as top scorer with 3-32 to his name, Brendan Lynch added 4-24, and Mick O'Dwyer was third highest scorer with 2-22. It was a magnificent year for the great O'Connell and later in the championship he would also finish as Kerry's top scorer with 0-15 to his name, followed by Mick O'Dwyer (0-11) and Brendan Lynch (0-8). Has any other midfielder in the history of the game finished as top scorer for his county in league and championship in the same year? It was an amazing experience to be so close to the legendary Valentia man in 1969, probably one of the greatest seasons of his career. He was the ultimate perfectionist, the prince of midfielders, the supreme athlete and one of a handful of Irish sports people who can be described in today's world as a 'living legend'.

One game he played in 1969 is more or less forgotten now, and yet he gave a display that probably matched any of his previous bests. It was the second leg of the National League final, played in Gaelic Park, New York. The final was played over two legs and both games ended in draws. So extra time had to be played the second day. New York had a great team around this time, including two Kerrymen reputed to be the best Kerry footballers to emigrate from the Kingdom: Jimmy Foley from Castlemaine and Mickey Moynihan from Rathmore, the New York captain. In the second leg of the final Kerry looked a beaten team. They were three points down with a few minutes to go. Mick O'Connell, who had been injured in the first leg, was introduced and in the closing minutes he scored three magnificent points to take the game into extra time. New York were demanding Kerry should stay on for another week so the third game could be played the following Sunday. Kerry players insisted on playing extra time and, while all the debating was going on, the players sought shade from the 110 °F heat under the railway line that runs high up and adjacent to the pitch. Water was being drunk by the bucket. Kerry, thanks to Mick O'Connell's amazing display, ran out easy winners in the extra time.

These two American matches had laid a perfect foundation for the rest of the season. Before Kerry had left for America, Waterford had been defeated in the first round of the Munster Championship, 1-18 to 2-7. Pat Moynihan from Gneeveguilla was a big success in the Kerry attack, scoring five points; however, he, together with Dom O'Donnell and Mick Fleming (1-1), would not feature in the All-Ireland final win over Offaly later in the year. Liam Higgins, Pat Griffin and Mick Gleeson would replace them in the forward division.

Next up for us was Cork in the Munster final, fixed for the Cork Athletic Grounds on 20 July. We were now training four times a week. Johnny Culloty and I, due to our work in St Finan's Hospital, were rostered for duty on that day. This was nothing new and it would require some swapping of Sunday duties to facilitate us. Indeed, I must add that we often took time off to play with club and county at our own expense. However, a nice little touch came during the week before the game when the chief nursing officer of the hospital informed us that we were being granted special leave on the day of the match to help the county. It was unique, he added, for the hospital to have the two Kerry goalkeepers as members of staff.

Now Kerry had beaten Cork in the National League in the Cork Athletic Grounds in April, 2-5 to 0-9, and it was a

In 1969, I was part of a team that won a summer relay race around Killarney – this was our third win in a row. My late brother Geni was also part of the team. *Back row (l–r):* Geni Fogarty, Pa O'Brien (coach) and Kevin Coleman; *front row (l–r):* Weeshie, and Tadghie Fleming. Kevin Coleman was a renowned, award-winning photographer with *The Kerryman* newspaper for many years.

highly fortunate goal from substitute Liam Higgins which won the day. In reality Cork had won everywhere but on the scoreboard and everyone knew that this Munster final (especially as Cork were playing at home) was going to be a very difficult battle. But Kerry had luck on their side again that day in 1969. I had the perfect view from the dugout and watched as we ran into an early four-point lead by the thirteenth minute. Two minutes later came the incident that would eventually decide the result. Cork was awarded a penalty.

Denis Coughlan took the kick; his low shot hit the butt of the post and rebounded back across the face of the goal. The Cork forwards rushed in to finish the ball to the net but Kerry's corner back, Seamus McGearailt, dived on the ball to prevent a goal. However, he had handled the ball on the ground and referee John Moloney had no hesitation in again pointing to the penalty spot. It was dramatic stuff. Donal Hunt took the second penalty, but captain Johnny Culloty saved brilliantly and pulled Kerry out of danger. Years later Johnny admitted to me that the ball had, in fact, crossed the line before McGearailt dived on it. However, Kerry were the better side that year and, irrespective of the penalty misses, I have no doubt but that we would have survived, whatever Cork had thrown at us. Billy Morgan was brilliant in goal for Cork that day, and I can safely say without fear of contradiction that the Nemo Rangers man was the best goalkeeper by a mile that I have ever seen. Celebrations were more or less non-existent for the players back then. The Munster cup with no name on it was thrown into the boot of the car, we had the team meal, then non-stop to Killarney, no drinking sessions and it was back to training the following Tuesday night.

Mayo would be our opponents in the All-Ireland semi-final. The following Tuesday evening at training that legendary New York figure, John 'Kerry' O'Donnell, was introduced to the players in the dressing room. Jackie Lyne and John Kerry had always been close friends but now Jackie informed us that John Kerry had been appointed as assistant trainer of the team. His announcement was greeted with a warm and generous round of applause because we all appreciated what the man had done for the GAA in America.

The legendary John 'Kerry' O'Donnell devoted his life to Gaelic games in New York. I befriended him when he was appointed assistant trainer to the 1969 All-Ireland winning Kerry team.

In my eyes he was an iconic figure, as I had heard so much about him. He did not suffer fools gladly and was always his own man. It was a well-known fact that he was never the flavour of the week with the head men in Croke Park and was generally a thorn in their side. He ran for president of the GAA at one stage, after nomination by Kerry, but his bid fell short. He famously referred to those who had promised to vote for him, but did not, as 'the rats that left the sinking ship'. His daughter, Kerry O'Donnell, spoke to me about her father some years ago and recalled her memories of this remarkable Kerry man.

> My father left west Kerry in 1920, met my mother (then Helen O'Callaghan from Brosna) in 1932, and got married in 1934 and had eight children. He took over Gaelic Park in 1945. The Wall Street Crash was a terrible time and thousands including Dad were laid off from the building trade. He was making ninety-nine dollars a week and now he was down to just seven dollars. Molly and Patsy Clifford were great friends of my parents and Molly kept them in a rooming house which she ran. He often told the story of walking down 139th Street to the public library; he had heard on the radio that they were selling apples for five cents and between them they couldn't come up with the five cents to buy an apple. But they were happy to just go down and see who was buying them. He didn't have things easy but I never heard him describe it as a hard life. I don't think that it was very different to other immigrant stories.
>
> They landed on the shores of Canada and America, worked very hard and made their way in life. He had travelled from Tralee with his uncle, I believe on a donkey and cart. They stayed overnight in Tralee. On to Cobh the following day, the ship

stopped at Southampton and then on to Montreal fourteen days later. He often spoke of this years later, especially when he flew Aer Lingus in a few hours coming back to Ireland. My father had a great sense of adventure as many had in those far off days, and I guess the life he had in later years made him forget any loneliness he might have experienced.

At the time Gaelic Park was called Innisfail Park and he was just involved peripherally at first as he played with the New York Kerry team and was also a delegate for the board there. Then in 1944 the lease of the Park was coming to an end. Paddy Grimes and Billy Snow had the lease at the time and were not interested in renewing. Gaelic Park is owned by New York City Metropolitan Transport Authority. It's built beneath the train yards and tracks. It was developed as a GAA pitch probably around 1938. My dad's big fear was if they did not renew the lease then the GAA would lose the ground to soccer as there were people very interested in coming in and taking over the ground. So my father and, I think it was, Barney Mulligan (I am not sure here) were approached and asked to take it over. Now this was a massive undertaking at the time. They agreed to do so and when they arranged to meet the solicitor to sign the agreement my father was the only one to turn up. The other man had backed down but my father decided to give it a go on his own. It was a very brave and courageous step by him. There was a huge fear that the ground would be lost to the GAA and this was the only reason he decided to step in and it all worked out very well for him of course.

That was 1945. Now it was just post-war time and it was quiet enough. The Park did provide a service for the people of the city and also to the soldiers coming home because a lot of them were

> Irish. Things began to improve, and the staging of the 1947 All-Ireland final in Gaelic Park, New York, was a huge boost for the sport as it left native Americans know a little bit more about Gaelic games. So everything grew from there. He never dwelt too much on promoting himself as the games were all important to him and the 1947 final added a huge profile to the games. The whole thing consumed him. The GAA was his life on a daily basis and indeed the same thing goes for many others in New York. He would often be on the phone at 5 a.m. in the morning and the phone would regularly ring in the middle of the night due to the time difference between Ireland and America. We would have a constant flow of visitors, especially from Kerry but also from all over Ireland. He was a great family man and always put us number one. I spent many happy days of my youth in Gaelic Park and I have wonderful memories of those days, meeting all the great players, and the hundreds of emigrants who attended games over the years. My father died in 1984, he was eighty-four years old.

And so Mayo stood between us and a place in the All-Ireland final. The intensity of the training increased and I loved the thrill of togging out three evenings a week and sprinting and running laps of the field in answer to Jackie Lyne's whistle. We stayed in the Skylon Hotel the night before the match. There was one enforced change in the team from the Munster final win. Mick Morris was injured; Micheál Ó Sé, later to become the renowned Radio na Gaeltacht GAA commentator, was drafted in at wing back and Donie O'Sullivan, the longest kicker of a dead ball I have ever seen, went to centre back. Kerry dominated for long periods but squandered a hatful of scoring chances. Mick O'Dwyer, Pat Griffin and two Mick O'Connell 'frees' had us ahead, 0-11 to 0-8.

Early in the second half the lead was stretched to five points with ten minutes left on the clock and then an unexpected Mayo goal changed the whole complexion of the game. Sitting in the dugout in Croke Park for the first time was an amazing experience. As Mayo came forward in waves of attack the tension was palpable. Jackie Lyne was like a cat on a hot tin roof as he ran from the sideline back to his selectors, who were frantically looking for ways to stem the Mayo onslaught. The high-fielding Mick Fleming was introduced. Joe Corcoran pointed for Mayo, to leave just one point between the sides. The tension was near unbearable during those last remaining minutes. Mick O'Dwyer kicked two wides and then Mayo had a wonderful opportunity to draw the game. Willie McGee – and I can still see this as clear as day in the mind's eye – jinked his way in for goal at the Railway End from under Hill 16 and it appeared as if he would goal. Corner back Seamus McGearailt later recalled that moment in time in an interview. 'Johnny Culloty roared at me, "Don't let him in," so I fouled him, preventing a goal which would certainly have seen us defeated as time was up.'

I had the perfect view of the free being taken. Joe Corcoran, Mayo's recognised free kicker, placed the ball to take what appeared to be an easy tip over free. However, he stepped aside and left it to Seamus O'Dowd. Din Joe Crowley stood between O'Dowd and the goal, hands raised in an attempt to distract the kicker. Now whether it was the massive pressure of the occasion or Crowley distracting him, the Mayo man pulled the ball wide to his right and it flashed inches wide. We were through to the final on the score 0-14 to 1-10.

It appeared as if Kerry were riding on their luck. Cork had missed two penalties in the Munster final and now Mayo had squandered the simplest of opportunities to send the semi-final to a replay. It was dramatic stuff and it was a fairly muted dressing room after the game as everyone fully realised that we had been very fortunate to come away with a win. And here was I with, in my own opinion, limited football ability but still part of a great Kerry team ready to contest the All-Ireland final against Offaly. Little did I think when I listened to that 1953 All-Ireland final on the side of Lower New Street, Killarney, on William McNeill's Bush radio that I would be part of such a wonderful occasion sixteen years later. It was the stuff of Kerry football dreams and mine had come true.

The run up to the final was everything I expected. We were training in the Austin Stack Park in Tralee and it was another glorious September. We were all in peak physical condition now and it was a tremendous feeling of satisfaction to be able to match my illustrious teammates as we jogged, sprinted and ran from one end of the field to the other. Huge crowds would turn up to watch the sessions; no such thing as locking gates and preventing Kerry supporters from studying form. There was also no such event as a special press night back then, and the photographers and journalists would simply turn up to training and get their interviews and pictures when the opportunity presented itself. I met legendary journalists such as Paddy Downey of *The Irish Time*s, John D. Hickey of the *Irish Independent* and Mick Dunne of *The Irish Press*.

Eamon Horan and John Barry were renowned *Kerryman* reporters and attended training most evenings. *The Kerryman* was the only local paper being published countywide at the time and they, too, had full access to the players and mentors. It was also a well-recognised thing for the journalists to visit the players at their place of work in those days, where they would capture their interview and have an accompanying photographer take pictures. Johnny Culloty, being captain, was of course in big demand and visits by journalists to St Finan's were common; the interviews would take place in the front hall or even outside the front hall entrance while patients and visitors passed in and out. It was really all 'off-the-cuff' stuff, with players far more accessible than today. But those journalists back then had a reputation and the players trusted them implicitly. Today there is a surfeit of journalists, and you have those who are continually searching for the so-called 'breaking news', writing anything, good, bad or indifferent, irrespective of the feelings of the player in question.

A major problem surfaced in the weeks preceding the final. Mick O'Connell was injured and was absent from training. There was consternation in the county and the local and national media got tremendous mileage out of it. Jackie Lyne and Johnny Culloty visited Valentia and conferred with Mick. He had begun treatment for muscle injuries and, as the preparations continued in Tralee, we were all in the dark as to whether O'Connell would play or not. Up until the morning of the match the doubt remained.

We travelled to Dublin by train on the Saturday and again stayed in the Skylon Hotel, where supporters were allowed to mingle freely with the players. That night it was off to a show in the Gaiety Theatre and bed by 11 o'clock. The team had been announced following a trial match the previous Monday in Killarney, and I was listed as sixth substitute. As there were just five medals for substitutes, I was fully aware that all my sacrifices during the year would be in vain if Kerry captured the All-Ireland. However, that was the way back then. Only two years later an extra medal was introduced to cover the reserve goalkeeper, alas too late for me.

I joined a few of my teammates on the sideline to watch the Minor final and soak up the atmosphere, a unique and wonderful experience. Cork beat Derry in that final, 2-7 to 0-11. Declan Barron, John Coleman, Connie Hartnett and Martin Doherty were the Cork stars, while Martin O'Neill (who would go on to become a top English Premiership player and manager) was corner forward for the Derry men.

The ultimate Kerry honour as I pose for the Kerry team picture before our victory in the 1969 All-Ireland final against Offaly. *Back row (l–r)*: John O'Keeffe, Pat Griffin, Mick Gleeson, Michael O'Shea, Mick O'Connell, Paud O'Donoghue (RIP), Liam Higgins (RIP), Mick O'Dwyer and Mick Morris; *front row (l–r):* Din Joe Crowley, Weeshie, Seamus Murphy (RIP), Tom Prendergast, Seamus McGearailt, Johnny Culloty (captain), Brendan Lynch, Eamon O'Donoghue (RIP) and Dom O'Donnell.

And so to the Senior final, and you could actually sense the relief in the dressing room when Mick O'Connell came in; it gave everyone a huge lift. Jackie Lyne gave a stirring pep talk and it was then team first out the door, substitutes next. I was directly behind O'Connell, the last man out as we ran onto Croke Park. It was evident that all Kerry eyes were watching, wondering, hoping and waiting for the Valentia man and when he appeared the roar that went up from the expectant Kerry followers would literally put the hair standing on your head. I have never heard or seen any player receive such a spontaneous and general acclaim for just appearing on the pitch on All-Ireland final day.

We won the toss and had been instructed to play with the strong wind, which we did. It was a terrible day for football and there is nothing more difficult than a fierce, swirling wind to spoil any game. Points from Mick Gleeson (2), Din Joe Crowley, Liam Higgins and young Brendan Lynch saw us ahead at the short whistle, 0-5 to 0-2. At the half-time break there was an air of calmness in the old dressing room under the Cusack stand, despite the fact that we would be playing against a near gale-force wind on the resumption. Jackie Lyne had seen it all, as a player for many years, and his experience was now vital – and he was adamant the team was in such great shape that they were well capable of holding out for a win. I remember distinctly the late Eamon O'Donoghue being instructed to fall back from his half-forward position to help out in defence. While this tactic is a common occurrence today, I believe Eamon was one of the first players to adopt this roving role on a constant basis. What remains etched on my memory is the cool, calm, steely determination of the Kerry players as they gathered around a table in the middle of the dressing room. Johnny Culloty said a few quiet words, as did Mick O'Dwyer, and then it was back out on the field where Kerry's destiny awaited them. Could we win the county's twenty-first title?

The second half was barely a minute old when we witnessed one of the great defining moments (and there were many) in the ongoing story of Kerry football history. Offaly were now attacking the Railway goal with the wind at their back. A long high ball was kicked into the Kerry square; full forward Sean Evans rose high, fielded, and all in one movement turned and shot hard and low for the goal with the right foot. However, Johnny Culloty, showing amazing positional sense, moved swiftly to his left, gathered the ball to his chest and saved. There is no doubt in my mind that if Offaly had scored here they would have gone on to lift the Sam Maguire. Tadge Crowley, the Kerry secretary, was sitting

The Kerry junior team with which I won a coveted All-Ireland medal in London in 1967. *Back row (l–r):* Mick Gleeson, Paudie Finnegan (RIP), Mickey Walsh, P. J. McIntyre, Patsy Joy, M. J. O'Shea, Colm O'Callaghan, Tom O'Sullivan (RIP) and Mick Aherne; *front row (l–r):* Donie Sheehan (selector), Weeshie, Pat O'Connell, Patsy O'Connor, Derry Crowley, Billy Doran, Pat Ahern and Gerry McCarthy; *sitting (l–r):* Pat Sweeney and Brendan Lynch.

close to the dugout and he turned to Jim Brosnan and said, 'That's the winning of this game.' And he was proved right. For the thousands watching the game, Culloty's save may have seemed as if it was pure instinct, however, there is a fascinating story behind the save that sent Kerry on their winning way to capture their twenty-first All-Ireland. And I was part of that story.

In the weeks leading up to the final when we had a free evening from Kerry training, Johnny and I would go down to the St Brendan's College field in the New Road and put in the extra bit of goalkeeping practice. At some of those sessions he instructed me to catch the ball with my back to the goal, turn and shoot to his left, all in one movement. We did this drill for all of one session, field, turn, and kick to his left. All in one movement. And he explained the reason behind the drill. 'That is the way Sean Evans might shoot; I have studied him and he always turns to his right foot, I want to be ready for that.' And when that moment came in Croke Park he certainly was ready. His years of playing in goal for the Kerry footballers and hurlers together with his time with Munster and Ireland had taught him every trick of the trade.

Offaly did cut the gap to one point at one stage but late scores from Mick O'Dwyer and Din Joe Crowley saw us deserved winners, 0-10 to 0-7. While Crowley was the hero of the hour, his midfield partner O'Connell was also superb and without him Kerry, in my opinion, would not have won. Wing back Tom Prendergast was also remarkable. The man from Keel was the best small man I have ever seen on a football field.

The after-match scenes were unforgettable. Thousands of Kerry fans rushed onto the field; it was particularly special to meet many of my own Killarney Legion clubmates, so proud to have two players and the trainer as part of the victorious side. What happened after that has become part of the wonderful cavalcade of All-Ireland winning memories down through the years. There was near bedlam in the dressing room as what seemed like hundreds of followers forced their way in. The then Bishop of Kerry, Eamon Casey, was there and offered up a stirring verse of 'The Rose of Tralee'. Reporters, TV cameramen and photographers battled for space to do their job as the Sam Maguire Cup was passed around over the heads of the milling crowd. This is a very much a snapshot from the past, since now access to the dressing rooms is closely guarded and such a scene would be impossible.

The Kerry Association in Dublin, as always, hosted the team banquet that night and the following morning, after a late, late night, we were all guests of honour at the Guinness brewery because Jackie Lyne was a lifelong employee of the firm. There was also a visit to the television studios in Montrose, where we viewed a film of the game and accepted excellent hospitality. But despite all of this and the great sense of occasion following the victory, at the back of all the players' minds was the thought of getting on the train and bringing the cup home to the Kingdom. This is what has inspired every single player that has ever worn the Kerry jersey, those magical childhood memories of seeing the Sam Maguire Cup paraded around the county.

Home, especially to a Kerry footballer, is where the heart is.

11

'Gossamer Lunacy': the Kerry build-up to an All-Ireland Final

The wonderful, late John B. Keane once talked to me about the phenomenon of the Kerry build-up to an All-Ireland final while a guest on my programme, *Terrace Talk*. He told me, 'A kind of a gossamer lunacy comes over Kerry people before an All-Ireland final. Young and old lose all sense of themselves; it's football for breakfast, dinner and supper, and everyone becomes an expert.' Beautifully said by one of Kerry's greatest and most loved sons.

For a few weeks of the year the excitement and anticipation of Kerry's involvement in the final will brush all other issues to one side. The opposition is discussed in great detail over big, frothy pints of porter in all the local GAA watering holes and, of course, there is massive debate on just who will, or will not, be on the Kingdom starting fifteen. How is that fellow going in training; is such and such a man injured? The debates are endless. And, boy, do the Kerry supporters know their football.

Back in the 1950s, and indeed even during my own era in the 1960s, things were slightly muted and not as colourful.

Everything has changed dramatically over the past decades. The schools of the county really get involved and classrooms everywhere are adorned with hand-drawn posters of the county players, all plastered on windows for passers-by to admire. Cars are painted green and gold and flags are, incredibly, unfurled in the most difficult places to reach. I have vivid memories of seeing four green and gold flags blowing proudly in the wind in 2004; there they were, all up on St Mary's Cathedral, Killarney, over 300 feet off the ground, proclaiming to one and all that Kerry football is indeed part of our religion. The steeple of this magnificent church, where Joan and I were married, was being repaired and the steeplejacks had erected the flags. It was a wonderful sight.

I had the honour of captaining this star-studded East Kerry team to county championship victory in 1968. We played in six county finals, winning four (1965, 1968, 1969 and 1970). We won the first All-Ireland club title in 1971 together with three Munster club championships (1965, 1968 and 1970). Thirteen of this team played for Kerry at some grade. *Back row (l–r):* John Saunders, Johnny Culloty, Tom Long, Din Joe Crowley, Tim Sheehan, Florry Mahoney, Donie O'Sullivan and Donie Sheehan (trainer); *front row (l–r):* Mick Gleeson, Mickey Lyne, Larry Kelly, Jerry McCarthy, Weeshie (captain), Jer O'Donoghue, Derry Crowley and Pat Moynihan.

Donkeys, ponies and sheep are also painted green and gold and songs are traditionally written for the occasion. Kerry jerseys are to be seen everywhere, worn by young and old; I have even seen a specially knitted *geansaí* on a three-year-old child. I knew a lovely Killarney lady who was seriously ill on the run up to one final, but she insisted that her finger- and toenails be painted alternately green and gold. Sadly, this fanatical Kerry follower has since died.

As the countdown continues, attendance at the team's training sessions becomes noticeably greater. It begins to seem as if the whole county is converging on Fitzgerald Stadium. Families arrive decked out in a blaze of green and gold, while the kids are in their element as they press their faces anxiously against the fence surrounding the playing field, pleading with the players for autographs and photographs. The excitement is palpable and in many ways this is also an important and totally infectious part of the handing down of the Kerry tradition. Let us hope that the tendency to have some training sessions behind closed doors, which I have seen creeping in lately, will not become a common occurrence. In my opinion it separates the fans from the players. It is a break from tradition and can only weaken the Kerry cause.

There is no better place to meet up with highly knowledgeable Kerry supporters than at one of these training sessions. If you are fortunate enough to fall into company with one of these men or women, you will come away with many golden nuggets of information and, more than likely, a greatly improved knowledge of the history of Kerry football. The most dedicated and knowledgeable followers tend to congregate in a particular area of the stand or terrace. All eyes will be focused on the players as they begin to go through their paces, with Jack O'Connor calling the shots and instructing the trainers as to what he expects from them. The three selectors will be standing back studying the players and, I presume, discussing the form being shown by the various members of the squad, but it is the man in the stand who will spot even the slightest little difference in a player's usual form. Body shape and weight will be discussed, as will running style, and the merest trace of an injury will be the subject of huge debate. And, horror of horrors, if a player goes down injured during one of the practice games. These Kerry experts know full well that injury is the catastrophe that can upset the best laid plans.

Attending training sessions is, and always has been, one of the great pleasures of many supporters in the build-up to an All-Ireland final. Of course in the 1950s and 1960s the training system was very different. The preparation of the team was obviously the best available at that time, but it has come on so much in the intervening years that there is almost no comparison. At that time it was customary to begin the session with laps of the field and the group of players would run bunched together in close contact, keeping outside the corner flags and not cutting corners. Following, perhaps, five laps of the field, the squad would divide up into separate groups of about ten. Each group would form a circle and, while standing in that circle, they would simply punch the ball from player to player, first with the right hand and then with the left hand. The golden rule was that when you received the ball you had to clutch it tightly to your chest every time. After, say, ten minutes of circle-punching, the squad would then spread out across the field in a straight line on the end line. On the first whistle from the trainer you were expected to break into a fast walk, on the second whistle you had to sprint as fast as you could, and on the third blast you slowed once again to the fast walk. This routine would be continued up and down the entire length of the field and was designed to train the players to be lightning fast from a standing position, thus getting to the ball ahead of an opponent.

Next might come piggyback jumping. Ten players would line up, one behind the other and say 5 yards apart, all bending down, with hands placed on knees. The man from the rear would then run, place his hands on the back of the crouching player just in front of him, and leap right over him; he would then run on to the next crouching player, and so on, until he had completed the line. He would finally crouch down at the front of the line while the new player at the rear took over, and the line of jumpers would continue around the field. The idea was to greatly strengthen all areas of the legs, thus giving the player the ability to out-jump his opponent for the high ball.

Huge emphasis was put on the art of high fielding. The squad of players would spread out to all corners of the field and, using a number of players, would then just kick the ball as high as possible to another teammate. The cry from the trainer would ring continuously around the pitch, 'Rise for it and field it over your head.' It is worth remembering that the football then was the old pigskin that would double in weight when wet and that the near-adhesive gloves now worn by all players had yet to be developed. A few more laps of the field would be added and these would often turn into a flat-out race between members of the squad; it was usually the same players who finished ahead of the pack with the few obvious smokers and pint men bringing up the rear.

Finally came the exercise that was the big 'sorting out' football exercise for many years – backs and forwards. It was the basis of great Kerry victories and it served to coach each player in relation to his particular position on the field of play. It served the county well. The regular goalie, six backs and six forwards all are marking each other. The subs are outside, driving in ball after ball, first a high one and then a low one, as faults are ironed out and teamwork and accurate hand-passing are polished to the highest level possible. Then to a jog, all together, around the field for a few more laps. In conclusion the entire squad would line up on the 50-yard line straight across the field. You had to wait like an Olympic sprinter for the trainer's whistle (the word 'manager' had not yet been introduced). On the whistle it was flat out for the end line where the selectors would call out the finishers, first, second and third.

So there you have it: a snapshot of training routine in the time of trainers like Con Brosnan, Dr Eamonn O'Sullivan, Dr Jim Brosnan, Jackie Lyne and Johnny Culloty. You may well say it was fairly primitive, but examine the record. There you will find the evidence of a county able to evolve and change its styles and methods, more so than many other counties. It is the record of Kerry's success.

Training teams was a huge part of my life. This outstanding East Kerry minor team won the Kerry Minor County Championship in 1972, defeating South Kerry in the final played in Killorglin. *Back row (l–r):* Pat O'Sullivan (Gneeveguilla), Donie Sheehan (Gneeveguilla), Dan Joe Sullivan (Glenflesk), Val Lynch (Glenflesk), Kevin O'Donoghue (Glenflesk), Jerome McCarthy (Glenflesk), Donal Brosnan (Killarney Legion), Tim O'Regan (Spa), Peter Gilhooley (Killarney Legion), John O'Mahoney (Spa), Jer O'Donoghue (Glenflesk), John Brown (Firies), Mike Howe (Killarney Legion) and Neilly Shea (Firies). *Middle row (l–r):* Weeshie, Joe McCarthy (Gneeveguilla), Tom O'Sullivan (Spa), Dinny Murphy (Killarney Legion), Dermot O'Sullivan (captain, Dr Crokes), Tadgh Moriarty (Killarney Legion), Michael Lyne (Killarney Legion), Eamon McDermott (Killarney Legion), Lawrence O'Donoghue (Dr Crokes) and Pat Kelly (Killarney). *Seated (l–r):* Unknown, Sean O'Sullivan (Glenflesk) and Donie Sweeney (Spa).

12

Bringing home the Sam Maguire: the end of a chapter for me

Our homecoming in 1969 was special and eagerly anticipated by the players – as always, for a winning Kerry team. At Rathmore Station the crowd was massive, since their own local hero, Din Joe Crowley, was the first Rathmore player to win an All-Ireland Senior medal. The late Father Kelly, uncle to former GAA president Sean Kelly, made a passionate and emotional speech. Then there was a thundering ovation as Mick O'Connell stepped forward, sending the crowd into raptures when he said, 'Well done to yer own Din Joe, the best midfielder in Ireland'; a little pause here before he added, 'after myself'.

Next stop was my own home town of Killarney and, as we eased into the railway station and the twenty-one detonators on the railway line exploded in joyous welcome, my mind wandered back to my childhood days in the 1950s – 1953, 1955, 1959 and also 1962 – when I had been part of that milling crowd on the platform, welcoming home the victorious captains aboard the old steam trains. Legendary names, magnificent captains, such as Jas Murphy, John Dowling, Mick

O'Connell and Sean Óg Sheehy, together with all their teammates. And now here was I, although just a peripheral player on this great Kerry team, still able to experience this once-in-a-lifetime journey into Kerry football history.

The station platform was a sea of laughing, joyous faces and, as the players alighted from the train, the supporters surged forward to raise Jackie Lyne and Johnny Culloty high on their shoulders, and then we were on board Galvin's lorry to begin the traditional journey through the packed streets of Killarney. Bonfires blazed at various places and the atmosphere was incredible; I shall never forget how moving it was to look down from the lorry onto the happy faces of the cheering Kerry supporters. Youngsters sitting on the shoulders of their parents and the Killarney Brass and Reed band leading the way down College Street, Henn Street (now Plunkett Street), Main Street and High Street. Eventually, after about two hours or so, we arrived outside the Park Place Hotel (now demolished), the recognised stopping point for the welcome speeches. The next day, as is the custom, it was a series of visits to the schools around Killarney. As we entered the Monastery School my mind wandered back to a day in 1955 when Tadghie Lyne and Johnny Culloty had visited us in that very same school. Now the wheel had turned full circle and I was delighted to be part of the group displaying the Sam Maguire to the excited, awestruck youngsters; I, too, was part of the handing down of the Kerry tradition. During the following weeks there were invitations to attend various functions in the company of team members, and our own club held a special reception to recognise our achievements and present Jackie, Johnny and I with mementoes of the win.

It was soon back to training because the 1970 National League commenced in November 1969. After the All-Ireland win Jackie Lyne had called me aside to discuss the fact that I had not received an All-Ireland medal. I assured him that I understood the rules governing the number of medals awarded. However, he told me that if Kerry went on to win the championship in 1970, he would do his utmost to see that I was one of the first five substitutes so that I might have a chance of getting that prized All-Ireland medal. This was a massive boost for me and I redoubled my training and set out to improve my goalkeeping abilities. I played in the first league game away to Mayo and was ready to deputise for Johnny whenever the occasion demanded.

In March 1970 we undertook that memorable around-the-world trip, including Australia, New Zealand, the Fiji Islands, Hawaii and home via America. I played in most of the games as Johnny suffered a knee injury, so I was now getting plenty of experience. On our return to Ireland, however, a serious injury was to intervene and my short-lived inter-county career would come to an abrupt end. While I was playing centre field with my club in an East Kerry League match against Rathmore, a player accidently stuck his finger in my right eye. The usual medical attention back then was applied: a drop of water from a bottle was splashed over my face with the advice, 'You'll be fine, keep going.'

I was not 'fine', unfortunately; as the days passed I noticed the vision in the injured right eye beginning to deteriorate. It was as if someone was slowly pulling a blind down over a window and I knew something was seriously wrong. Expecting to be given some eye drops and told to return in a few weeks, I visited an eye specialist in Killarney. He certainly alarmed me greatly when he insisted that I immediately enter hospital in Cork for observation. Following a series of tests it was discovered that I had a detached retina. The retina is the back part of the eye that contains the cells that respond to light. This type of injury is now treated easily and quickly by laser, but in 1970 the only option was a long and delicate operation. I spent two weeks in hospital and was advised to avoid any contact sport, since a bang on the head or a collision of any sort might again detach the retina.

For the time being I kept my place on the East Kerry team and the divisional side as we went forward to retain the Kerry County Championship and complete the three-in-a-row. I was also on the side that won the All-Ireland Club Championship in Croke Park, defeating Bryansfort County Down in the final. However I was seriously shaken. I had suffered many and various injuries to bones, muscles and ligaments over the years, but the problem with my eye was a completely different challenge. The thought of the retina becoming detached once again or, even worse, suffering an injury to the other eye, proved too much psychologically and I regretfully accepted that my playing days were over. It is said that when the man above closes one door he opens another and this was certainly true in my case. I would go on to take up refereeing, a career that would last close to fifteen years and see me handle three All-Ireland semi-finals and an All-Ireland Under-21, as well as six Kerry County finals, club finals, National League finals, Railway Cups and Munster Championship finals. I would travel the length and breadth of the country, winter and summer.

That year of 1969 had been for me a glorious and unforgettable glimpse into life as a Kerry footballer. Granted it had been short and sweet, but I was lucky. Not every Kerry lad with the typical football obsession can dream the dream and see it come true. Kerry did go on to retain the All-Ireland the following year, beating Meath in the final thanks to a memorable goal scored by Din Joe Crowley. And once again I missed out on winning that coveted medal. Donie O'Sullivan captained the side and John O'Keeffe won his first Senior medal as a player – he was a sub the previous year.

In the following year of 1971 Cork hammered Kerry in the Munster final in Cork, 0-25 to 0-14. Jackie Lyne retired as trainer and Johnny Culloty took over that position and led

Kerry to the 1972 final. A late and extremely fortunate Offaly goal forced a replay, which the Leinster men won easily, 1-19 to 0-13. It was the end of a wonderful period in Kerry football history. I believe that this group of players assembled by Jackie Lyne in 1968 was as good as any that had left the county. Donie O'Sullivan and Brendan Lynch went on to be part of the 1975 winning side when Mick O'Dwyer began the era of near complete dominance that lasted until 1986.

In 1994 that winning Kerry team of twenty-five years previously was invited to Croke Park on All-Ireland final day, as is the tradition, to be honoured and introduced to the supporters at half-time. Weeks before, when it had first been announced in the media that the 1969 team would be honoured, I had begun to look forward eagerly to meeting up with all the men with whom I had trained and played back then. A lot of water had flowed under the proverbial bridge in those intervening years and it would be a great opportunity to recall past times and renew old friendships.

The week before the final dawned and I was still awaiting my invitation from the Kerry County Board. When Thursday came, and still no letter in the post, I realised that I had been ignored and forgotten. I was in a bit of a dilemma as to what course of action I should take. Since I am not the type of person who is inclined to push himself forward or kick up a fuss, I just decided to keep quiet and accept the situation, upsetting as it was. However, one man stepped in and did his best to rectify the snub. Near neighbour and great friend, the late Murt Galvin, had been treasurer of the county board for many years and he rang me on the Thursday before the event, wishing me well for the weekend. When I told him the situation he was dumbfounded and then became furious. He later told me that he immediately rang up Croke Park, but they informed him that it was the responsibility of the Kerry County Board to decide who was or was not invited. Murt then contacted the County Board and was told that as I had not received a medal in 1969, I was not entitled to be amongst those travelling up to Dublin.

It is worth mentioning that in recent years I have often noticed up to thirty former players on the field when the victorious teams of the past are being honoured at Croke Park. But in spite of the fact that I had given my all for the county in my brief career and then served the county as a referee for many years, I was ignored for the sake of a train fare. The whole experience of 1969 had been magical for me, but to be cast aside like that all those years later was one of the most painful experiences of my sporting life. And, to this day, no one has ever contacted me to explain this hurtful decision.

13

Paddy Kennedy and Phil O'Sullivan: jewels in the Kerry crown

Paddy Kennedy. The name keeps coming up wherever football is discussed. Ask anyone who knows anything at all about the game, 'Who was Paddy Kennedy?' The answer invariably will be, 'Wasn't he the great Kerry midfielder of the 1930s and 1940s?' Or else pose this question while in company of the knowledgeable follower: 'Who was the greatest footballer of them all?' And the answer might be – Paddy Kennedy or Mick O'Connell. Even now, years after his death in May 1979 at the young age of sixty-two, the name Paddy Kennedy is immediately associated with great fielding, sheer class, and graceful movement on the field of play, together with great modesty and pure love for the green and gold. I have always regretted not having had the privilege of seeing the Annascaul man play, or of having the honour to meet him and shake his hand. And so, on a cold and wet October day back in 2009 in the company of Paddy's son Brian, I found myself standing at the graveside of this Kerry legend in Bohernabreena cemetery in County Dublin and gently laying a little green and gold flag by the headstone on which is written the inscription:

> God rest you Paddy Kennedy,
> your reward you've surely won.
> When duty called, you gave your all,
> both off the field and on.

My great friend Christy Riordan (CR Video and DVD Productions, Cahersiveen) and I were on a quest to document the achievements, in some small way, of all winning Kerry captains. We traversed the length and breadth of the country interviewing Kerry winning captains together with friends and relations of those captains who had died. It was a humbling experience as we delved in to the lives of legends that had played such a massive part in the story of Kerry's football greatness. *Secrets of Kerry: A Captain's Story*, a four-hour DVD, was the result of that amazing journey and it consumed my life for nearly three years.

Our journey eventually brought us to Dublin where Paddy Kennedy had lived, reared his family and died. The Kennedy family was lavish in their hospitality and we spent a wonderful afternoon in their company discussing the career of the great Kerry midfielder. Paddy's wife, Lyla, is the proud owner of her husband's six All-Ireland medals: five Seniors in 1937, 1939, 1940, 1941 and 1946 and the Minor win from 1933. These six precious pieces of gold are now linked together, forming a magnificent bracelet that is worn on all the great GAA and family occasions.

Annascaul-born Paddy won a county championship with Kerins O'Rahillys in 1939 and four championships in Dublin: three with Foxrock Geraldines and one with the Garda, which he joined in the late 1930s. He left the force some years later to take up a position as a mineral water company representative. His name, as expected, provided a massive boost to the company's sales; he was also the manager of the Crystal ballroom in Dublin up until the mid-1970s. His vast collection of honours included ten Munster Senior Football Championship medals, the first in 1936 and the last in 1947. In 1941 and 1946 he helped Munster to Railway Cup victories.

When I visited Paddy's family, his niece Emma was also there to talk about her great pride in her uncle, as was Knocknagoshel-born Moss Walsh, brother of the late Kerry great Eddie Walsh. As well as being friends with Paddy, Moss had been a teammate when they both lined out for Dublin club Geraldines. Paddy's two lovely daughters, Eilish and Helen, have wonderful memories of their father. They recall him teaching them the art of his legendary high fielding out in the back garden – the spring from a standing position and the wide-open arch of both hands to grasp the ball. Both girls later went on to represent their school and Ireland in basketball. Their skills saw them travel all over Europe. 'No doubt it was Dad's coaching that helped us on the road to play with Ireland,' Helen informed me.

Speaking to sons Brian and Paul it is so obvious that they are very proud of their famous father. Both played football and Brian recalled the many occasions when comparisons were made between themselves and their dad: 'It made it very difficult; the usual comment was, "Sure, you will never be as good as Paddy."' This, of course, is a common problem when the sons of former Kerry stars play with their fathers' clubs. Paul is the proud owner of a Kerry jersey worn by his father. Not just any old jersey, let me add, but the one worn by Paddy in the famous 1947 Polo Grounds final in New York when Cavan beat Kerry. Now much smaller, having been washed a few times, it has the huge number 15 on its back. Paddy played in the corner that day, as he had not fully recovered from an ankle injury sustained the previous year in the great final replay victory over Roscommon. He was, of course, the Kingdom captain for that memorable win.

All Kerry high-fielders are inevitably compared to Paddy. Both his sons recall how, despite being elevated to the status of a national hero after his retirement, he would explain away the phenomenon in his usual modest way by saying, 'Sure only for Mick O'Connell and the comparisons that they are making between us, I'd be forgotten long ago.'

It certainly was an unforgettable experience to spend a day in company with the family of a Kerry legend. On the morning of Paddy's funeral mass Mick O'Connell rose early in his Valentia Island home. He drove to Dublin and before mass began he walked up the centre aisle of the church, shook hands with the grieving family and said, 'It's one of my great regrets in life that I never got to know Paddy Kennedy, I would love to just have shaken his hand.' When mass was over Mick drove back to the island. One legendary Kerry midfielder bidding his farewell to another.

One week after our meeting with the Kennedy family, our journey brought us to Cloyne in County Cork, birthplace of the great Christy Ring, where we spent a fascinating few hours in the company of a charming lady now in her ninetieth year. Annie Hegarty has a memory crystal clear and as sharp as a razor, and her recollection of events stretching right back to the 1920s is simply amazing. Our great good fortune in being put into contact with Annie helped us discover some wonderfully intimate details about one of the legendary Kerry captains of that decade.

Phil O'Sullivan from Glenmore in Tuosist captained Kerry to win the 1924 All-Ireland. He also lays claim to the distinction of being the person who invited his college friend, the late Kerry trainer Dr Eamonn O'Sullivan, to train the Kingdom for the first time in preparation for that 1924 final. Annie Hegarty, his niece, is a direct link to that 1924 Kerry victory and one of the few remaining people who saw Phil play with Kerry. She remembers seeing him in the local field after Sunday mass in the summer, training and coaching the Tousist footballers. She also tells the story of how he travelled to America with the Kerry team in 1927 and met and fell in love with Kathleen O'Mahoney from Tipperary, who played the piano at a function for the visiting Kerry team. Annie informed us that Phil, who was a beautiful singer of old Irish melodies, was prevailed upon to sing a duet for the huge attendance with the beautiful young Tipperary girl, and so began an affair that would eventually end in marriage. Phil and Kathleen did not have a family and Annie was clearly emotional as she informed us that in 1952, when Phil died at a young age, there was no one present at his funeral.

Today Phil O'Sullivan, the 'Master', the man who led a star-studded Kerry side to victory over Dublin in 1924, lies at rest in Calvary Cemetery, New York, far from his beloved Glenmore where his father and later his sisters taught in the local school. Indeed it was in this school, now used as a youth hostel, that Phil was born in 1897. Years later Kerry emigrants from Tuosist and the surrounding area came together and erected a marble headstone to mark his grave. In 1965 the Tuosist GAA club named the local sports field the 'Phil O'Sullivan Memorial Park', a fitting tribute to this great Kerry sportsman. Annie Hegarty's recollection of her uncle and his times is precious and our lengthy interview with her is, in my opinion, a wonderful contribution to Kerry football, Tuosist and history in general.

14

My life behind the walls of the mental hospital

The old mental hospital system was indeed a heartbreaking one, with people sometimes 'buried alive' for forty years or more, many for the most obscure reasons; only their hospital files can tell their life stories. Two sad and poignant events that I experienced at first hand paint the picture of just how tragic the situation could be for patients back then.

The first happened sometime in the 1960s. I was on night duty in the infirmary ward of the hospital. It was here that patients who were seriously ill or suffering some other illness or injury were treated. It was a Monday night, my week had just begun, and an old man who had been a patient in the hospital for more than thirty years was dying. Always a very traumatic experience when one of your patients lies on his death bed. I made him as comfortable as possible and watched over him carefully as his life ebbed away. He took his last breaths around four in the morning. He had a peaceful death. A priest had administered the last rites the previous evening. I remember this particular patient for two special reasons. During his life in the wards I had had many conversations with him and he had informed me that he had worked in a meat plant in Chicago as a young man. Not feeling able to cope so far away from home, he had returned to Ireland after a few years, and his family had had him admitted to St Finan's 'for a rest'.

He thus became just another number, another statistic and eventually became institutionalised, abandoned and deliberately forgotten. That morning after he died, my job was to inform the doctor on duty and the man's nearest relatives of his death. When I opened his bulging file in search of a contact phone number or address I quickly discovered there would be no need for either. Clipped into his file inside the front cover was a note printed in large lettering: 'When John dies we are not to be contacted, the local Killarney undertaker, M. D. O'Shea, will handle all burial arrangements.' The message was clear. The family did not want to be associated with a relation in the Killarney Mental Hospital and probably younger members of the family did not even know they had a relation in the hospital. I attended his burial two days later and helped lay him in an unmarked grave.

Some years later, this time on day duty, a second sad experience came as another sharp reminder that many patients were forgotten about back in those strange times. I was in charge of a ward when a patient died suddenly. Once again he was buried without a relative at his funeral. Some weeks later three adults, two girls and a man, came to my office obviously upset and distressed. They had discovered completely accidently through friends that the man who had died was, in fact, their uncle. They had grown up without knowing that this lovely, gentle person even existed. They asked to read his file, and did this following a doctor's permission. Then they quizzed me as to this man's life, his personality, his habits, and so on. The two ladies wept openly as I recounted as far as possible exactly what kind of a person their unknown uncle had been. As in the first case I have outlined, their parents had kept his existence completely hidden from family and friends. Just two brief memories that signify in graphic detail the sad plight of patients in the 1950s and 1960s. There are many more and it would take a book on its own to recount my thirty-eight years behind the walls of Killarney Mental Hospital.

There were more than 20,000 people locked up in mental institutions during the 1950s and 1960s, many more than in any other form of institution. They became overcrowded, insanitary, and many people died when admitted to the so-called 'asylums'. In many ways they were 'dumping grounds' for social problems and, in most cases, when people went in they never came out alive again. It was a case of people being locked away for ever. Of all records of life in Ireland in that era, the records of these hospitals give the deepest insight into the hidden misery in society during those years.

The system was at its peak when I entered the nursing profession. Statistically, Ireland was even ahead of the old Soviet Union in terms of the numbers per head of the population who were incarcerated. For most of the 200 years of its existence Ireland's mental hospital system had never stopped expanding. Its size and scale was massive by international standards. How did this happen? Was it an epidemic of mental illness or, as it was referred to in my youth, 'insanity'? I do not think so. It was certainly far too easy to have a person admitted then and this must have been taken advantage of in some instances. However, patients were often admitted in a clearly disturbed state or in a deep state of depression and, occasionally, there were patients who were admitted in a chronic schizophrenic state after spending a prolonged period at home without receiving any form of treatment whatsoever. In this era before modern drugs and enlightened care in the community, incarceration was sometimes the only option for these patients. Their condition would then be addressed in the hospital by one of the following range of treatments: electroconvulsive (or electroshock therapy, as it was then known); insulin shock therapy; sedation; occupational therapy; psychotherapy; or (in a very extreme case which I saw performed unsuccessfully just once) cerebral surgery, which involved destroying some of the nerve-fibre connections in the frontal lobes. Very few patients, as you can imagine, accepted this last form of treatment and thankfully it was soon discontinued.

And as to the much-debated electroconvulsive therapy or ECT? This was used as a treatment for a small number of severe mental illnesses. It was originally developed in the 1930s and was used widely during the 1950s and 1960s for a variety of conditions. I would have assisted at this on a regular basis, both in the hospital and at clinics in Tralee and other venues in Kerry. It was not a pretty sight, as ECT consists of passing an electrical current through the brain to produce an epileptic fit – hence the name, electroconvulsive. On the face of it, this sounds bizarre. Why should anyone ever have thought that this was a sensible way to treat a mental disorder? The idea developed from the observation that, in the days before there was any kind of effective medication, some people with depression or schizophrenia who also had epilepsy seemed to feel better after having a fit. In patients without epilepsy the seizure can be brought on by passing an electrical current from an ECT machine across the person's brain in a carefully controlled way. An anaesthetic and muscle relaxant are also given, so that the patient is not conscious when the ECT is administered; the muscle spasms that would normally be part of a fit – and which could produce serious injuries – are reduced to small, rhythmic movements in the arms, legs and body. By adjusting the dose of electricity, the ECT team will try to cause a seizure between 20 and 50 seconds long. Any improvement in the patient's condition is due to the effect that the fit has on the body, not to the electric current used to induce the fit.

Present at the procedure would be the anaesthetists, hospital doctor and a number of nurses, depending on the quantity of patients receiving ECT on any given day. That number could range from five to fifteen. This form of treatment was graphically displayed in the 1975 film *One Flew over the Cuckoo's Nest.* Jack Nicholson brilliantly played the part of Randall Patrick McMurphy in the film and he was shown, in graphic detail, being administered ECT as a response to his uncooperative behaviour towards nursing staff in the hospital where he was a patient. The use or misuse of ECT is still a topic for much discussion today and, I suspect, will be for a long time to come.

There were certainly people in St Finan's well enough to go home who were not welcome there. Others wished to stay because they could not face their home communities; the stigma attached to being an ex-inmate at the hospital was huge. But it must, of course, be stressed that there were also many cases where family and friends kept in constant touch with patients and would visit on a regular basis. However, even in these cases I always had the feeling that the one subject generally avoided when talking to relatives was 'taking the patient home'. I also feel it is important to be clear that life inside the hospital was, for many who were admitted, far better than that which they had left outside. In almost all the country areas of Kerry back in the 1950s and 1960s the rural electrification scheme had not yet brought the magic of electricity to the parishes. And it must be remembered that very few houses had running tap water, relying instead on wells and rainwater collected in barrels from the gutters of their homes. And so, for many a patient from a very rural area, life would literally improve overnight when they were admitted. Everything not available in their homes was now at their fingertips.

One comment made to me by a long-stay patient summed up in no uncertain terms just how comfortable life could be for many. When I asked him one day why he never spoke about being discharged home to his family, his reply was short and to the point: 'Why should I leave here? I have three good meals, a bed, blazing fire, laundry, light and nurses to look after me night and day.' This, then, is the other side of life behind the walls and I sometimes get angry when I hear certain radio programmes or watch television documentaries that dwell on some of the depressing and frightening tales about the old hospitals that have come to light. Yes, of course, it was a harsh era; but one needs to have worked in these institutions to appreciate that there were two sides to the story. The good these hospitals did is rarely, if ever, highlighted.

The routine on the ward of a mental hospital back in the 1960s was rigid and, with over seventy patients in residence, Ward 5 was very over-crowded. Each morning the night nurse would hand over to a day staff of five at 8 a.m. sharp, and the day staff would get the patients up, wash them and generally ready them for breakfast. Bathing and showering took place once a week, but we shaved the patients with the old Mac's Smile razor blades twice a week because most were unable to shave themselves. One very quickly became a bit of an expert at this job.

The question arises: how did the patients pass their day? What type of life did these patients lead? One could say that the day was built around mealtimes, occupation times and recreation times. In those days the St Finan's kitchen was feeding over a thousand patients, not to mention the staff who took their three meals in the staff dining hall, and so it was always a fierce hive of activity. Male and female patients ate in separate dining halls back then, although in later years they would all eat together. There were also meals that were delivered to the infirmaries and secure, locked wards in specially heated containers. I well remember serving those meals on the secure wards; the only eating utensils were the tin mugs and tin plates. The patients sat at long tables, maybe twenty at each table, and it was important to be always vigilant as it was more than likely that one of these highly disturbed people would cause a problem at mealtimes.

Vegetables were all supplied from the hospital farm, which was worked by a body of patients who were rewarded for their contribution to hospital life. In my early days pigs and cattle raised on the farm were slaughtered and the patients always received the best of food. Male patients worked on the farm (forty to fifty men at peak times) and a further twenty-five to forty men would be engaged in other forms of occupational therapy, such as basket-weaving, chair and fence making, painting, using the hospital's printing press, odd-jobbing, and working in the garden, kitchen or laundry. Female patients worked in the kitchen, laundry and occupational therapy. The maximum employed at any time was between 200 and 250 patients, leaving a balance of 700 patients unoccupied.

For those patients who did not work, recreation time was the focus of their day. At the eastern side of the hospital was situated the 'male airing court', an open space of about two acres enclosed by a 6 foot iron railing. It had two goal posts, a handball alley, and a covered shelter. When the daily routine of cleaning, bed-making, shaving and bathing was completed, the patients who were not occupied in work were escorted to the airing court where they remained until lunch. After lunch, these patients were again escorted back to the court, where they remained until teatime. The whole court was supervised by about twenty staff, and the difficult and aggressive patients were closely monitored. Nurses were stationed at various points around the grounds and it was often I was assigned to the position behind the handball alley, a blind spot where a patient might attempt to scale the railing and head for home.

Fifteen to twenty patients played football, three or four played handball; some played cards or pitch and toss, while others read newspapers. The majority walked around a pathway situated close to the perimeter fence. Most patients kept to themselves, many had their own specially worn path on which they walked continuously, up and down, up and down, oblivious to those around them and lost in a world of their own. The majority of patients used this time to exercise and enjoy the fresh air.

The airing court was an integral part of the hospital for 150 years, but with the emergence of more enlightened attitudes and the advent of drug therapy, the airing court disappeared around 1963 or 1964. All that remains today is the handball alley – a monument to the many men who spent their days in its shadow. In 1964 part of the airing court was converted into a golf putting green and a small pitch and putt course. The remainder was landscaped, and today is a beautiful open space.

The female section of the hospital had two airing courts; the first was for the difficult and aggressive patients and was small, accommodating a maximum of about sixty women. The second was for the chronic long-stay patients, who contrasted with the first and tended to be more contented and easy to manage as a result. Both were dismantled around 1964 and are now landscaped gardens.

The importance of these airing courts for the well-being of the patients cannot be overestimated. In this era of full custodial care for the mentally ill, it was always very evident to me that some patients began to suffer greatly when the long, dark winter days set in and bad weather prevented those precious hours outdoors. They would become restless, more noisy and agitated. The majority of the patients, however, were unfortunately institutionalised, having spent many years in the hospital; they had grown used to this annual change in their daily routine.

A lot of paperwork was involved in the job because it was vital to update each patient's file daily. These records had to contain all the necessary information on the patient's mental and physical wellbeing, and especially changes in behaviour, sleep patterns, eating habits and medication. The night nurses had to be particularly observant of patient sleep patterns, since this was vital information for the doctor when he prescribed medication. This was administered either by tablet or injection form. Side effects from these medications, especially in the early 1960s when I was a young nurse, could be sudden and dangerous and, here again, continuous observation and recording was crucial.

Upon arriving for duty at 8 a.m. each morning, I was expected to update myself on the special aspects of the ward I was to work on: the total number of patients; which patients were sick or feeble; those liable to have epileptic fits; those with suicidal tendencies; and those who may be dangerous or harbour escapist ideas. Indeed, we frequently dealt with new admissions who had indicated suicidal tendencies to friends or relatives. Consequently, I often spent days or nights on end sitting at a patient's bedside on a duty that was referred to as 'being on special'; on no account were you allowed to leave the patient on his own.

The nights in particular were very long and trying. Even when visiting the bathroom the patient had to be closely watched, as the danger of attempted drowning in a bath of water was a distinct possibility. It would take just inches of water in a bath to allow a fatality. Articles of clothing such as neckties, bootlaces, stockings and so on, could potentially be used in a suicide attempt and I have seen this myself, thankfully not with fatal results. The most likely item of clothing, in my experience, was the cord of a dressing gown and I always removed these from the patient where danger might threaten. But attempts at suicide by drug overdose were far more common; patients would fail to take their daily medication, instead concealing it and building up a lethal supply. I have also seen patients attempting to cut their throats or wrists with scissors, knives, or other type of blade but thankfully, due to the very professional observance of the nurses on the ward, we avoided a fatality.

Night duty would begin at 9 p.m. and finish at 8 a.m. and the number of days or weeks you served on nights varied. As the hospital slept, the lights were dimmed and the quietness of the night descended; the urge to close your eyes and drift off to sleep was powerful but night duties were quite busy. 'Non-special' night duty (a duty that was not a suicide watch), when I would be responsible for maybe a hundred patients, consisted of making regular rounds of all my wards and ensuring that all patients were comfortable. I would distribute night medication and chat and talk to the men before they slept. An occasion would often arise when a patient became disturbed and was unable to sleep; then a doctor would be summoned, stronger night sedation would be prescribed and, hopefully, this would work. Usually around 7 o'clock in the morning I would go on my last round, checking that all my patients were alive and well. It was always an upsetting occasion if you discovered a patient had died suddenly during the night. Once again the doctor would be called, relatives notified and forms filled up. That was always a very difficult day to try and get a few hours' sleep, and I have never been very good at sleeping during daylight hours in any case.

I have vivid memories of looking down on the sleeping town of Killarney from the big old Victorian windows of the hospital as the hours dragged slowly by. When I started work at 9 p.m. the picture from the window would resemble a giant Christmas tree because all the houses were lit up. Then, as the hours passed, the lights went out one by one until eventually the town was in near darkness. However, there were always a few homes that remained lit and I often wondered why a particular house kept its light on. Perhaps someone was ill there, a baby was being fed, a member of the household suffered from insomnia? Or perhaps it was simply the case that someone could not sleep without the light on. Of course I would never know. Then, as dawn broke on a winter morning, the scene would change once again. It was always the same houses from which you would first see the chimney smoke curling up as another day unfolded and, as figures could be seen moving around their houses, I would be preparing to head for home and get a few hours' sleep. I never liked night duty. It interfered too much with my sporting life.

Life working in a mental hospital was a continual learning experience, with new and challenging situations every day. And every patient was different, having to be handled in a different manner. You had those who resisted, those who were highly suspicious or aggressive, those who were very depressed or highly agitated, and then there were those who simply were unduly indifferent to life in general. I found that self-control had to be cultivated on a daily or nightly basis: these unfortunate patients were very sick people and it was important never to view difficult or tiresome behaviour as an insult or personal affront, but as a sign of the patient's illness. There were, unfortunately, occasions of violence when assigned to a ward where the most difficult and troublesome patients lived. It might be a case of a man refusing to take his medicine, or assaulting a nurse or another patient, or refusing to apply by the rules of the ward – or simply that the unfortunate person was very unwell. If this was the case, then that patient had to be manually restrained. It might require four or five nurses to achieve this and it was always, for me, very upsetting. There was the great danger that one might be injured, bitten or spat upon and, of course, the danger that the patient himself would be hurt during such an episode. So that they were well prepared for these tricky situations all of the nurses were sent to Cork at some stage or another to undertake a course in manual restraint. But then, to see a man who had been so difficult slowly recovering from his illness was really a gratifying and rewarding experience; his personality would change dramatically, he would move to a less strict ward and, eventually, could be discharged.

St Brendan's Ward in St Finan's Hospital was a 25-bed unit and was the busiest ward of all. Patients were admitted and discharged on a continuous basis. Men from all over Kerry with alcohol and drug addiction, schizophrenia, depression and numerous other psychiatric illnesses would be admitted, on most occasions accompanied by their families. At other times I, with other nurses, would be sent to their homes on what was referred to as an 'escort'.

This was the part of the job that I hated most of all. A taxi from Killarney was generally our mode of transport and it was our duty to enter the home of the person who was due to be admitted. Admittance forms had already been signed by the family and local doctor. You never knew what to expect as you entered a house in some far-flung area of Kerry. The patient might have to be restrained and, if this was not considered safe for us, the Gardaí would accompany the nurses and assist. I have been involved in some very sad occasions when the patient you were to escort to hospital had been 'signed in' by his family, unbeknown to himself. When it was then explained to him and he realised he was being admitted, the seriousness of the situation would dawn on him. It might take a long time to persuade him to come with us and I have seen the patient and families crying bitter tears as he left.

Watching a father or son being taken, against his own free will, from the home in which he has been born and reared is terribly upsetting. It was not unusual to see a patient jumping out a window or escaping out a back door when he realised what was about to happen. On one occasion I recall arriving at a farmyard to collect a poor unfortunate man who had been unwell for some time and there he was parading, military style, around the haggard with a pitchfork held over his shoulder. Needless to say that was an occasion for the Gardaí to be called. I have seen men being admitted to the hospital by Gardaí, bound hand and foot; unfortunate patients who had become violent so that restraint such as this had been unavoidable. On most occasions when they arrived under our care in the ward and medication had been administered, they would eventually become calm. It was one of the most pleasing aspects of the job to see patients slowly recovering under the expert care of doctors and nurses. Each patient differed; it might be days for one, weeks or months for another.

I must stress that in my thirty-eight years as a psychiatric nurse I never personally witnessed any patient being wrongly committed to the hospital by the family. It would be the last resort for a family to sign one of their loved ones into what was referred to as 'Killarney'. The phrase 'he is gone to Killarney' was the easiest way of conveying news of a family member who was mentally unwell.

I cannot speak for the past, however, and I would suspect some patients back in the 1930s, 1940s and maybe even the 1950s were 'signed in' following a row at home over land, property or a dispute over a will. In situations such as this it often happened that the person admitted was from that day left alone, abandoned and forgotten. I have sometimes sat and read through patient files reaching back many years, and the reasons given for admission could be very trivial: a minor family row, refusing to get out of bed or reports from neighbours that a person was dangerous or simply behaving strangely.

It was a chastening experience to nurse these unfortunate people who had been residents in the hospital for maybe forty or fifty years before I began work there in 1962. While some patients did attend occupational therapy departments within the hospital and some patients worked daily in the hospital farm or other sections, for many it was a case of nothing to do and all day to do it. Doctors and nurses were always striving to improve the plight of the long-stay patient but, as is well known even in today's world, the money provided for psychiatric care is often meagre. I have vivid memories of gentle, kind, unassuming men who I befriended in the various wards. Some had been farm labourers, shop assistants, fishermen, and there were two brothers from Killarney town who had served in the English army in foreign lands. Their backgrounds were many and varied, but all had now one thing in common: they were totally institutionalised. The hospital was their home and they would live and die there. They paced the day room, smoked their rat-tail tobacco and Woodbine cigarettes, listened to the radio, walked in the airing court morning and evening when weather permitted, or just sat and stared during long, dark and dreary winter days.

This was the way of mental hospitals before massive changes took place in the late 1970s and 1980s. I have seen those changes taking place and now, thankfully, it is much more difficult to have a person admitted to a psychiatric unit. There are very rigorous rules and regulations to follow. On the other hand, I must say that in later years I have known of people who badly needed time in a psychiatric unit due to their mental condition or continuing deterioration of mental and physical health as a result, for example, of chronic alcoholism; But their families are sometimes refused admission, with the result that the person's health continues to deteriorate.

The old stigma surrounding mental illness and the mystique attached to the large, old grey buildings of St Finan's is now fading into the dim and distant past; thankfully a whole new era has dawned for psychiatry in County Kerry and beyond. But I have many snapshots in my head, pictures of times long gone that will probably never be erased from my memory. I can still see those long corridors, old wards sometimes thick with cigarette and pipe smoke, patients – many forgotten by relatives and friends – sitting alone in overcrowded wards, muttering and singing to themselves. There are many whose names I can recall but, sadly, many more whose faces are clear but whose names I have long since forgotten. And, of course, I can still remember the names and faces of my nursing colleagues, many gone to their eternal reward. Men from all corners of Kerry who nursed side by side with me morning, noon and night and who strove to make life that little bit more comfortable for patients for whom this life behind the walls was the only life they knew.

15

1976 Munster Senior final: the greatest game I ever saw

The greatest game of Gaelic football I have ever seen was the replay and extra-time of the 1976 Munster Senior football final between Kerry and Cork. Most observers have said that the greatest game ever in the history of the GAA was the 1977 All-Ireland semi-final, when Dublin beat Kerry by scoring two late goals, however, I cannot agree.

Many years later I can still recall that magical day at Páirc Uí Chaoimh as if it were only yesterday. I will never forget the closing minutes of that match as both sides strove for victory and we watched the players give their all in sweltering conditions. The supporters in the stand were on their feet and the Kingdom followers were chanting, 'Kerry, Kerry, Kerry'. I have never heard this before or since at a Munster final. The tension in the air, the thunderous cheering of supporters from both sides and the non-stop action on the field as the play surged from end to end; it was just magnificent to watch. One man just a few rows from me could not take the tension any more and simply collapsed in his seat. The medics came rushing to the scene and he was eventually whisked off to an ambulance. I later learned that he was a Kerryman who was known to me. He had suffered a mild heart attack and made a full recovery. Now an old man, he has never attended a game since.

Years later, when I secured a copy of a book entitled *Rebels: Cork GAA since 1950* by the renowned *Irish Examiner* journalist Michael Moynihan (Gill & Macmillan, 2010), I went straight to the chapter covering that game. Michael Moynihan gives his readers a wonderful insight into the minds of the Cork players involved in that mighty struggle for Munster supremacy ahead of the 1976 Munster football final replay. In his chapter entitled 'Watershed', he writes: 'It's usually dangerous to isolate a single game as the fork in the road for a team, or even a player, but the participants in the 1976 Munster football final, particularly the men in the red jerseys, are unequivocal in their belief that this was a turning point in fortunes.' For me, Moynihan's words copper-fastened the belief that there was something very historic about that game.

Cork still had the spine of the team that had won the 1973 All-Ireland title, while Kerry were the reigning champions after shocking Dublin in 1975 with a team of young bachelors. They had wintered well and celebrations were widespread as this brilliant side, under Mick O'Dwyer, took the field for the defence of their title. In many ways, this match defined the future of Kerry football at the time and it would also prove to be the most controversial game I have ever witnessed. Cork came out the worst from that controversy.

Cork defender John Coleman recalls, 'The extra-time defeat to Kerry was a turning point; a hundred and ten minutes of sheer tension, the likes of which you couldn't imagine and which knocked the stuffing out of the Cork team for all time.' The great Cork dual player Jimmy Barry Murphy is even more forthright: 'It was the defining moment of our careers. My personal opinion would be that we were robbed of a Munster title that day. I'd go so far as to say that a whole generation of

Cork footballers had their careers seriously affected by decisions made that day.' Barry Murphy's statement is, in any man's language, pretty dramatic stuff.

It was the first Munster final to be played at the newly opened Páirc Uí Chaoimh on the banks of the Lee and there was chaos before the game had even begun, because no one was familiar with the new stadium. Some 10,000 people got in for free and a mass of supporters crowded onto the sidelines, nearly invading the pitch. The game had to be held up as Tipperary referee John Moloney attempted to push the spectators back. Pat Spillane of Kerry got a belt of an umbrella and was told not to venture into that area for the remainder of the game, while Kerry goalkeeper Paudie O'Mahoney had great difficulty running up to kick-out the ball as fans were crowded around his goal. It was an amazing scene. There were no health and safety regulations back then – it was every man for himself.

The first game had been a dull affair, but the replay and extra time made up for every single disappointing Kerry v. Cork game I had seen since 1955. Pat Spillane, whose point sent the teams into extra time, reflects decades later on what happened: 'It was daylight robbery, we were haunted. We got the rub of the green in a couple of refereeing decisions, Declan Barron's goal especially.' I have vivid memories of those incidents. With just five minutes left Cork were four points ahead when a Sean Walsh effort for goal was saved on the line by Brian Murphy, the Cork corner back. But the umpire decided that Murphy had stepped back over the line with the ball. The goal was awarded. I would swear myself that the decision was wrong. Cork swept upfield, where Declan Barron, the magnificent Cork midfielder, rose majestically high in the Kerry square to punch the ball to the net. But the goal was ruled out for a square ball. It was a very marginal decision. If I was asked I would say it was a legitimate goal. This was a swing of six points to Kerry; Cork were stunned, they never recovered and in extra time Kerry surged to the title, 3-20 to 2-19. Kerry went on to beat Derry in the All-Ireland semi-final but lost a classic decider to Dublin. However, they had survived Munster and a defeat here would probably have finished their great run.

There was a fascinating sequel to that famous (or infamous) final. In 1983, I refereed an opening game at Páirc Uí Chaoimh, the Munster Minor final between Cork and Tipperary. After the game I was togging off and the late John Moloney, then one of the greatest dual referees of the time, was alongside me getting ready to officiate in the Senior final. We were chatting away when a well-known Cork official stuck his head around the dressing-room door and remarked to John, 'Hope you give us fair play today, Moloney.' It was evident he was referring to the 1976 controversy. I could see John, a gentleman of the highest calibre, was visibly upset.

In *Rebels*, Michael Moynihan employs the words of Cork's Dinny Allen to describe the closing moments of that Seniors final in 1983: 'Páidí Ó Sé was right behind me but I picked it off the ground. I just didn't have the energy to get my toe under the ball. I picked it straight in front of Moloney, but Páidí wrapped his arms around me and the whistle went for a free in. I don't know if Moloney felt sorry for us for '76, or what, but he gave the free when it should have gone the other way. Amazing, given what came out of it.' Tadgh Murphy got the ball and goaled off the butt of the post and Kerry were beaten. I also believe Murphy was in the Kerry square when he gained possession of the ball and a free out should have been awarded. Decisions had now gone Cork's way.

That Munster final replay of 1976 was the greatest game of Gaelic football I have seen since my first final in 1955. It was man for man, there was no swarming, crowding or game-suffocating tactics; it was football as it should be played. I could well be accused of living in the past, but I would take those games of the 1970s any day of the week in preference to the basketball-style affairs we see today.

16

Assault and battery: some refereeing experiences

Much has been written and spoken about football over the decades, but one subject above all others has continued to cause heated debate and controversy – the standard of refereeing. (I should add that this certainly does not apply to hurling.) Any publication on the GAA and Kerry in general should, I feel, touch on this because in all the games I have witnessed, played in, or been involved with as selector or trainer, the role of the man in the middle invariably comes up as a hot topic.

Strangely enough, Kerry would not be that well known for supplying referees to the inter-county scene. The cause, no doubt, being Kerry's continuous involvement in the final destination of honours during most decades. Jack McCarthy (1930) and Gus Cremin (1956) have handled All-Ireland Minor finals. At Under-21 level Tommy Sugrue (1988), Aidan Mangan (2001–2004) and myself (1980) have been in charge. For All-Ireland club finals Tommy Sugrue (1990) and myself (1980) have refereed. At Junior level Dan Ryan (1936), Paul Russell (1948), Tommy Sugrue (1987) and Muiris O'Sullivan

(1995) have been the men in the middle. At Senior level it was not until 1934 that a Kerryman was appointed to officiate at an All-Ireland Senior final, and that was Jack McCarthy; two years later the Kerins O'Rahillys man was handed the honour for the second time. Dan Ryan was appointed in 1949 and in later years the excellent Tommy Sugrue served in 1988, 1992 and 1994.

Renowned Killarney publican Jimmy O'Brien presents a set of jerseys to Kerry inter-county referees in 1979, *(l–r):* Tom Brennan, Jerome Conway, Jimmy O'Brien, Eamon O'Sullivan, Sean O'Connor, Bart Moriarty, Weeshie, and Andy Molyneaux, Secretary Kerry County Board (RIP).

I spent close to fifteen years travelling around the country, handling league and championship matches and, having played in six Kerry Senior County Championship finals with East Kerry (winning four), I also had the privilege of refereeing six Senior County finals in the county. I must, however, admit to being bitterly disappointed when, after refereeing the All-Ireland Senior semi-finals of 1981, 1982 and 1983, I was not handed the honour of officiating the 1983 final between Dublin and Galway. Kerry for once was not involved.

Preparing to referee the 1982 National League game in Cork as I meet the Dublin and Cork captains for the toss of the coin. Billy Morgan (Cork) is on the left and Tony Hanahoe (Dublin) is on the right. Billy Morgan was best GAA goalkeeper I ever saw. Both men captained their counties to win the Sam Maguire Cup, Billy Morgan in 1973 and Tony Hanahoe in 1976 and 1977.

It was a sign of the times and the new manner in which referees were appointed at that period when, to my shock, an official entered my dressing room following the 1983 semi-final between Galway and Donegal. I will never forget his words to me: 'You did a great job today, now when you go back to Kerry make a few phone calls around and pull a few strings and you could get the final.' I was shocked by this attitude and, never having been a person to ask for favours of any description in my sporting life, needless to say I did not follow his advice and this may well be the reason I was not appointed for the final.

That 1983 All-Ireland final will live long in the memory for all the wrong reasons. Conditions were atrocious and the rain fell in torrents. John Gough of Antrim was the appointed referee. The match eventually exploded into ill temper and violence and four players – Brian Mullins, Ray Hazley and Ciaran Duff of Dublin and Thomas Tierney of Galway – were sent to the line. The decisive goal came for Dublin when Barney Rock gained possession. Joe McNally of Dublin was lying injured on the ground close to the Galway goal and was being attended to by a posse of medical men and officials. I think the match should have been halted. Barney Rock, however, took advantage of the mix-up and, seeing the Galway goalkeeper Padraig Coyne off his line, lobbed the ball in superb style from far outfield over the keeper's head into the net. It was the decisive score and the Dubs, who were affectionately tagged the 'Dirty Dozen', held out for a famous win.

The following week I wrote to Croke Park, informing those responsible for the appointment of referees that I was no longer available to referee. I continued in Kerry for a number of years following this. I still feel that Gough was too inexperienced for such an occasion and those in Croke Park ultimately responsible for his appointment were to blame for the happenings on the field, not the Antrim official.

A group of Kerry referees gather in 1983. I served as first chairman of this committee for five years. *Back row (l–r):* T. J. O'Connor, Mick Sullivan, Eamon O'Sullivan, Tom O'Connor, Richie Williams, Noel O'Connor and Timmy Carmody; *middle row (l–r):* Gerry O'Riordan, Jerome Conway, Bruddy O'Grady, Tom Keane, Tom Brennan, Gerry Gleeson and John O'Connor; *front row (l–r):* Mick Galway, Weeshie, Mick O'Neill, County Board Chairman Frank King, Bart Moriarty (referee's secretary), Dave Geaney, Liam Sayers and Gerry McCarthy.

'Let us have uniformity in the application of the rules,' is the message coming from Croke Park on a continuous basis. And, while managers and trainers feel it is the very least they might expect from our referees, it is, in my opinion, something we can strive to achieve – but will never reach. The rules of Gaelic football are far, far too numerous and complicated for that. And one thing is sure: during all championship matches we will continue to see some hotly debated referee decisions, with yellow and red cards flashed right, left and centre. While most of the cards will be deserved, there will be others which will have managers hopping in anger and frustration on the sidelines up and down the country. And you can be full sure that some poor, unfortunate man in the middle will be verbally assaulted by some sideline mentors following these 'win at all cost' matches.

The 'experts' on RTÉ's *Sunday Game*, newspaper journalists, radio commentators and those who analyse matches will continue to voice their opinions on the referee in any given game. So, in defence of our referees, let me pose a question. How many of the present inter-county managers and media reporters have ever refereed an inter-county match? Let's make it a little easier. How many of them have ever refereed a local championship or league game in their own county? Let's make it easier still. How many of the above mentioned have read, from cover to cover, the *Official Guide* on the playing rules of Gaelic football? Very few, if any, I would wager. And yet some of these people will rage at the referee, question his ability to be a referee, and even verbally abuse and castigate him in the media following their team's defeat. It goes without saying that constructive criticism is always a healthy thing – if you know the rules.

Of course there are referees who are simply not up to scratch and make blatant mistakes, however, this should not give any person – whether mentor, player or spectator – the right to assault either verbally or physically the man in the middle. Managers, selectors and players make more mistakes in games than any referee. In the mad scramble of today's world of player sponsorship, win at all costs, inter-county player grants and exotic foreign trips, the plight of the referee is sometimes forgotten, in my opinion. In my own experience, having been involved in every aspect of club management and as a player, refereeing is easily the loneliest role. I base this observation on my experience as an inter-county referee for close to fifteen years who has handled games at all levels in the four provinces, including those three All-Ireland semi-finals in Croke Park and a potentially explosive National League final between Armagh and Down.

While most of my refereeing career was totally enjoyable and I would do it all again if the clock was turned back, there is a very dark and dangerous side to the job. A dark side that I have not experienced in any other area of GAA involvement. Unsigned, threatening letters, Garda escorts off the field, team managers ready to give you a savage verbal assault and, worse of all, cowards waiting in the tunnel or on the sideline to attack you when their team loses. I have experienced all of this and more.

One such experience in the late 1970s has left a particularly strong mark on me. I was assigned to referee a National League game in Páirc Uí Chaoimh. A cold, wet, dark February Sunday, Cork against Kildare. Late in the game my umpires awarded a goal to Kildare as they deemed a Kildare shot had marginally crossed the line. Cork lost. It had not been my decision but I had full confidence in my umpires and allowed the green flag to be raised. Some of the Cork players were incensed and sections of the crowd, despite being far away from the incident, proceeded to boo us off the field as the match came to a conclusion. Then it happened. As I was walking into the tunnel under the stands that led to the dressing rooms, I caught a flash of movement out of the corner of my eye. My next recollection was being surrounded by officials as I lay on the cold cement floor of the tunnel. A so-called fan had waited, hiding in the milling crowd, until I was abreast of him. He had lashed out at me and caught me square on the chin, the perfect knock-down. Then, like the coward he was, he ran off through the tunnel. I was helped by some very kind Cork officials to the dressing room, groggy and sore.

There was a lot of coming and going to the dressing room and enquiries about my well-being, as I slowly regained my composure. About twenty minutes later a Garda sergeant came in and informed me that they had apprehended the man responsible. Did I wish to press charges as this was a very serious assault in their opinion? It was then that I made a decision I have since regretted. I decided that an on-the-spot apology (recommended, I must add, by the Garda sergeant) was sufficient. The person was brought into the dressing room by the officials, informed me that he had had big money on the match result, had lost his head and had struck me. He duly apologised, walked out the door and I never heard from him since. I believe to this day that I should have pressed charges and sent a message to those who behave in that way. I let down my fellow referees in not doing so.

Two years later, another National League game, this time in Tullamore. Again, a dark, rainy, depressing kind of a day. A huge and very vocal crowd present. Offaly with the magnificent Matt O'Connor (what a player!) are leading Down by two points, time up. I award a penalty to Down. Martin Furlong makes a brilliant full-length save, diving low to his right; Offaly win by two points. As I walk through the milling crowd around the gate on my way to the dressing room, a man rushes forward and strikes me savagely in the face with an umbrella – then quickly vanishes into the crowd. Now, escorted to the dressing rooms with an ugly swelling developing on my cheek, I am approached by two gardaí. The culprit has been arrested and I am required to attend the Tullamore Garda station before we begin the journey home. No simple apology accepted this time. I had learned a harsh lesson due to the first assault.

I gave a lengthy statement at the station and, when finished, I asked to see the person who had struck me. Locked up in a cell, sitting on a chair, he was feeling fairly sorry for himself. 'So why did you strike me?' I inquired. 'Well, Down were beaten and I had to take it out on someone, so you were the obvious person,' he replied. Two months later he was up in court in Offaly, he got a hefty fine and a twelve-month suspended jail sentence.

I should stress that I enjoyed my time with the whistle and that there were far more good times than bad. However, those two assaults left a bad taste. The most disappointing aspect was the complete lack of interest in my welfare demonstrated by both the Kerry County Board who had nominated me as an inter-county referee and by Croke Park, to whom I forwarded my report. Neither body contacted me, one way or the other, and I was left to my own devices to sort out problems arising from the two incidents. We were never, in the course of any seminar or meeting I was required to attend during my career as a referee, advised as to the appropriate course of action in such circumstances. Physical assault such as this affects not only the referee himself, but also his family. I am utterly convinced that an individual who commits such an act should be brought before the courts and taught a salutary lesson. This, I believe, would quickly stamp out such unacceptable behaviour.

We hear about the players and managers and the time they put into the game, but let us not forget the men in the middle who are out, four and five evenings a week, travelling the country and their own counties, and frequently at the receiving end of abuse you would not dish out to a dog. Yet while I have often heard the Gaelic Players Association and Croke Park vigorously pushing the idea of grants for so-called 'elite' players, I have never once heard referees mentioned as potential recipients for such grants – not once. However, the referees themselves must examine their responsibilities. When did you last see a player get a red card for foul language? I maintain that if such language by players and mentors were to be punished without exception (as it is in some other sports) then many problems might be solved. 'Beaten by a referee' is the meanest excuse any fifteen men could advance.

17

Radio days: my late vocation and national honours

It is amazing how a simple five-minute phone call can change the course of one's life to such a great extent, but that is exactly what happened to me when I answered the phone one afternoon in St Brendan's Ward at St Finan's Hospital twenty years ago. There followed a short discussion and the result is that, from that day to this, I have been deeply involved with one of the top local radio stations in Ireland.

When I took that call, little did I realise the many wonderful opportunities the job would hand me and the personalities I would meet and interview. I would travel to New York and follow the Kerry banner down 5th Avenue in the St Patrick's Day parade. I would sit in the magnificent Michael O'Hehir broadcasting area of Croke Park and take part in every single broadcast of every game that Kerry would play there, right from the station's first live All-Ireland final broadcast in 1997. Three All-Ireland GAA McNamee Awards would come my way, as well as the ultimate honour of being named Ireland's Sports Broadcaster of the Year. It has really been a fairy-tale journey and, as I look back and recall these glorious twenty years with Radio Kerry, I still feel like pinching myself to see if I will wake up and discover it has all been a dream. Yes, it has been that life-changing and I am fully conscious of the fact that very few people are fortunate enough to enter a profession late in their life that would bring them such wonderful satisfaction.

Accepting my second national GAA McNamee award in 1998 from Eamon O'Sullivan from the Kerry County Board *(left)*, and GAA president Joe McDonagh *(centre)* for my Radio Kerry programme *Terrace Talk*. The programme was again recognised for its excellence in 2005. While secretary of my club Killarney Legion in the 1970s, I was honoured twice with McNamee awards for my work as public relations officer.

I am pictured here in 1997 in Randall's Island, New York, with two of my Killarney Legion clubmen, Denny Lyne *(right)*, who captained Kerry in the Polo Grounds in the 1947 All-Ireland final against Cavan, and Teddy O'Sullivan *(left)*, who was midfield that day. Surviving members of the team were invited to attend a commemorative National League game between the two counties and I was there, with Liam Higgins, to broadcast the game live to Ireland for Radio Kerry.

The station was established in 1989 and began broad casting in 1990. Its magnificent high-tech headquarters are in Tralee, with studios also in Killarney and Cahersiveen. Radio Kerry broadcasts twenty-four hours a day and employs approximately seventy people, between full-time and part-time staff. Its management team is one of the hardest working you will find anywhere and their enthusiasm and professionalism are a wonderful case of 'leading by example', to such an extent that all the other staff members literally leave no stone unturned as they strive morning, noon and night to provide their listeners with only the very best programming. The 2011 line-up of Paul Byrne (Chief Executive), Fiona Stack (General Manager and Programme Controller), Melanie O'Sullivan (Events and Marketing Manager), Marie Sweeney (Finance Manager), Pat Reidy (Sales Manager) and John Herlihy (Training Centre Manager) combine to provide the bedrock for this superb station. Trevor Galvin is Station Engineer and I always marvel at his knowledge and expertise; I would go as far as to say that without him Radio Kerry broadcasting would probably grind to a halt.

And one simple phone call twenty years ago from the then head of Radio Kerry sports, Tralee man Seamus O'Mahoney, launched me on a path to work with this terrific team. His request was short and sweet: 'Can you phone in a one-minute report of your club's county league game to the Sunday sports programme tomorrow?' And, he quickly added, 'Begin with the score, give three highlights of the hour and then finish with the score.' Seamus later added me to his expanding sports reporting team. I continued to cover all local games and two years later he asked me to sit in as station analyst with the late Liam Higgins for a Munster Championship game as Kerry played Cork in Fitzgerald Stadium, Killarney. The game was, of course, live on air and I hesitated, wondering if this was too much to take on. Seamus must have noted my hesitation as he quickly added, 'Just speak about what you see on the field in front of you, it's simple really, with your experience as a player and referee you'll have no problem.' He made it sound so easy. And so I sat in with Liam. It was the beginning of a magical period. For the next ten years we would travel all over Ireland bringing the thrills and excitement of Kerry's league and championship matches to Radio Kerry listeners at home and abroad through the internet.

The station's service is superb. Eight hours of sport every weekend from the sports team lead by Joe O'Mahoney and Garry O'Sullivan provides up-to-the-minute news of all the many and varied sports for which Kerry is renowned, not just Gaelic games I must stress. Fourteen years ago in 1997 the then Chief Executive of the station, Paul Sheehan, offered me the opportunity to present a one-hour Monday evening sports programme, from 6 until 7 p.m. It was a daunting experience since I had literally no training of any description, however, I jumped at the opportunity. And so *Terrace Talk* was born. So popular did it become that it was later extended to its present format of two hours. Eamon O'Sullivan, the PRO on the Kerry County Board at that time, sat in with me for the first year or so. It was initially intended that the programme would deal with only GAA matters but after a year or so I quickly realised that if *Terrace Talk* was to last and be successful its coverage of sport would have to expand greatly. And so today that is exactly what I do. I cover every single sport, no matter how marginalised it might be.

Over the years the programme has developed a huge following, both locally and (thanks to the internet) worldwide. While local Kerry sports are the main background of the programme, I also cover national and international events and have had many world renowned sports stars chatting to me. Presenting a live two-hour show takes a lot of planning and preparation and I believe the real secret of its success is the fact that most of the interviews conducted are recorded outside the studio and not by telephone. I have a strong belief that to get the very best from the person you are interviewing it is vital that you sit face to face with them as much as possible.

I have to admit that *Terrace Talk*'s success has been far beyond my wildest dreams. Every year the National PPI Radio Awards are presented at a gala function at the Lyrath Hotel in Kilkenny. The awards recognise the arts and skills of radio production and programming. *Terrace Talk* has been shortlisted on three occasions, a tremendous honour in itself. However, in 2008, in the presence of close to one thousand people, I was absolutely stunned when it was announced that Radio Kerry's *Terrace Talk* was the winner of the category 'Best Sports Programme'. To make the success even more rewarding was the fact that *Terrace Talk* finished ahead of the hugely popular RTÉ Radio 1 *Drivetime Sport* and Newstalk's *Off the Ball*. Two of the country's best sports shows. To come out as the number one sports programme in the thirty-two counties was a massive tribute to Radio Kerry and its entire staff, but it seems to me that it is a particular tribute to Paul Byrne and Fiona Stack, who literally give me close to complete broadcasting freedom each week. Of course at times I am open to correction but generally interference from above is minimal. With the support of an exemplary and dedicated back-room team, *Terrace Talk* has reached the pinnacle of its popularity. Andrew Morrissey, a Nemo Rangers GAA club man, is the producer, Sinead Prendergast operates the desk and is responsible for sound, and Eileen Moynihan will often log in over one hundred phone calls from our dedicated listeners as she mans the reception.

While winning that PPI award was hugely satisfying and completely unexpected, an even greater honour was to come my way. Two years later in 2010 I was again shortlisted, but this time the station had nominated me in the category, Sports Broadcaster of the Year. Two men for whom I have always had huge admiration were shortlisted with me: Newstalk's Ger Gilroy and Eoin McDevitt. That night the three of us watched as our names were flashed up on the huge screen and, if I had been stunned two years previously with the win, I was absolutely speechless when I got the nod ahead of the two Newstalk lads. I had been chosen against all the odds as PPI Sports Broadcaster of the Year in Ireland. The huge Radio Kerry contingent present had further cause for joyous celebrations when Sean Hurley, my colleague, also won a gold award and, to cap a historic Kerry evening, the station was announced as winner of best Local Station of the Year, its third time coming out on top for this hugely prestigious award.

When I look back and contemplate these two PPI awards, I still wonder if it has all been a dream because on those winning occasions I spoke and mingled with some of the legendary names of Irish radio. Here was I, with no formal training whatsoever, in the company of other nominees such as Pat Kenny, Joe Duffy, Ray D'Arcy, Philip Boucher-Hayes, Sean O'Rourke, Ian Dempsey, Oisin Langan, Dave Fanning, Cian McCormack, Des Cahill and representatives from stations all over the thirty-two counties. To add to the enjoyment of these wonderful occasions, both Marian Finucane and Jimmy McGee were also present to receive their Outstanding Achievement Awards. Jimmy Magee and Micheál Ó Muircheartaigh are people I admire greatly as supreme masters behind the mike, both of whom have been guests on my programmes.

My programmes *In Conversation With* and *Terrace Talk* have afforded me the amazing opportunity to interview, face to face, well-known personalities from all aspects of Irish life. Sportsmen and women, Olympians, world champions living at home and abroad, politicians, authors, painters, bishops, priests, nuns, refugees, community activists. The list is endless. Here in Kerry Brendan Kennelly, Con Houlihan, John B. Keane (he told me never to lose my Kerry accent), Padraig Kennelly, the Healy Rae family, Mick O'Connell, Mick O'Dwyer, Mick Galway and politicians of all parties have been special. If you visit my terracetalk.com website, which people from all corners of the world do, you can still listen to and enjoy these historic interviews. Alan Groarke, a Moyvane man living in Colorado, is responsible for the management of this massively important website.

Four Taoisigh, Enda Kenny, Brian Cowen, Bertie Ahern and Charlie Haughey, have all given their time to me; indeed, the Charlie Haughey interview, conducted in the home of

Haughey's great friend Tom Fitzgerald of Dingle, was the very last radio interview this controversial politician ever gave. So it is hugely historic for that reason. This unique opportunity was afforded me when he was on holiday in west Kerry. Liam Higgins set it up with the assistance of Tom. I found it a most daunting experience. Charlie was at the centre of massive controversy at the time, his health was in serious decline and the interview was agreed on the condition that politics would not be discussed. I fully understood the situation and was just delighted to meet the man. We had breakfast with him at Tom's home as he gently questioned me in relation to my political beliefs and interests. On reflection I realised he was sounding out what kind of a character I was. It was a fascinating experience; I remember feeling that it was as if this man could look right into your mind and know exactly what you were thinking. I found him very courteous, polite and helpful and we spoke about his football interests (his brother Jock had won an All-Ireland with Dublin), his views on Kerry and his memories of being in France at the finish of the Tour de France when Stephen Roche won – and so much more.

A career in broadcasting and winning the highest honours available to someone in the profession has never been part of my plan. As a result of my work on Radio Kerry I have been invited to speak at functions near and far, launch books, visit Maynooth College to lecture on the 'power of radio', open festivals, art exhibitions, and a hundred and one other events. The experience I have gained behind the mike has resulted in visits to New York, Texas and London, where I conducted many interviews for my great friend Christy Riordan as we documented the lives of emigrant sportsmen and women. All of this may not have been part of the Kerry dream I had been chasing for half of my life – but it has been an exciting rollercoaster of a ride I would not have missed for the world.

18

Great sadness and tragedy in my family

The sharp, shrill ringing of the telephone, as if far away in the distance, awoke me from a deep sleep. It was 2.30 a.m. on Sunday 4 August 1996. The ringing continued relentlessly as I roused myself to answer the call. Immediately I knew that this could only be bad news, but little did I realise how terribly tragic this call would prove to be. It was my brother, Geni, a year younger than me. In a steady, calm and measured voice he said, 'Karen has been involved in a road accident, Weeshie, and we are here in Tralee General with her.' I asked how serious was it, and would she be all right. He hesitated before he replied with words that I will never forget: 'It's very serious, Weeshie, and she might not live.'

Within minutes I was on my way to Tralee. I was shown to the intensive care ward and the minute I saw Karen I realised just how seriously injured she was. This beautiful, laughing, vibrant, 21-year-old girl was lying silent and still, her head swathed in bandages; only the continuous hum of the machine that was keeping her alive disturbed the near silence of the ward, while the nurses busied themselves

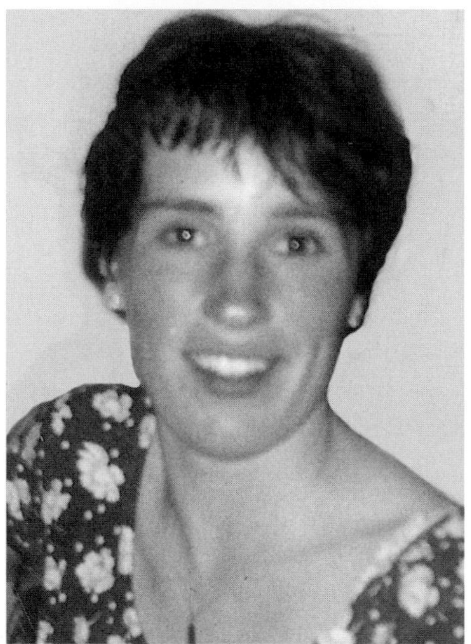

My beautiful 21-year-old niece Karen Fogarty who died in a tragic road collision on Sunday 4 August 1996.

around the bed. Geni, his wife, Maureen, and their other daughters were sitting by the bedside holding Karen's hands; all of them, as you can imagine, were confused, upset and bewildered. Sometime after this Karen was pronounced dead. From that hour on the lives of the family would be changed forever. While Karen's death was a terrible tragedy, the circumstances surrounding the fatality added enormously to the grief of Maureen, Geni, Anne, Clare and Susan.

Karen had been killed in a hit-and-run collision. She and her boyfriend, Gerard O'Donoghue, had walked the short distance from Killarney town to his home on the Muckross Road. Karen kissed Ger goodnight at 12.30 a.m. Dressed in all the bright clothing and luminous lights necessary for night cycling she began the familiar two-mile journey home. However, just moments after leaving Ger, Karen was hit from behind and fatally injured. She really had no hope of survival. Karen's boyfriend had heard the sound of the collision and he was first on the scene; Geni and Maureen arrived shortly after this and accompanied the ambulance to Tralee. One can only imagine their shock and anguish as the terrible events after the collision began to unfold.

Detective Sergeant Paul Downey was the man assigned to investigate the tragedy. Sixteen years after Karen's death Paul, now retired from the force, recalled for me the events of that terrible August weekend. His daughter Deirdre had been a very close friend of Karen and on the Saturday before her death Paul recalled Karen visiting his home. He told me: 'I will never forget her beautiful, beaming smile as she hopped on her bike and said goodbye.' He then told me that he had become very emotionally involved in the case, something which he rarely allowed occur in his line of work.

Paul and the Killarney Gardaí had moved quickly to apprehend the driver. He had raced away from the scene, concealed his car in a field some distance from his home in Muckross, and was then either driven by others or made his own way to Kilgarvan where, in an attempt to evade arrest, he took refuge with friends. The Gardaí quickly discovered the whereabouts of the car and some shrewd detective work led them to the house in Kilgarvan where the driver was hiding. It now became clear that he was preparing to flee to England to avoid the consequences of his actions. The man, who was in his early thirties, was arrested and charged with Karen's death. He was later found guilty and sentenced to three years' imprisonment and banned from driving for life, but he could apply to the court ten years later to have his licence reinstated.

Maureen and Geni had had four beautiful daughters: Anne, Clare, Susan and Karen. They lived in one of the most beautiful areas of Killarney, Muckross. Karen had a tremendous love and enthusiasm for life, which she took from her parents . They had given her a happy, solid upbringing and instilled in her the many virtues for which everyone loved her. Geni, recalling his daughter, said, 'Everything Karen did, she gave 300 per cent. Any task or duty she was asked to perform, she did it to the very best of her ability.' She had tremendous energy and loved cycling. Her father recalled a journey she undertook to Dingle; a return journey of approximately eighty miles. 'I remember one day in the pouring rain she said she was going to see her friend Siobhan Moore in Dingle. She got on her bike and cycled all the way to Dingle, stayed overnight and cycled home the following day. On her return she cycled to Killarney to a job interview and later that evening she was off rowing.' She was a tremendously fit young lady: cycling, running, and especially rowing on the Lakes of Killarney were her favourite pursuits. She trained all year around.

Shortly after her death the annual 211th Killarney Regatta was held; had Karen lived she would have been competing for her third successive Senior Ladies Sixes Championship with the club she had loved so much, Muckross Rowing Club. That day was a very poignant occasion for the family because Muckross were the overall winners, dominating the day's events. Karen's sisters, Susan and Clare, collected the trophy. Their sister had given a huge part of her life to Muckross and had served as coach, public relations officer and secretary.

The apple never falls far from the tree and, in Karen's case, her passion for rowing came from both sides of the family. Her father, Geni, had played football at Under-21 level with Kerry, represented his county at basketball and had also been a winning oarsman with the local St Brendan's club. Karen's grandfather on Maureen's side of the family was Pa Doyle, a famous Killarney boatman renowned for his trips on the Lakes of Killarney and to the Gap of Dunloe. Karen had been a trainee confectioner at the time of her death and had made arrangements to begin a new life in Dublin. She had recently landed a job with Cooks Restaurant in South

Williams Street and was planning to join the famous Neptune Rowing Club, of which her friend Denise Casey from Muckross was already a member. Sadly this would never be.

It is impossible to comprehend why such a beautiful young life was cut short so tragically; the grief of her family is even harder to imagine. I once asked Geni and Maureen how they had coped following the terrible tragedy and Maureen replied in an instant: 'It was our faith that kept us going; without it life would have been so difficult.' My memories of my beautiful niece are many and varied, but I particularly treasure the image of her laughing, beautifully dimpled face that could literally light up a room when she entered. She was always on the go, always looking ahead and planning for the future. My last memories of her are in relation to her work as a trainee confectioner, delivering big trays of confectionary around the shops in Killarney. Her route would bring her through Plunkett Street and I still see her in my mind's eye every time I drive down that street. The day after Karen's funeral I sat down and tried to express my own emotions in a tribute to this lovely young lady, tragically killed at just twenty-one years of age.

Smiling, laughing, dimpled cheeks,
Vibrant, busy scaling peaks.
Waving, greeting young and old,
Face of beauty, still and cold.

Cycling, always on the go,
Music, meetings, never 'no'.
Work her favourite, aprons white,
Trays and traffic, what a sight.

Muckross rowing, lakes serene,
Just twenty-one, what might have been?
Time and tide, days too short,
New job waiting, soon to start.

Cycling homeward, traffic speeding,
Father, mother, sisters grieving.
Romance, boyfriend, last goodbyes,
Her moon, her stars, her love-filled eyes.

Void of darkness, hearts so broken,
Special person, love unspoken.
Memories vivid, never end,
On waking, sleeping, of time not spent.

Rest above the lakes she loved,
Watch forever from above.
Anger, grief, great confusion,
Friends, tears in huge profusion.

Nights of sadness, days so barren,
Busy, laughing, lovely Karen.

In December of that year, 1996, Karen's selfless spirit was beautifully commemorated by her community when a hall in the Muckross Community Centre was called after her. The Karen Fogarty Hall was blessed and dedicated by Kerry's bishop, Bill Murphy. Bishop Murphy said the centre was a wonderful place to associate with Karen's memory as it was infused with her spirit of enthusiasm, commitment and zest for life. He said that in her short life Karen had acquired a wisdom that most people only acquire through lifelong experience and that this realisation had helped him appreciate the phrase, 'Those whom the Gods love, die young.'

In March of the following year Karen's memory was further commemorated when the club she loved so dearly, Muckross Rowing Club, dedicated a new racing boat to her memory in a moving and nostalgic ceremony. The boat is painted in the club's traditional lemon and white colours and would race under the banner the *Karen Fogarty*. Geni and Maureen officially christened the new four-seater, which was built in England, and it made its competitive debut at the Neptune Regatta in Dublin the following month. Karen's two sisters, Clare and Susan, together with two of her former teammates, Denise Coffey and Eimear Fitzpatrick, rowed the boat in its debut outing on Killarney's Lakes following a blessing performed by Father Michael and Cannon Brian Lougheed.

Two years after Karen's death her club further honoured her memory in a very special way. She had been a member of the first Muckross crew to win a national rowing title (the Women's Novice Fours Sprint Championship of Ireland in 1993 and 1994). In 1998 the club commissioned a trophy to her memory, to be presented to the Women's Novice Eights Champions of Ireland each year. The Karen Fogarty Memorial Trophy is a miniature replica of an eight, with oars in silver mounted on a teak base. It was made by Brian de Staic of Dingle, one of Ireland's foremost jewellery designers who specialises in interpretations of Celtic history and culture. Fittingly, Muckross were the first winners of this trophy in 1998 and, to add to what was a memorable occasion, Karen's sister Susan was a member of the winning crew. It has been won since then by nine different clubs: Carlow R.C., Queen's University Belfast, University College Cork, Commercial R.C. Dublin, Galway R.C., Neptune R.C. Dublin, the University of Limerick, University College Dublin, and University College Galway.

Waterford-born Detective Sergeant Paul Downey, the man who led the successful investigation and eventual prosecution into Karen's tragic death, is now retired and living in Killarney. He is a renowned artist and his magnificent paintings, especially those of sporting times, are in huge demand. Paul's paintings pulsate with life and are breathtakingly beautiful. He brings the viewer to the heart of the action. The adrenalin is at its peak. Every muscle is extended to breaking point. This is no place for the faint-hearted. His paintings of rugby have included games played by Munster, Ireland, the All Blacks, Wales, Slade and the Saracens. One of his rugby paintings was presented by the Munster Branch IRFU to Peter Sutherland at their pre-match function for Munster v. Gloucester in 2002. Downey's football and hurling paintings hang in Croke Park, his horse-racing paintings have been used as prestigious race prizes, his cycling paintings hang in the homes of cycling experts, a collection of his sporting and landscape paintings hang in many offices, including the Kerry Group and Kerry County Council. Downey is also capable of freezing a split second – sky, light and colour – in his impressionistic landscape paintings. And Paul's name is linked forever with my family under those most tragic of circumstances as the man who successfully prosecuted the person responsible for the death of a fabulous young lady.

Fourteen years after Karen's death on 1 April 2010, her father, my younger brother Geni, died. He was laid to rest alongside Karen in Adhadoe cemetery, which is located high overlooking the Lakes of Killarney, the place both of them loved so much. Geni had developed non-Hodgkin's lymphoma and, despite fighting and battling with tremendous fortitude and courage for two years, he finally succumbed to this deadly disease. I was fortunate to have been at his bedside with Maureen and the family when he took his last breaths. That very day, for some unknown reason, I had felt compelled to leave my home in Killarney to pay Geni a visit, never expecting that the end was so near. On my way to Tralee Geni's son-in-law, Cathal, contacted me on my mobile urging me to come quickly. Luckily I was halfway to Tralee and, minutes after reaching his bedside, the man with whom I had shared my life since we were kids on the side of New Street back in the 1940s and 1950s died. To commemorate Geni and as a tribute to his love of snooker, the family later donated a perpetual cup, which will be presented to the winner of the Kerry Snooker County Championship every year.

Just two short months later on 30 May the cold hand of death once again reached out for a member of my family. Dermie, my older brother, died of prostate cancer. He had been married to Kenmare lady, Tessie McCarthy, and they had a family of five: Richard, Katherine, Sheila, Gerald and David. Tessie had also died of the same disease two years previously, following an exhausting thirteen-year battle with the illness. She was a wonderful lady and never once did I hear her complain during those long years of treatment and fight for life. Dermie was hospitalised shortly after Geni's death. His illness was sadly terminal and it was the first time I had occasion to visit a hospice for the dying. Marymount Hospice in Cork city is an amazing place and the help and care Dermie received there in his final weeks was a massive consolation to his family. The nurses and staff were unbelievable and I never ceased to be amazed at their generosity of spirit and willingness to ease Dermie's suffering during those very difficult final days.

There was one beautiful moment towards the end that gave my brother a massive boost, and it came from a most unexpected source. Dermie had been a fanatical fisherman all his life and both he and Geni knew the Lakes of Killarney like the backs of their hands. Also a massive follower of snooker, Dermie would travel on a regular basis to the World Snooker Championships at the Crucible in Sheffield with his friends. On one occasion, when the legendary Steve Davis was visiting Killarney with his girlfriend, Dermie entertained them and brought them on a boat trip on the lakes. He loved telling the story of how Steve had stood up in the bows of the boat as they approached Ross Castle and declared, 'I have been fortunate to travel the whole world but never have I seen such beauty as I have seen on the Lakes of Killarney today.' Now it was a Tuesday, two weeks before Dermie's death. Joan and I had been sitting all day with him in the day room of Marymount Hospice when a very excited young nurse entered and said, 'Dermie, you have a visitor.' With that the door opened and in came the six-time world champion and one of the greatest snooker players who has ever lived, the easily recognisable Steve Davis. Not having been forewarned of the impending visit, both Dermie and I were stunned into silence. It was a very poignant moment as Steve put his arms around Dermie who, like me, was visibly overcome by the moment. Two great friends of Dermie had arranged the visit. Connie O'Sullivan (Kerry's 'Mr Snooker') and Sean McMonagle, the two men who had always been his travelling companions to those Sheffield championships. Nurses were crowding around, autographs were signed by the champ, photographs were taken and then Dermie and Steve were left on their own for twenty minutes. Just one brief visit, one moment in time, but one that I will cherish forever. It was the last time I saw my eldest brother alive.

I experienced a range of emotions in the months following the two lads' deaths because now I was the only remaining brother of four in the Fogarty family. That scourge of humanity, cancer, had also been responsible for the death of my third brother Jimmy in 1998 and, just like my father and Dermie, it was prostate cancer to which he, too, finally succumbed. Jimmy had emigrated to England back in the 1950s when thousands were forced to take the boat across the water. Manchester had been his first destination and when he lived in Oldham I would visit him; he took me to my first game in Old Trafford to see the Busby Babes playing. That great Manchester United side were in their prime before the Munich air crash decimated the club. We would stand behind the goal at the Stretford end among the mass of swaying, crowding, fanatical supporters. My passion and love for this great club was well and truly fostered back then with those regular visits and, to this day, I retain a great and constant interest in all their games and visit Old Trafford, the 'Theatre of Dreams', at least once a year. Jimmy married Mary Kildunne from Sligo and they had two boys, Sean and Kevin. He eventually settled in Shrewsbury – a beautiful place – and when he died it was there he was buried.

I can recall vividly each moment of my last visit to him, which was very poignant for both of us as he had only weeks or days to live. As he lay seriously ill, I sat on the side of his bed and we said our last goodbyes. The room was in semi-darkness, Jimmy was comfortable and pain-free, and the pump attached to his body would click and hum into life every so often, ensuring that the morphine kept at bay the terrible pain prostate cancer can inflict. The illuminated dial of the bedside clock showed 4.10 p.m. My flight home was in two hours' time. We spoke quietly about our families, our work, and his reasons for emigrating. Then, looking towards the window, he whispered something I will never forget. 'You know, Weeshie, if only I could fly out that window, fly over to Ireland and look down on Killarney with its lakes and mountains just one last time I would die a happy man, but maybe my soul will pass through Killarney.' I said goodbye, left the room and cried bitter tears. Two weeks later I returned to Shrewsbury to attend his funeral.

Death seems to have been a constant companion all my adult life. Only six short years after my father's death in 1964, my older sister, Kathleen Ann, had become seriously ill. It was a very traumatic time for the family, especially my mother and Kathleen Ann's husband, Jim Broderick. She had been complaining of severe headaches and double vision for a number of months following the birth of her first baby daughter, Deirdre, but back in the early 1970s the early diagnosis of serious brain illness was in its infancy in many

Basketball played a huge part in my life and was a tremendous way of keeping fit in winter. The Busby Babes was the top team in Kerry for a number of years, winning Killarney, Kerry and Munster senior titles. The club was founded in 1957 and called after the great Manchester United side that crashed in Munich in 1958. Matt Busby, Manchester United manager at the time, sent us a set of jerseys that had been worn by the team. *Back row (l–r):* Pat Sommers, Tommy 'Bracker' Regan, Enda Curtyane, Paudie O'Connor and Weeshie; *front row (l–r):* Tadghie Fleming, Geni Fogarty and John Keogh. Paudie O'Connor was one of the greatest players to come from Kerry and is the only Irishman to have been selected on a European All-Star basketball team. Tommy Regan played hurling and football for Kerry.

The first ever Busby Babes Killarney basketball team, pictured in 1957 – we went on to dominate Killarney and Kerry basketball for a number of years. *Back row (l–r):* Mike O'Shea, Danno Keeffe, Michael O'Connor, Lui Nolan and Nolie O'Connor; *front row (l–r)*: Donie Courtney, Weeshie, Mick O'Sullivan, Jimmy O'Leary and Sean O'Shea.

respects. She was seen by various specialists and consultants, but they all failed to diagnose the brain tumour that would eventually lead to her premature death. Her condition gradually deteriorated and it was heartbreaking to see her suffering so much. Her second baby daughter, Fiona, was born during her illness. Finally, one evening in August 1971, Jim and I drove Kathleen Ann to Dublin and she was admitted to St Vincent's Hospital where surgeons immediately performed a brain operation and discovered the tumour. She never recovered from the operation and, as with Karen's death, my last memory of Kathleen Ann is of her body, motionless and serene, in the intensive care ward. Her head was swathed in bandages, only the gentle hum of the life-support machine breaking the silence as the nurses and doctors busied themselves around the bed. It was a long, sad night for all of us present; my brother Jimmy had flown in from England to be with us at the end. The following morning, after a consultation with the family, the doctors switched off her life-support machine and my beautiful, gentle sister who had devoted herself to a career in nursing and had worked in Manchester and Killarney was pronounced dead.

A few years later Jim remarried. Joan Daly had been a great friend of the family, loved by all, and I was greatly honoured when they asked me to be best man at their wedding. It was a bittersweet day for all involved; Kathleen Ann's two little daughters Deirdre and Fiona, who had been just two years and ten months old respectively when their mother died, now had Joan as their mother. While rearing their own family, Jim and Joan ensured that Deirdre and Fiona received only the best and most loving care and attention as they grew up. They did a magnificent job. Both ladies are now happily married with their own families and, while they have similarities to their father, I can see amazing resemblances to their mother in their smiles, the way they walk, their determination, certain mannerisms and their generosity.

All those family deaths have left a massive void in my life, however, I get great consolation when I think of the enormous strength and faith my mother possessed, despite all the heartache she endured. It is always said that no parent should have to bury one of their own children. But my mother stood at the gravesides of her husband, brother, sister, daughter, son and niece. Her generation had something special; their great faith saw them through heartache and loss. I have learned a lot from her. My eldest sister Sheila is now my only remaining sibling. She was also forced to emigrate in the early 1950s and entered the nursing profession in Manchester. She later married Jerry Mulholland, who sadly died a young man; they had three children, Richard, Gerald and Sarah. Sheila lives in Birmingham and I eagerly look forward to my yearly visits to her; she, in turn, is a regular visitor to Killarney.

It does seem as if death has been at my shoulder all of my life; I even feel guilty at times because I am the only surviving member of the family who is left at home in Killarney. But as the years pass and I attend their funerals, I know I am fortunate to have so many wonderful memories of absent family and friends.

Nurses' gradation at St Finan's Hospital, Killarney in 1966. *Back row (l–r)*: Tadgh O'Reilly (tutor), Cait Moynihan, Joan Murphy, Joan Fogarty and Kathleen Ann Fogarty (my late sister who was acting tutor in the hospital during this period).; *front row (l–r)*: Doreen Corcoran (Assistant Chief Nursing Officer – ACNO), Dr Jack O'Connor (Registered Medical Superintendent – RMS), Dr Des Kelly (Assistant Medical Officer – AMO) and Tom Lynch (ACNO).

19

On the trail of Eamon Fitzgerald

It was a lovely June evening in 2002 and Joan and I were spending a few days at the beautiful Cahernane Hotel near Castlecove in south Kerry. We stopped to pay a visit and say a few prayers at the little church there, the Church of the Precious Blood. When we entered, the magnificent colours of the stained-glass window on the gable end of the church were lit up by the golden rays of the setting sun. As I stood and gazed at these magnificent windows, one name emblazoned on a pane of the glass caught my attention. Somewhere in the back of my mind that name rang a bell. The inscription read: 'In Memory of Eamon Fitzgerald, Behihane. Donor, Daniel McGillicuddy.' Little did I realise that this one name was about to lead me on a voyage of great discovery, nor that this voyage would lead me to encounter many new people, among them Bob Tisdall, Ireland's great 1932 Olympic gold medal winner in Los Angeles.

My curiosity had got the better of me and I called into the Black Shop public house, which is just alongside the church, knowing that the landlord and my great friend, Brendan

A rare and previously unpublished photograph of Kerry Olympian and footballer Eamon Fitzgerald taken while he was training in Killarney for the All-Ireland final in 1930. (*courtesy Mons. Liam Brosnan Collection*)

Galvin, would explain all. And he did. Eamon Fitzgerald was a legendary footballer and athlete from the area; he had represented Ireland in the 1932 Los Angeles Olympic Games and won All-Ireland medals with Kerry. I listened enthralled as Brendan and his wife, Carmel, retraced the life and times of Eamon. While it was a wonderful Kerry sporting story, it had, in many ways, a very distressing ending. Brendan concluded, 'It's very sad, Weeshie, as Eamon is simply completely forgotten and has never once received the credit he deserved from the Olympic Council of Ireland or from our own county here in Kerry.' Brendan had done his best to keep the memory of this great athlete alive, as he explained. 'The only memories of Eamon now are that stained-glass window in the church and across the road here I have a little stone plaque with his name on it; at least that keeps a little interest in his career, but in general he is completely forgotten. He was buried in Dublin, in Deansgrange cemetery I believe, but that is all I know.' Brendan also told me that Daniel McGillicuddy, who was responsible for having Eamon remembered on the window, had been a great friend of the athlete and had had to sell three of his cattle to pay for it. And so I vowed there and then to discover and retrace the life and times of Eamon Fitzgerald. And what an amazing story it would prove to be.

Eamon (Ned Seán Óg) Fitzgerald was born in Behagane, Castlecove, in 1903. His father, John, was a farmer and his mother was a McCarthy from Upper Liss, Castlecove. Eamon grew to be over six feet tall, was of slim build, and from an early age displayed great athletic potential. His second cousin, Jim Murphy, remembers him 'as a very loose man who jumped over fences and gates around the area with great ease'. Jim also recalls Eamon coming home to the area on holidays wearing plus fours and always immaculately dressed. Eamon's football ability was quickly recognised and he won a Junior All-Ireland with Kerry in 1924 when

Longford were defeated in the final. He lined out at corner forward and that very same year he collected the first of his four All-Ireland Senior medals, as a substitute when Kerry beat Dublin in the final. A golden era for Kerry football was about to unfold and Eamon would become a vital part of the success.

The Kingdom won four successive All-Irelands between 1929 and 1932 and Fitzgerald was magnificent in the forward line of the 1930 and 1931 sides. Eamon's teammates during that glorious era included all-time greats Con Brosnan, John Joe Sheehy, Paul Russell, Danno Keeffe, Dan Spring, Jack Walsh, Tim O'Donnell, Miko Doyle and many more – and the Castlecove man was equal to the best. He also won Railway Cup medals in 1927 and 1931 and it is worth mentioning that the winning side in 1931 was composed entirely of Kerrymen. That great Kerry scribe, Paddy Foley, described him in *Kerry's Football Story* as 'a wonderful high jumper who could literally sweep the ball out of the clouds'. As his 'best-ever' Kerry side, Paddy chose the team that won the All-Ireland in 1930 and toured America the following year; it was a team that included Eamon. In the course of my research I interviewed a pleasant Cork man, Pierce Ryan, who described Eamon as 'a second Mick O'Connell', the ultimate honour. He also recalled that Eamon was a fluent French speaker.

How Fitzgerald combined his brilliant football career with his magnificent achievements in athletics must be rated as one of the most fascinating of Kerry sporting stories. His success in the hop, step and jump was amazing. While attending University College Dublin in 1930, he won the National Irish title with a leap of 48 feet 1¾ inches, an Irish record at the time; in 1932 he jumped 48 feet 2 inches, which qualified him to represent Ireland in the Olympics that year. This amazing man was about to write himself into the pages of sporting history, becoming the only Kerryman to hold both an All-Ireland football medal and to compete in the Olympics.

On 13 July 1932 four Irish athletes set out on a 6,000-mile journey from Cobh to compete in the Los Angeles Olympics. They had trained for three weeks on the sandhills of Ballybunion, here in Kerry. They would become one of the country's most successful Olympic teams ever as they won two gold medals, but an unfortunate injury prevented Eamon from joining this elite band of Olympic medallists. Dr Pat O'Callaghan from Knockanroe just outside Kanturk in County Cork would retain his gold medal for hammer-throwing, which he had first won in 1928 at the Amsterdam Olympics. The second member of the four-man team was Sri Lankan-born Bob Tisdall. He qualified for the 400-metre hurdle as he had been raised in Nenagh, County Tipperary. His first job had been running a passenger boat on the Shannon. A relative newcomer to the sport, Tisdall stunned the sporting world when he won that gold medal in a world and Olympic record time of 51.67 seconds. However, the record was not ratified as Tisdall had knocked the last hurdle on his surge to the tape and into the history books.

Throughout my life the name of Bob Tisdall has signified a faraway, heroic figure who brought glory and honour to Ireland. Little did I think, even in my wildest dreams, that I would someday interview him and that it would be the name of Eamon Fitzgerald that opened the door and enabled me to contact him. It was September 2003 and my research into the career of Eamon continued. By that year only one member of the 1932 Olympic team was still alive – Bob Tisdall. I contacted the Irish Olympic Council, who were very helpful and gave me a contact number in Nambour, Queensland, Australia, where Tisdall had retired to grow fruit and raise cattle.

I telephoned him from the Radio Kerry office. I must admit that I was very apprehensive because I knew that this legendary Irish sporting figure was ninety-seven and I wondered how his health was. I need not have worried and my heart literally skipped a beat when his cultured, soft-spoken voice answered my call all the way on the other side of the world: 'Hello, this is Bob Tisdall, who am I speaking to?' It was a magic moment for me and, to this day, I still listen to that tape of our conversation and cherish it greatly. He was so polite, gracious and eager to answer all my questions. It was a fascinating interview that covered a lot of ground. When I brought up Eamon's name, he spoke with great clarity: 'Eamon was older than I and, as far as I can remember, a tall lanky fellow and very good company. He wouldn't go out of his way to make you laugh. Unfortunately he got injured on his way out to Los Angeles and only for that would probably have won a medal. Of course I was aware he was a Kerryman but I did not know he had won All-Ireland medals with Kerry, he never spoke about that.' As the interview drew to a close I asked him what message he had for the people of Kerry in relation to Eamon. 'Well I can only say he was one of the nicest people I have ever met and I am sorry I didn't know more about him for you but it is such a long time ago; please don't let him be forgotten.' Then it was time to say goodbye and I thanked him for speaking and wished him well. I can still hear his last words to me: 'Thank you for remembering me and God bless you.'

The following year, on 27 July 2004, Bob Tisdall died. To the best of my knowledge my interview with him was the very last he gave. His death marked the end of one of the most remarkable eras in Irish sport and, sadly, it meant that each one of that magnificent four-man Irish Olympic team of 1932 had gone to their eternal reward. The fourth member of that 1932 team to accompany Eamon Fitzgerald to Los Angeles was a County Clare man, Michael 'Sonny' Murphy from Kinaboy. Sonny represented Ireland in the steeplechase, although he would collapse with heatstroke in the course of the race. Dr Pat O'Callaghan had tried to persuade him not to take part as he felt he was not well enough after training every day in the phenomenal heat; but Sonny was determined to run, for his family and his community. He started the race well, moving into third place, but then the crippling heat and the blistering pace forced him to push his body far beyond its limits and he collapsed on the track. Sonny, one of the bravest of all Clare men, died on St Patrick's Day 1936 while yet a very young man. He was buried in Deansgrange cemetery in Dublin where his Irish Olympic teammate Eamon Fitzgerald is also buried. Years later Sonny's final resting place was discovered by a Clare woman, Deela Maddock, who later told me, 'There wasn't a stick or a stone marking it – it was a disgrace.' And so it was not to be until sometime in the late 1990s that Michael 'Sonny' Murphy – yet another forgotten member of Ireland's most successful Olympic team ever – was ultimately remembered. A stone was erected at his grave in a ceremony attended by Olympians Ronnie Delany, Fred Teidt, Eamon Coughlan, Brendan O'Reilly, Harry Perry and many more friends and relations.

And so back to Eamon's story. In 1932 he was in superb physical shape and was highly fancied to win a medal at the Olympic Games. But events were to conspire against the man from Castlecove. After the long journey by ship and train, the team stopped to put in some training and to spend the night in Devour, Colorado. Dr Pat O'Callaghan spoke about what happened next: 'We all went down to this high school to get in some training. Eamon was at the long-jump pit, but after the second jump he injured himself and was limping badly; his heel swelled up and he was in bad shape. He rested for a few days and, despite being in great pain, he qualified for the final of the hop, step and jump.' Dr Pat then went on to recall what happened during those final jumps. 'I came down to the last row of seats to be near Eamon between jumps in the final and I gave him a pain-killing injection; it worked to some degree but unfortunately he could not reach his very best. It was a great shame because I am certain he would have brought a medal of some colour back to Kerry.' Chubel Nambu of Japan won the gold medal, setting a new world record, Eric Svenson of Sweden won silver, and another Japanese man, Kenkichi Oshima, took the bronze. Eamon's best jump of 49 feet 6¾ inches was just 1 inch behind the bronze medal winner and, amazingly, it would have won gold in seven of the previous nine Olympics. Those 1932 games had an entry of twelve nations in the treble jump and in the final the Kerryman had faced the best from America, which had three men in the final together with athletes from Japan, Holland and Sweden. Subsequently, Eamon won the Irish Triple Jump Championship of 1933 and 1934 and, to confirm greatness, he tied for the high jump title with another Kerryman, Garda Con O'Connor. As an athlete he was also highly accomplished when competing in the 220- and 440-metre events, as well as in discus and javelin throwing.

Amazingly, I was to discover that Eamon's education at UCD had been paid for by none other than the very same Lady Albina Broderick who had been involved with St Finan's and of whom I have already written. After settling in Castlecove in 1908 and founding her cooperative movement, she had also provided financial assistance for the education of the young men of the area and Eamon Fitzgerald had been one of those to benefit greatly as a result of her generosity. It is doubtful if, without her financial aid, he could have gone on to achieve all that he accomplished in life. Eamon also attended school at St Enda's (now a museum), founded by Padraig Pearse in Rathfarnham; later, when he qualified as a teacher, he taught there. A phone call in August 2004 put me in touch with Pierce Ryan from Michelstown in County Cork who had been a pupil of Eamon's at St Enda's. He had vivid memories of the great Kerryman, as he explained to me.

> I was a pupil at St Enda's in 1932 and 1933 when I was just twelve years of age. There were about seventy pupils there and seven teachers, one of whom was Margaret Pearse, Padraig's sister. I have great memories of Eamon Fitzgerald. He taught us French and was a beautiful speaker; he also played football with us. He was highly skilled, a natural footballer and could field a ball with one hand and had a tremendous leap; he was like Mick O'Connell. He never spoke about his participation in the Olympics of that year. On one occasion when the teachers were out a few of us, as boys will do, were opening presses in a room which Eamon used for storing his books and in one press we were astounded to come across a lot of silver cups and medals, all of which we later learned he had won for athletics all over Ireland. But we knew very little about him. I had tremendous respect for him and that is why I am in Kerry to remember him. He was a gentleman, quite helpful and was always encouraging . . . Well, Weeshie, I was in Kerry for a few days; I called to the County Board offices in Tralee to ask about Eamon and what had become of him. I was most disappointed when I was told that nothing was known about him. I was then put in touch with you and delighted to hear your story of discovery. I am surprised that there is not some more.

Eamon had also taken an active part in the War of Independence and was imprisoned for a period in Droichead Nua. He contracted TB in the 1950s, was engaged to be married, but due to his failing health declined to do so. My investigations were now centred on Eamon's last years alive. After he retired from teaching he lived a quiet life in Dublin. The wonderful Dan Keating from Ballygamboon, Castlemaine, who had worked as a barman in Dublin and whom I befriended before his death at the age of 105, recalled meeting Eamon on his daily walk and supplied me with information relating to Eamon's death. 'He died in 1958 in Dublin when only fifty-three years of age,' Dan recalled. 'The funeral was a very sad occasion as there were only a handful of people present; myself and John Joe Sheehy, who had travelled from Tralee, shouldered his coffin and helped lay him in his grave.'

Eamon had been buried in Deansgrange Cemetery following mass at the Church of the Good Shepherd. My next task was to visit Eamon's grave and, with that in mind, I contacted a football friend in Dublin. Eugene O'Sullivan from the Glen, Ballinskelligs, was then a detective stationed in Dublin and also chairman of the Kerry Association in Dublin; he readily agreed to check out Eamon's final resting place and to inform me as to where I should go. Weeks later Eugene was back. Together with his friend and colleague, Detective Sergeant Jim Martin, they had located the grave but, sadly, he reported that it was completely overgrown, dilapidated and the writing on the headstone was completely faded. Eugene, to the best of my knowledge, was the very first person to kneel at the grave of this legend since his burial in 1958.

It was, indeed, a very sad situation but something special was about to happen. Eugene and the Kerry Association in Dublin took on the task of having the grave rededicated. They very willingly accepted the financial costs and, one Saturday in May 2004, the memory of Eamon Fitzgerald was finally honoured in a very appropriate way. On the day of the rededication the sun shone brilliantly from a cloudless blue sky as close to two hundred people met at Eamon Fitzgerald's graveside; a far cry from the handful who had attended the funeral in 1958. Father Gaughan led the prayers and other speakers included Kerry County Board Chairman Sean Walsh, legendary Olympian Ronnie Delany, and President of the Irish Olympic Council Pat Hickey; Carmel Galvin spoke on behalf of the Castlecove community, many of whom had travelled for the occasion. To conclude the speeches I explained to those present the way my quest had begun when I first saw that stained-glass window in Castlecove. Then Brendan Galvin, who had fought so hard and long to keep Eamon's name alive, laid a special stone plaque on the grave together with earth and flowers from Eamon's home place in Behihane. A lovely poignant gesture. Micheál Ó Muircheartaigh was in attendance, as was Listowel Olympian Jerry Kiernan and President of the Irish Athletic Association Michael Heerey. Breda Barrett represented the Kerry Athletic Board and Sean O'Dwyer, a Corkman who eventually had broken Eamon's Irish hop, step and jump record was also at the graveside. Ann and Tony Donnelly, cousins of Eamon, had made the journey for the occasion. Jimmy Magee was also present.

There was a very special link with the burial in 1958 because 102-year-old Dan Keating had travelled from Kerry to be present. He had been one of the original handful of people at Eamon's funeral all those years ago. He simply lit up the occasion and was in constant demand with journalists and photographers. A great friend who was always urging me to sit down and write this book, author and broadcaster Colm Keane, was there with his wife, RTÉ newsreader Una O'Hagen. They were accompanied by their lovely young son, Sean, who sadly died later as a result of cancer. In many ways I found the whole occasion a very emotional one, the climax of a journey that I had almost felt it was my destiny to undertake. But now the road that had begun two years previously in the Church of the Precious Blood had come to a magnificent and highly satisfying conclusion. Eamon Fitzgerald would no longer rest in his grave as one of Kerry's forgotten sporting heroes. Instead he might now be remembered as, arguably, Kerry's greatest ever sporting son. Was that visit to the church a complete accident and or (as I believe) divine intervention? Judge for yourself.

20

Liam Higgins: Kerry's radio hero

One glorious September day in 2006 Kerry beat Mayo, 4-15 to 3-5, to capture their thirty-fourth Senior All-Ireland football title. But it is not the memory of another Kerry triumph that I cherish so fondly amongst a multitude of action-packed, golden moments that day. Triumphant it may have been for Kerry, but it was also one of the saddest, most traumatic days of my sporting life. For this was to be the very last day that I spent at Croke Park with my great friend and Radio Kerry commentator, Liam Higgins.

Liam was dying from oesophageal cancer and he had, literally, just weeks to live. But yet, unbelievably, as Kerry and Mayo took the field on that Sunday, he was prepared to sit behind the microphone and broadcast the All-Ireland final to the thousands of listeners in the towns and villages of his beloved Kerry. I sat beside Liam high up on the Hogan Stand in the magnificent Michael O'Hehir commentary position among the hundreds of press, radio and television personnel.

Liam had shone for Kerry on many occasions in both league and championship on the sacred green sward of Croke Park, but that day in 2006 was to be his greatest day of all.

Just four months previously on a sad day in May he had received the terrible news: death was inevitable and the doctors told him that he had just months to live. His partner Helen recalls: 'At first he was, as expected, devastated, but being the amazing person he was, after a few weeks he bravely came to terms with his illness.' Helen says that the Munster final in Killarney on 9 July was a defining moment in his last months. 'He was, at first, not going to attend the game and we all thought he would just retreat into himself and sit at home. How wrong we were. He made up his mind to live the remaining months of his life as best and as actively as he could.' And that is exactly what Liam did. He attended and commentated on the 2006 Munster final. Kerry and Cork drew that day in Killarney, Kerry lost the replay, and he and I then followed our county as we broadcast games against Longford in Killarney, Armagh in Croke Park, the semi-final against Cork and, eventually, to that final September victory over Mayo.

The decline in his health became very noticeable as the summer unfolded. The position of the cancer in his body prevented him from eating properly, and even drinking became a big problem. He was in and out of hospital as the doctors monitored his deteriorating condition. Liam and I discussed his cancer on just one occasion, and he was adamant that he would fight to the very last breath, whenever that might be. His final words to me on the subject of his illness were short and sweet, 'God, Weeshie, it's an awful way to go.' After that there was a kind of mutual unspoken agreement between us that further discussion was unnecessary.

Some years previously we had travelled to a Kerry game in Portlaoise and afterwards we had visited one of the local public houses for a drink and a bite to eat. Liam fell into conversation with an old friend from Lispole. The pair had not met for a number of years and enjoyed a long and deep discussion. On our way home later he was silent for a few miles, in deep thought as he often would be, then he explained. 'That man I was talking to has prostate cancer and has just a short time to live. I'll tell you one thing, if I was told I had incurable cancer, I just could not handle it and I would prefer to be dead.' When the cancer struck Liam himself, these words came readily to my mind and I feared for his final few months. I need not have worried. To this day I continue to marvel at his bravery, his stoicism, and his acceptance of what lay before him. It was, quite simply, awe-inspiring to see how he handled himself. He continued to travel all over his native county, fished in Dingle Bay, met friends and family on a regular basis and put his private affairs in order, leading a normal life (as far as was possible) right up the very end.

That September day in Croke Park, as Kerry met Mayo in the final, it was evident that the end was very close. The fact that Liam had even survived the journey to Dublin was a miracle in itself. He had been admitted to Tralee General Hospital the week preceding the final. On the Thursday of that week I visited him and, in spite of the fact that he had weakened considerably since I had last seen him, he was still adamant that he would be by my side in Croke Park. It seemed to me that this was a near impossibility, given the way he looked. But when I rang Helen later that day, she said that he was resolute in his decision and had instructed her to book a flight and a hotel.

Then his lifelong friend and confidant, Páidí Ó Sé, rang me in a very emotional state. 'Is it true, Weeshie, that Higgins is broadcasting the final?' Páidí asked. I explained what Liam had told me when I visited him and Páidí was literally dumbfounded. 'We must stop him. Sure, the man is dying on his feet and will need a wheelchair to go anywhere. I would hate to see him in such a state in Dublin.' Nevertheless, Liam signed himself out of hospital, Helen accompanied him on the flight from Kerry Airport at Farranfore on the Saturday and they booked into the Dublin Airport Hotel. 'First, I believed he wouldn't make Farranfore,' recalled Helen, 'and then I was afraid something would happen to him on the flight, but he never once complained, he was unbelievable.'

The All-Ireland final was due to start at 3.30 p.m. We took our seats in our broadcasting positions high up on the Hogan Stand. Trevor Galvin and Stephen O'Mahoney were Radio Kerry's sound engineers that day. They, of course, were conscious of the enormity of the occasion and in later years they continued to speak of the tremendous courage, calmness and professionalism Liam displayed on that day. Just minutes remained before we were due to go live on air. I turned to him and, trying to keep my voice as casual as possible, asked, 'Are you okay Liam? Any problems?' He looked me in the eye, gave that little chuckle of laughter that had become so familiar to me and replied, 'Not a problem, boy; I have this little pump attached to my side here and if I get a dart of pain all I need to do is give myself a shot of morphine and I am floating on air. Christ, it's great stuff and it's keeping me going.'

Kevin Casey was the Radio Kerry sideline reporter that day. The Kerry team was limbering up at the Canal End watched by Kerry legend Johnny Culloty who was now a selector for the county. Kevin approached the Killarney Legion man for a last-minute comment. 'So what's your final word, Johnny?' he asked. Culloty paused for a second, looked the reporter in the eye, then pointed to the Hogan Stand and uttered the wonderful line: 'If the Kerry players have the same heart and spirit as Liam Higgins up there then there is no way we are going to be beaten.' It was a remarkable and poignant moment as Johnny, who had captained Kerry to their twenty-first All-Ireland win in 1969 with a team that included Liam at full forward, paid that final magnificent tribute to his former teammate. And that was how Liam Higgins broadcast his final game from Croke Park. He was superb and, as always, his gift as a natural communicator came shining through. The consummate professional, Liam's deep knowledge and love of the game was evident in every word he uttered as he moved beautifully from the Irish language into English. After the match, a Kerry win, we were about to hand back to the studio in Tralee but Liam posed the question, 'Who was your man-of-the-match today Weeshie?' I paused for a moment, looked him in the eye and said, 'There were two stars here today Liam, Seamus Moynihan and yourself.' Once again he gave that beautiful little chuckle, we handed back to the studio and our last moments together in Croke Park drew to an end.

It had always been our normal routine when flying to games in Croke Park to return to the Airport Hotel and have a drink and some food. Not so, of course, on this occasion. Liam was collected by his family as soon as the final whistle sounded and I then made my way to the same hotel to await the flight home. All the Higgins family were seated just off the main bar, including Liam's mother Nell. Liam was now surrounded by those he loved most. I was sitting at the bar on my own. Helen approached me, we spoke of how ill Liam appeared following the exertions of the day, and she invited me to join the group. Liam then passed by, stopped and said, 'Sorry I can't join you for the usual, Weesh, but I must go to my room and lie down, I am exhausted.' I watched him, helped by Helen, leave the bar and suddenly the enormity and great sadness of the moment hit me like a ton of bricks. I went to the restrooms and there the tears literally came in torrents. All the pent-up emotions of the day engulfed me. I found it difficult to fully believe that this was our last time together in Dublin and that this proud west Kerry man who was so passionate about his county, who wore his heart on his sleeve, was just days from death. Liam's brother Joe, the renowned politician, had followed me and his reassurance and words of great comfort helped me compose myself but the flight home was one of the saddest of my life.

We had one last final hour together. A Kerry county semi-final was played in Austin Stack Park, Tralee, the following Sunday. To the amazement of friends and family, Liam once again insisted that he be brought to Tralee to take his place for the Radio Kerry broadcast of the game. Once again the morphine was literally keeping him alive, this time it was in liquid form and at times during the game he took little sips from a bottle that he described as 'great stuff'. The final whistle sounded; I followed him closely as he descended the stairs of the commentary box. He looked so ill and weak. I knew for sure that we would never sit together again. He died at home, peacefully in his sleep, one week later with Helen at his side. An impeccable one minute's silence was observed at the Kerry football final seven days later. It was one of the most poignant matches I have watched.

St Mary's Church in Dingle could not accommodate the huge crowds who attended the requiem mass for the late Liam Higgins on the Tuesday afternoon following his death. For over three hours on the previous evening hundreds of mourners paid their last respects to Liam and his family at O'Connor's Funeral Home on the Mall Road, Dingle. In a rare departure from other funerals his coffin was shouldered to the church from the funeral home. CBS teachers and students, as well as some students from the Presentation Convent, formed a guard of honour on the Mall in front of the CBS where Liam had taught for almost forty years. There were moving tributes, in song and word, during the funeral mass, which was celebrated by Father Pat Moore. Liam's brother Joe spoke of Liam's love of football, which the family had played in Ballineetig. He recalled how, as a youngster, Liam would give a running commentary on the game, even as he was playing. I was afforded the great privilege of speaking about my late, great friend's indomitable spirit. And I again recalled my astonishment and admiration of Liam's decision, while very ill, to commentate on that year's All-Ireland final from Croke Park. In a very moving final tribute the congregation heard an excerpt from Liam's final radio commentary at that September All-Ireland final. His remains, donated to medical research, were later removed to Cork. Liam was just sixty-one at the time of his death.

This late, late vocation in radio has literally consumed me, just as it consumed Liam. Now in the autumn of my life's journey, I am in many ways still chasing that Kerry dream, but the horizons opening up are new. I can peer back through time and see myself as a twelve-year-old, sitting on the footpath outside McNeill's little shop in Lower New Street, listening to the magical and captivating voice of Michael O'Hehir broadcasting that epic 1953 All-Ireland final. That was the first time I heard a sports event on radio. And then more memories come flooding back. Getting out of bed with my brother, Geni, at the crack of dawn to listen to crackling broadcasts of the great heavyweight boxing matches, coming all the way from America. The great fighters brought into our little kitchen on the Bush radio. Rocky Marciano, the 'Brockton Blockbuster', world heavyweight champion; he won forty-nine fights in a row and retired undefeated. Joe Louis, Don Cockell, the English man Jersey Joe Walcott, and the great Archie Moore; all visited our home through the magic of radio. And then there was Ronnie Delany racing the 1,500 metres in the 1956 Melbourne Olympics, the voice of the British broadcaster fading in and out, and the wonder, the awe and bewilderment as Delany crossed the line to win the gold. The greatest sporting memory of my life and I was not even there.

Years later when I talked to Delany in Dublin I told him that story and he gave me a wonderful piece of advice: 'Whenever you are broadcasting a match, Weeshie, always visualise that you are speaking to a man sitting on his own by the fireside in his home somewhere deep in the heart of Kerry.

Remember that you have the priceless gift of being his ears and eyes at the match, always cherish that. Only the radio has this power.' I will never forget those words. In that moment I could see that the wheel of life had turned full circle for me and that I had found a dream I had never set out to capture. Somebody up there likes me.

21

My favourite fifteen Kerry footballers, 1955-2012

Picking my best Kerry team since 1955 right up to the present day was always going to be next to impossible, but any publication concerning Kerry football would be incomplete without one's best-ever fifteen. The county has produced so many brilliant players that, really, it comes down to the toss of a coin for most positions. For me many of the chosen men were simply automatic choices and, having seen every Kerry footballer since 1955, I was able in my own mind to recall and compare players through the years; eventually my decision was reached following long deliberation. Indeed, it is my belief that the fifteen I have settled on would be capable of starring in various other positions at the highest level. I count myself very fortunate to have seen, played with, commentated on, befriended and interviewed many of the legendary Kerry footballers of the last fifty years. It has been an amazing experience and I can still see in the mind's eye all those men whom I first saw playing under Captain John Dowling in 1955, right up to the exemplary men of today who are led by Colm Cooper. I was once told that distance lends enchantment to the view as one peers back through the mists of time. I suppose I saw some of those players from the past through the rosy spectacles of a boy, but my youthful impressions persist. Those Kerrymen will forever remain my heroes on the green sward of Croke Park.

Goalkeeper, Johnny Culloty

Club: Killarney Legion
Senior career: 1955–1971
Championship appearances: 44
League appearances: 68
Scored: 1-1 in Championship; 7-9 in National League
Munster Senior finals: played in 12 finals; won 10, lost 2
All-Ireland Senior finals: played in 9 finals; won 5, lost 4

Right Full Back, Seamus Murphy (RIP)

Clubs: Camp; Lispole
Senior career: 1958–1970
Championship appearances: 41
League appearances: 51
Scored: 0-10 in Championship; 2-4 in National League
Munster Senior finals: played in 11 finals; won 11
All-Ireland Senior finals: played in 8 finals; won 4, lost 4

Full Back, John O'Keeffe

Club: Austin Stacks
Senior career: 1970–1983
Championship appearances: 49
League appearances: 90
Scored: 0-9 in Championship; 0-7 in National League
Munster Senior finals: played in 16 finals; won 12, lost 4
All-Ireland Senior finals: played in 10 finals; won 7; lost 3

Left Full Back, Paudie Lynch

Club: Beaufort

Senior career: 1971–1983

Championship appearances: 39

League appearances: 60

Scored: 0-7 in Championship; 2-32 in National League

Munster Senior finals: played in 13 finals; won 10, lost 3

All-Ireland Senior finals: played in 9 finals; won 6, lost 3

Right Half Back, Tomas O Sé

Club: An Gaeltacht

Senior Career (to 2012): 1998–2011

Championship appearances: 82

League appearances: 85

Scored: 3-32 in Championship; 1-28 in National League

Munster Senior finals: played in 12 finals; won 9, lost 3

All-Ireland Senior finals: played in 8 finals; won 5, lost 3

Centre Back, Seamus Moynihan

Club: Glenflesk

Senior career: 1992–2006

Championship appearances: 61

League appearances: 94

Scored: 0-5 in Championship; 4-38 in National League

Munster Senior finals: played in 12 finals; won 8, lost 4

All-Ireland Senior finals: played in 6 finals; won 4, lost 2

Left Half Back, Mick O'Dwyer

Club: Waterville

Senior career: 1957–1973

Championship appearances: 48 (of which one as a substitute)

League appearances: 93
Scored: 6-129 in Championship; 16-291 in National League
Munster Senior finals: played in 13 finals; won 11, lost 2
All-Ireland Senior finals: played in 10 finals; won 5, lost 5

My two midfield choices were easy, even though Kerry is renowned for great midfielders. I never saw the legendary Paddy Kennedy playing, but the old-timers tell me that he was as good as Mick O'Connell. The ultimate honour. Those midfield men whom I have watched throughout their careers include: John Dowling, Din Joe Crowley, Darragh Ó Sé, Ambrose O'Donovan, Donal Daly, Jer D. O'Connor, Sean Walsh and William Kirby. Mick O'Connell was the most amazing footballer I ever saw. He was unique, he was different, he was oozing with class, style, athleticism, and that very rare ingredient, charisma. There will never be another Mick O'Connell. In my year on the Kerry winning panel of 1969 I had a close and personal view of the Man from Valentia. He was the county's top scorer from midfield that year with 0-15. Enough said.

MIDFIELDER, MICK O'CONNELL

Club: Valentia Young Islanders
Senior career: 1956–1973
Championship appearances: 56
League appearances: 73
Scored: 1-121 in Championship; 7-131 in National League
Munster Senior finals: played in 16 finals; won 12, lost 4
All-Ireland Senior finals: played in 9 finals; won 4, lost 5

And now for Jack O'Shea. He was quite simply the greatest Gaelic footballer I have ever seen. No words of mine could do justice to that magnificent career. He was a giant on the field and his record speaks for itself. What other midfielder has scored the unbelievable total of 27 goals and 165 points in their career? And remember that today's players have more games under their belts since the introduction of the qualifying rounds.

Midfielder, Jack O'Shea

Clubs: St Mary's, Cahersiveen; Leixlip

Senior career: 1977–1992

Championship appearances: 53

League appearances: 102

Scored: 11-55 in Championship; 16-110 in National League

Munster Senior finals: played in 18 finals; won 12, lost 6

All-Ireland Senior finals: played in 8 finals; won 7, lost 1

Right Half Forward, Maurice Fitzgerald

Club: St Mary's, Cahersiveen

Senior career: 1988–2001

Championship appearances: 45

League appearances: 62

Scored: 12-205 in Championship; 11-237 in National League

Munster Senior finals: played in 12 finals; won 6, lost 6

All-Ireland Senior finals: played in 2 finals; won 2

Centre Forward, Tom Long

Clubs: Ventry; Dr Crokes, Killarney

Senior career: 1956–1964

Championship appearances: 26

League appearances: 43

Scored: 5-22 in Championship; 11-30 in National League

Munster Senior finals: played in 6 finals; won 5, lost 1

All-Ireland Senior finals: played in 4 finals; won 2, lost 2

Left Half Forward; Pat Spillane

Club: Templenoe

Senior career: 1974–1991

Championship appearances: 56

League appearances: 81

Scored: 19-123 in Championship; 13-103 in National League

Munster Senior finals: played in 17 finals; won 13, lost 4

All-Ireland Senior finals: played in 10 finals; won 8, lost 2

Right Corner Forward, Colm Cooper

Club: Dr Crokes, Killarney

Senior career (to 2012): 2002–2011

Championship appearances: 67

League appearances: 50

Scored: 19-240 in Championship; 11-137 in National League

Munster Senior finals: played in 9 finals; won 7, lost 2

All-Ireland Senior finals: played in 7 finals; won 4, lost 3

Full Forward, John Egan

Club: Sneem

Senior career: 1973–1984

Championship appearances: 41

League appearances: 65

Scored: 14-59 in Championship; 21-59 in National League

Munster Senior finals: played in 14 finals; won 11, lost 3

All-Ireland Senior finals: played in 8 finals; won 6, lost 2

LEFT CORNER FORWARD, MICKEY SHEEHY

Club: Austin Stacks

Senior career: 1974–1987

Championship appearances: 49

League appearances: 74

Scored: 29-205 in Championship; 22-251 in National League

Munster Senior finals: played in 17 finals; won 14, lost 3

All-Ireland Senior finals: played in 9 finals; won 7, lost 2

To date, he is Kerry's all-time top scorer.

22

My choice of the greatest living Kerry sports legends

Kerry is renowned worldwide for its natural beauty, magnificent scenery and the brilliance and tradition of its footballers. It is my experience that no matter where you travel in the world and meet up with sporting people, especially Kerry people, the number one topic of conversation will be Kerry football. And it will be football and no other sport. I have travelled from New York to San Francisco, from Melbourne to Auckland, from London to Glasgow and all around Ireland, and I can say that seldom have I heard any other sporting son or daughter of Kerry, apart from a footballer, brought up for discussion. I have sat in great GAA watering holes debating Gaelic football for hours on end and I have rarely heard praise being lavished on any of our great sports stars outside of football. Kerry footballers and their supporters literally turn a blind eye to the legendary sporting greats this county has produced. And, for me, this is a sad state of affairs.

Recently, as part of my research for this chapter, I sat with a group of friends and in the course of conversation posed the question, 'Where in Kerry did Jerry Kiernan, Ireland's great marathon runner, come from?' No one could answer. Then I mentioned the name Damian Foxall, the world renowned sailor from Castlecove, and again vague answers. So I asked who was the only Kerryman ever to climb to the top of Everest? Blank stares in return. Photographic exhibitions in praise of Kerry footballers are a common occurrence in the county. Local newspapers produce special supplements at various times to record some big football event but never have I seen an exhibition of photographs strictly in honour of the so-called 'minority' sports in Kerry.

In 1984 when the aforementioned great runner, Jerry Kiernan, finished ninth in the Olympic marathon (an event at which it was acknowledged we had seen the greatest field of runners ever assembled), it was a footballer who was nominated sportsperson of the year at an awards function in County Kerry. A terrible injustice and a slap in the face for the man who was the talk of the athletic world at that time. There is none so blind as he who cannot see; footballers rule the roost when honours and praise are handed out. Yes, when a Kerry athlete from an arena other than football hits the world stage, we certainly hear about him or her – but their star wanes quickly. Examine all the Kerry GAA books that have been published in the last twenty years; I am 99.9 per cent certain that there will not be one mention of a Kerry man or woman from another sport. No recognition, not a word of praise and no credit where credit is due. But then again, in fairness, that is the way people are reared in Kerry; it is football first and foremost, from the cradle to the grave. Nevertheless I find it sad that all our great sportsmen and women are not awarded the praise they so richly deserve on a continuous basis.

This chapter is therefore in praise of all those Kerry sportspeople still living in 2012 who have achieved greatness in their chosen sport – outside of Gaelic football. Of course, there are many others that I might have included. Soccer players such as Gordon Kerins, Billy Dennehy, Sean Carey,

Tom Johnson, Peter O'Brien, Johnny Conway, Elisha Dowling, John Doyle, Maurice Goosie O'Rahilly, Dermot Lyne, James Sugrue, David Hennessey and Peter McCarthy. In the world of basketball there would be Paudie O'Connor, Buddy Burrows, Charlie Hanlon, Kieran Donaghy, Michael Quirke, Paddy Culligan, Hugh O'Brien, Derry O'Shea, Pat O'Shea and many more. Snooker was once a major sport in the county and Ger 'Shy' Nolan from Castleisland was one of the best, as was Tom Murphy, Hawley Walsh, Noel 'Chakie' Whyte, Geni Fogarty, Arthur Drugan and Killarney lad Danny McGoff. I hope that some day a mightier pen than my own will take on the task of writing the complete history of Kerry sports stars.

I have had the great privilege of interviewing each and every one of the names that follow and their stories are now recorded for future generations. Enjoy this tribute to great Kerry men and women; I think you will be surprised at what they have achieved at local, national and international level. To me they are living legends.

GILLIAN O'SULLIVAN, *Kerry's only lady Olympian*

Gillian O'Sullivan is one of Ireland's greatest athletes. She represented Ireland at European, World and Olympic Games in the 20 km race walk. When she retired from race walking in April 2007 at just thirty years of age following a long battle with injuries and illness, she left the legacy of her magnificent career and a hugely impressive list of achievements. She was the reigning world record holder in the 5000 m, a record she set in Santry in 2002 at the Irish National Championships. She was also the Irish record holder in the 3,000 m, 5,000 m and 10,000 m and holds the 10 km and 20 km Irish road records.

Gillian's best performance came in 2003 when she took second in the 20 km walk at the World Championships in Paris. She also had a fourth place finish at the 2002 European Championships and came tenth at the Sydney Olympics in

With Gillian O'Sullivan, Kerry's only lady Olympian, in Killarney in 2003 on a night when Gillian was honoured for winning the silver medal for the 20 km racewalk in the World Championships held in Paris. Injury ended what would have been a magnificent career for the lady from Minish, just outside Killarney, who retired in 2007.

2000 in the same event. A very gracious lady and so generous with her time. I had the honour of interviewing her on a number of occasions at her home in Minish just outside Killarney and, after her retirement, in the Radio Kerry studios when she told me:

> To retire from competing was always going to be a huge decision for me but I have put a lot of thought into it and I feel now is the best time to move on.

> Athletics has been so good to me but it has got to the stage where with some of the problems I've had I didn't feel I could get back to the heights I hit in 2002 and 2003, and to leave now I can be happy with everything I have achieved and not have any regrets. I want to thank Athletics Ireland, the Irish Sports Council and the Olympic Council for all their help and support throughout my career. For the future I have no immediate plans but I would certainly love to be involved in athletics at some level down the line and maybe I will look at getting involved in coaching.

I spoke to Liam Hennessy, Chairman of the Athletics Ireland High Performance Committee and, as expected, he was full of praise for her outstanding career: 'Gillian is a huge loss to us but her place in the history of Irish athletics is assured. From her excellent performance in Sydney to her moment of true greatness in Paris she has been one of Ireland's best. These are my abiding memories of Gillian along with that of a supremely talented athlete with a burning determination to succeed. On behalf of Athletics Ireland and myself I want to wish her all the best for the future.'

There is no doubt in my mind that, but for her premature retirement, Gillian would have won a medal of some colour in the Olympics. She was the first, and so far the only, Kerry-born lady to participate in the Olympics. Gillian is now a qualified personal trainer (NCEHS, 2006) and also a qualified teacher (BA, H.Dip.Ed., 1998); she is married and based in Cork.

Maureen Harrington, *world cross-country star*

Maureen Harrington is, in my opinion, one of the most unacknowledged sporting greats this county has seen. A remarkably successful athlete, she has had a wonderful career and, at the time of writing, she is still taking part in races around the county from her home in Kenmare. Her achievements are amazing and speak for themselves. Indeed her greatest admirers have been known to refer to her as Kerry's answer to Sonia O'Sullivan and, whether you agree or not with this high praise, few people will argue that she is not one of the most exciting female athletes to emerge from the Kingdom. Maureen is from Tousist, the very same parish from which the great winning Kerry captain of the 1920s, Phil O'Sullivan, came.

Maureen wrote herself into the annals of the Kerry legends when she was a member of the Irish women's team that won the country's first bronze medals at the World Cross Country Championships in 1997 and again in 2002. A magnificent achievement by this very unassuming and private lady. Her teammates on those winning sides included Sonia O'Sullivan, Catherina McKiernan, Valeria Vaughan, Una English and Pauline Curley, all legends in ladies' athletics.

So just how talented is this amazing Kenmare lady? During the 1990s she won seven Kerry Senior Cross Country Championships and five Munster Senior Cross Country Championships. At All-Ireland inter-counties her record is two wins and five second places. In the All-Ireland inter-club championships her record stands at two wins, three third places, and a fourth, fifth and sixth.

In her stunning career, the Kenmare lady represented Ireland on eight occasions in the European Cross Country Championships and in ten world championships. She ran in the international marathon in Seoul and has competed in numerous international grand prix races. Amazing statistics – and who can argue with those?

DAMIAN FOXALL, *star of the sea*

Unquestionably Ireland's finest ocean-racing sailor and Kerry's least acknowledged sporting great, Damian now lives in France with his wife Suzy-Ann, son Oisín and daughter

Neave, and his name is whispered with awe among sailing's elite. Damian was born and reared close to the village of Caherdaniel on the Iveragh Peninsula where his parents had moved to from England. Foxall's childhood was spent messing about with boats in Derrynane harbour in the company of his younger brother, Rupert. In the competitive world of professional sailing it is not all about catching the wind. Endurance is the name of the game. Ocean racing means sleep deprivation, sharing wet, cramped conditions below deck, eating barely edible freeze-dried food and, worst of all, leaving family and friends for months at a time.

In his new book, *Ocean Fever*, Damian traces his adventures from Derrynane to racing around the Southern Ocean. Foxall left school and Ireland early to pursue his ambition. He did everything from labouring on construction sites to flipping burgers to pay for his sailing. His restless spirit saw him move to the Canaries and a chance meeting led to his first job as a sailor on a passage to the Caribbean. He was soon racing with the world's best sailors and adventurers, such as Alan Gautier, Steve Fossett and Tracy Edwards. In 2007 and 2008, with co-skipper Jean-Pierre Dick, the Kerryman won the 25,000 mile Barcelona World Race and in 2009 he was part of the crew of the *Green Dragon* that took a creditable fifth place in that year's Volvo Ocean Race.

In a career of highs the 2008–9 Volvo Ocean Race is right up there, particularly the moment when the fleet arrived in Galway in May 2009 because that city had been chosen to host a leg of this most gruelling race. As Foxall recounts in *Ocean Fever*, the crew expected to be greeted by a few die-hard supporters as it was 3 a.m. in the morning. It was, in Damian's words (and as any great Kerryman would sum it up), 'like All-Ireland final day. We could see the sheer scale of 9,000 people gathered at three o'clock in the morning. We never expected this.' On the dockside was Foxall's wife,

Suzy-Ann, smiling and with tears in her eyes as she passed their then eighteen-month-old son, Oisín, up to him.

High risk, extreme weather, and monumental challenges in the world's harshest environment are all in a day's work for him; but in his heart, as he puts it himself, Kerry will always remain 'the place called home'. When Damian returned to Derrynane following that Barcelona World Race, Christy Riordan and I were present as a massive crowd of people paid tribute to one of their own. Bonfires blazed, there was music and dancing, and a pig was roasting on the spit in the marquee erected at the Blind Piper Pub as Damian and his wife were paraded through the village. It was a memorable occasion and then Damian very graciously sat down with us and I interviewed him about his life and times.

And on Monday 2 July 2012 Damian was on board the French yacht *Groupama* which won the world-renowned Volvo Ocean Race. The race involved a nine-month voyage across four oceans and ten countries, including South Africa, China, New Zealand, Brazil, the US, France and Portugal. More than 20,000 people turned out as Damian Foxall and the crew of *Groupama* sailed into Galway in the early hours of the morning. This amazing Kerry sportsman from little Caherdaniel in the south of Kerry said that after fifteen years of work and nine months spent travelling 40,000 miles with the team, the achievement was 'a childhood dream, an adult's dream'. What a man, is he Kerry's greatest ever sportsman?

EUGENE MORIARTY, *steeped in a cycling tradition*

Eugene Moriarty was born into a cycling family in 1974. His grandfather, Gene Moriarty, had been the first of the family to become immersed in the tradition, becoming well known as one of Kerry's grass-track stars in the late 1940s and early 1950s; his father, Tadgh, is one of Ireland's great cycling sports administrators. Eugene himself started racing in the Kelly-Roche era of the early 1980s at nine years of age. He quickly came up through the under-age ranks with many successes countrywide, winning under-age Irish titles for the Listowel club under his first coach, Jimmy Healy. He moved on to the international stage at sixteen when selected for the Irish Under-18 team to race in France. He had many successes at this level with Kerry Group Rás hero, John Mangan, now as his coach. He won a prestigious international two-day event in Manchester, one of the biggest ever wins for an Irish cyclist at Under-18 level.

Eugene finished his early education at Scoil Realt na Maidne and St Michael's College in Listowel and he moved to Trinity College Dublin, where he graduated with BSc (Hons). When he was just twenty years old, he competed in his first Rás Tailteann on the Ciarraí Og team under another Kerry cycling legend, Gene Mangan. Since then he has lined out in the Rás fifteen times and he has many top-class results in Ireland's most famous bike race. His record as a team rider is well known: he was on seven winning teams in the Rás; two winning Irish international teams in 2000 and 2004; and five winning inter-county teams for his adopted county of Meath in 2002, 2003, 2005, 2007 and 2009. His best individual inter-county placing was ninth overall in 1999. He holds a record thirteen Cú Chulainn awards as top county rider on stages also. He has never won a stage, but was second twice and third three times, and has many other top-ten placings. He has worn the King of the Mountains jersey in two different Rásanna and has also won 'best climber' in the Tour of Ulster.

On the international scene the Listowel man has worn the green jersey of Ireland well over one hundred times and he has been placed in races in France, Holland, Greece, Egypt, Malaysia, Australia, New Zealand, Britain, Japan, USA, and other far-flung countries. But his finest hour in the Irish jersey came when he took fifth place in the World Amateur Cycling Championship in 1999 in Uruguay. His performance qualified Ireland for a place in the 2000 Sydney

Olympics. Initially he was assured of his own place at the Games by the powers that be, but was sensationally denied entry afterwards. He again lined out in the World Championships in Switzerland in 2003.

On the home front Eugene won Rás Mumhan in 2001 and was second overall in the Tour of Ulster the same year; he has also won stages in Rás Connachta, the Meath Grand Prix, the Tour of Monaghan and he won the Gene Moriarty Cup (bestowed in memory of his grandfather) in Listowel in 1996, making County Senior Champion as well. He was awarded the Kerry Sports Star of the Month on three occasions. Eugene won All-Ireland medals on the Road, Hill Climb and was Irish Senior Criterium Champion in 2005, and also won team medals with his Cycleways team.

A legendary Rás Tailteann-winning Kerry cycling team of the 1950s pictured outside St Mary's Cathedral in Killarney before the start of a stage. I was fascinated by these iron men of the road in my youth and, in later years, had the honour of interviewing and befriending some of these boyhood heroes, Gene Mangan *(front row, third from right)*, Paddy O'Callaghan *(front row, first from right)*, Paudie Fitzgerald *(front row, third from left)*, and Johnny Switzer *(front row, fifth from right)*, all of whom are included here. Gene Mangan was the youngest ever Rás winner – he won three days before his nineteenth birthday.

These days Eugene lives and works in Amsterdam where he still races, but he comes home to ride in all the big events in Ireland. His record on track and road can stand equal to all the great men who have gone before him and he is certainly a worthy successor to his grandfather and father Tadgh.

Frank Conway, *star athlete from Dooks*

Look back to the year 1989 and ponder on what Frank Conway achieved in America at that time. In the entire history of athletics only two Kerrymen have run the mile in under four minutes: Jerry Kiernan, the great Listowel man and TV analyst, and Frank. Just three years before 1989 Frank had been awarded a full athletic and academic scholarship to Providence College in America, under the guidance of Ray Tracy, brother of Olympic silver medallist John. His progress on the track in that short time had been simply phenomenal. He ran an indoor mile in Harvard in 3:56.6 minutes and improved his world ranking to fifth fastest. He won the Millrose Games mile, beating Olympic Champion Peter Rono in the process. He won New England titles in the 1,500 m, 3000 m, and 800 m, and captured a number of US regional titles (east coast). He was ranked as one of the top two indoor college milers and, to cap a sensational year for the man from Dooks, he was nominated College Athlete of the Year.

Frank began his running back in intermediate school in Killorglin, where he was a pupil from 1980 to 1989. He joined the famous Iveragh Athletic Club in Cahersiveen and had his first big win when he left the field trailing in his wake to capture the Kerry Colleges Cross Country Championship. He has high praise for the club and the men who set him on his running career. 'Brian McCarthy, a teacher in Killorglin, Mike Cahill, Ross Bay (a county councillor) and Lorcan Murphy, Cahersiveen, were just a few of the people who looked after and encouraged me during my young days,' he told me when we met one Christmas at Ger O'Connor's beautiful home in Dooks. During those schoolboy days Frank won a host of school competitions in Kerry, Munster and Ireland but one victory remains etched on his memory. He recalls, 'I won the All-Ireland Schools 2000 m Steeplechase in record time and, believe it or not, that record still stands today, one of the longest-standing school records.' He was now running in all the big cross country championships and was chosen to represent Ireland on many occasions. He was quickly spotted by the American college scouts and in 1986 he was offered and accepted the scholarship to Providence College.

After arriving in America he suffered illness for a time and returned home to rest. While in Ireland he won the prestigious Cork City Mile in February 1987, but by mid-November he had returned to full fitness and went back to the States. The following year he beat the great Peter Rona over one mile in the famed Madison Square Garden, New York. Today Frank Conway is deeply involved with the Kerry Athletic High Performance Development Squad, which numbers eighty-five top Kerry athletes, including some outstanding middle-distance runners.

After his glittering career on the running tracks of America and Europe, it was an amazing experience to sit and talk with him for hours about his life and times. Sadly, his career came to an early end following an ankle injury and his failure to qualify for the Olympic Games. He had not yet reached the summit of his powers and, who knows, but for that injury, Dooks, the village of Glenbeigh and the Iveragh Athletic Club could have celebrated their very own Olympic medallist. Nevertheless, he is still a Kerry legend and will be for the foreseeable future until some whizz kid comes along and runs the mile in under 3:56.6. Until that day he remains Kerry's fastest man on the track.

Jerry Kiernan, *Kerry's first man to run the mile in less than four minutes.*
Jerry Kiernan was born in the little village of Brosna in north Kerry, where his father was a member of An Garda Síochána. A very promising footballer in his youth, he won a Kerry Minor County Championship medal with Feale Rangers and also played for St Michael's College, Listowel. However, his great love for athletics was born as he watched the best runners in the world compete in the Tokyo Olympics of 1964. He was simply, as he says himself, 'born to run'. He won his first medal in Duagh when he finished second at a local sports meeting. Little did he realise that this was the beginning of what was to be one of the greatest running careers of any Kerryman to date. In fact Jerry's ninth place finish in the Los Angeles Olympic Marathon is the second highest placing ever achieved by an Irishman. That same year John Treacy won the silver in the very same race.

As a youth Jerry won all the major under-age titles, Kerry, Munster and All-Ireland; his career was blossoming. He left Kerry at eighteen years of age to begin a teaching career in Dublin and joined the famous Clonliffe Harriers Athletic Club, with whom he won a host of All-Ireland championships. His ability at a range of distances was astonishing. He was fractionally outside the world record for the ten miles, running this in 46.5 minutes. Jerry ran in four Dublin City Marathons, winning twice and setting the record time in 1982. Then, in a classic mile race in June 1976, the Kerryman became the very first from the county and only the seventh Irishman to run under four minutes for the distance. Rod Dixon was the winner.

The Kerryman competed all over the world despite his commitment to his teaching career. Half-marathons, full marathons, 10 km, the mile or 3,000 m (he held the then Irish record for this distance), Jerry took them all in his stride. He excelled at cross-country running and won All-Irelands at

Under-18 and Under-20 levels, winning the Senior title in 1984. He was a regular on the Irish team, winning close to sixty green singlets: a magnificent achievement for this Kerryman. When the book of Kerry's greatest athletes is finally written, Jerry Kiernan will be right there at the very top.

In the Los Angeles Olympic Marathon of 1984 he proved beyond a doubt that he was equal to the world's very best. Finishing ninth, despite cramping a lot towards the finish, was an astonishing achievement when you consider that this was one of the greatest fields of marathon runners ever assembled: Carlos Lopez of Portugal won the gold in a new Olympic record time, John Treacy was second for Ireland, and Charlie Spedding of England was third. Other legendary names in the field of 105 athletes running shoulder to shoulder with the Brosna man that blistering hot day in Los Angeles included: Alberto Salazar (USA), Takeshi So (Japan), Rob de Castella (Australia), Joseph Nzau (Kenya) and the legendary Toshihiko Seko (Japan). We can only speculate what Jerry Kiernan would have achieved if he had gone to America and become a full-time athlete. The minds boggles.

JIM CULLOTY, *riding into history*

Jim was born in the heart of Killarney town and grew up right next to Fitzgerald Stadium, the home of Kerry GAA. He played with my own club, Killarney Legion, as a youngster and I have vivid memories of tying his boot laces when I was ten. He developed a great interest in horses at a young age and, as they say, the rest is history. Jim Culloty rode into history when he partnered Best Mate, owned by Jim Lewis and trained by Henrietta Knight, to win three consecutive Gold Cups in 2002, 2003 and 2004, matching the record of the legendary Arkle.

Jim's career lasted almost a decade, during which he rode a total of 394 winners. He rode 13 winners in one week as an amateur during the 1996 season and in 2002 he won the Grand National on Bindaree. He is now retired and living in

County Cork where he is a trainer and runs the J. H. Culloty Racing Stables at Mount Corbett House in Churchstown. His is an amazing success story. Truly one of the legendary Kerry sports heroes.

John O'Dowd, *the only Kerryman to summit Mount Everest*

John O'Dowd from Waterville reached the summit of Everest on his first attempt in May 2008 and became the first Kerryman to achieve this amazing feat. John has established himself as one of Ireland's premier high-altitude mountaineers, with a string of notable successes under his belt. (It may be worth stressing that mountain climbing was registered as a sport back in the 1950s.)

I was lucky enough to interview him just after that success, when he had arrived back home in Tarmons, near Waterville, surrounded by the mountains he knows best. He is a builder by trade and his family has lived in Tarmons for three generations. When the bug first began to bite he joined the Killarney Mountaineering Club, eventually travelling far and wide as his climbing skills developed. He has climbed in Alaska, the Himalayas, the Alps and the Andes, not to mention mountains in Scotland and England. John's extensive experience evidently served him well on his Everest conquest. He is married to Mary and they have three children, Imelda, Rebecca and Gabriel.

The team that conquered Everest included a Frenchman, a Dutchman, two British men and six Americans. They set off in early April and John was away from home for six weeks. What was it like, I asked him, to stand on top of that 29,029-foot peak, the highest in the world? He replied that it was an experience he will never forget:

> I stepped onto the summit at 7.30 a.m. and remained there for twenty minutes. It was amazing, just seven

> people can stand on the summit at a time and the view is stunning; you can see, on a clear day, for up to 300 miles. It's confusing, a little frightening and you feel very elated. My first thoughts were of home and how far I had come since I began climbing the mountains around Waterville. The scariest part for me was approaching through the ice falls. Massive blocks of towering ice which are moving all the time. The whole experience gave me the urge to climb even more.

This shy and unique Kerryman was given a hero's welcome back home, and rightly so. His achievement demanded courage, bravery, ability, fitness and determination, all of which John O'Dowd possesses in spadefuls.

JOHN GRIFFIN, *Tralee's champion athlete*

I had the great privilege some years ago to interview two amazing sporting brothers from the town of Tralee. The careers of John and Paul Griffin are astonishing and their list of local, national and international achievements is simply unparalleled for one family. Quiet, unassuming, courteous young men, they must be considered as two of Kerry's greatest sportsmen.

John was born in Ballymacelligott in July 1959. He grew up in Strand Road and now resides with his family in Ballinorig, Tralee. He is a grandson of that renowned barber, the late Foster Griffin, and is a son of Billy, a former champion track cyclist. His siblings Stephen and Liam were also involved in athletics, while the youngest, Paul, is an international cyclist. John took up athletics at sixteen years of age and won the Kerry Community Games Marathon in 1975. He joined St John's Athletic Club, Tralee, at this time. His first national Junior cross-country title came in 1977 and he then went on to represent Ireland in the 1978 World Junior Cross Country Championships in Glasgow. His victories in

County, Munster and national titles in both cross country and road are too numerous to list.

John ran his first marathon in 1981, finishing in fifteenth position. He was now well and truly bitten by the marathon bug and moved into an amazing phase of his sporting life. He has completed a total of twenty-nine marathons and has finished first twice, second twice and third twice; he is the only athlete to have finished in the top three on six occasions. He has been placed second in the Belfast Marathon twice, and also claimed third spot in the same race. John's fastest marathon was in London in 1991, a world cup event in which he achieved a time of 2 hours, 14 minutes and 42 seconds. He was the first Irishman across the finish line. The following year he had another superb run in London and was again the first Irishman across the line.

This Tralee man has had a magnificent career, but perhaps his most memorable achievement was winning the Dublin Millennium Marathon in 1988 in a time of 2 hours, 16 minutes and 2 seconds. He won Dublin again in 1989 and also won the Irish National Marathon of the same year, which was held in his hometown of Tralee. He won three national half-marathon titles in 1991, 1993 and 1994. Another top achievement was the Ballycotton '10', the most prestigious road race in the UK and Ireland. John has claimed this title on no less than four occasions, and has also been placed second twice and third twice. He has run in many international races, both individually and on Irish teams, and that has taken him to the UK, Holland, Belgium, Italy, Yugoslavia, Spain and the USA. In 2009 at the age of fifty John won the Dingle Marathon.

JOHN LENIHAN, *king of the mountains*

One of the bravest and most charismatic sportsmen Kerry has ever seen, John Lenihan first laced his racing shoes in 1977 to finish second in his local parish community games.

He won his first international cap for Ireland in Junior cross country in 1979 before joining John Treacy on the 1981 Irish Senior team, and was selected as a member of Ireland's training squad for the 5000 m in the 1984 Olympics after running 13:55 in Cork City Sports. He won Munster track and cross-country titles, has finished in silver and bronze position at national Senior level, and has twice been the winner of the Irish road half-marathon title, with a personal best of 63:5.

He ran 28:40 for 10 km and 47:19 for 10 miles before turning to mountain running, in which he was twice winner of the Isle of Mann Manx Mountain Marathon, six times winner of the Sligo Warrior Mountain Race and also won the Snowdon International Mountain Race in Wales, before going on to win the world Senior mountain-racing title in Switzerland in 1991. John has won the annual Carrantuohill Mountain Challenge nineteen times and currently holds the course record of 45 minutes to the summit from the bottom of the hydro road, not to mention a decent time of 25 minutes to the summit of Caher.

He has represented Ireland in track, road, cross-country and mountain running, and was awarded Kerry Sports Person of the Year in 2001 and Irish Sports Person of the Week in 1991. In the course of this stunning career John has set records on nearly every summit in the land and won races throughout Europe, at one point calling northern Italy his second home. Now retired from running as a result of injury, Lenihan says, 'I'm a farmer, not an athlete.'

He keeps a dairy farm on the land where he grew up, six miles outside the small town of Castleisland. When I visited him there, I arrived by way of roads that became increasingly narrower and steeper; the adventure ended (with a flourish) on a half-mile climb up his driveway in first gear. Perhaps a hint at the origin of his hill-running skills? Milking keeps Lenihan busy morning and night, but he still manages to run forty to fifty miles a week, enough to best most on any mountain; enough to best all on Carrantuohill, the peak he can point out across the valley from the field above his farm. Until you have witnessed John Lenihan racing at breakneck speed up the side of a mountain, long, flowing locks billowing in the wind, you cannot say you have seen the best of Kerry sport in action. We may never see his like again.

JOHN O'GRADY, *Kerry's greatest dual player*

The history of Kerry GAA is simply littered with celebrated accounts of players who have written their names into the pages of history, but here I want to write about a player who has excelled at football *and* hurling; the latter is always the poor relation in Kerry, a notoriously football-mad county. While Cork is renowned for its dual players, Kerry has also seen some brilliant men who have represented their county in both sports. Names that readily spring to mind include Niall Sheehy, Billy McCarthy, Sean and Declan Lovett, Mickey Joe Quinlan, P. J. McIntyre, Johnny Culloty and John Bunyan. There are, of course, many others.

However, one man stands out for me and he is John O'Grady from the historic north Kerry club of Ballyduff. So why does John deserve a place amongst my all-time Kerry sporting greats? Well, as they say, let his record speak for itself. He is the holder of four Senior hurling county championship medals with Ballyduff (1972, 1973, 1976 and 1977) and he also trained them to win the title on a fifth occasion. He is unique in the fact that he has won Senior football county championship medals in Kerry *and* Cork, both achieved in the same year of 1972. In that special year of his sporting life he helped the north Kerry divisional side, Shannon Rangers, to victory in the Kingdom and (because he had taken up third-level education at University College Cork) he also helped the UCC team to the Cork Championship. Add to that the fact that he has won the Fitzgibbon and Sigerson Cup medals. Now throw in a London County Championship with St Gabriel's (he worked there during the summer holidays when the rules and regulations were laxer). Finally you have a little insight into the man's passion for both football and hurling.

In 1973 he was still playing for UCC when they recaptured the Cork football county championship, to be beaten by only one point in the All-Ireland club final by Bellaghy of Derry. The famed Cork club, Blackrock, was quick to spot the brilliant Ballyduff hurler who was now living and working as a vet in Bantry (with whom he won a Cork intermediate medal). He threw in his lot with the Rockies and starred for them as they gathered up both the Cork and Munster crowns. In 1979 he lined out with Tom Cashman at midfield and enjoyed that rarest of experiences for a Kerryman, when the team won the All-Ireland championship in thrilling fashion, beating Ballyhale Shamrocks of Kilkenny, 5-7 to 5-5. Hurling legends on that team included John Horgan, Frank Cummins, Pat Moylan and Ray Cummins. And the Kerry dual player was equal to the very best. Not many men have played in both hurling and football All-Ireland club finals.

John gave fourteen years of dedicated service to the Kerry hurling team and was twice voted Kerry Hurler of the Year (1973 and 1978). He lined out for Cork in a number of tournament games, however, many shrewd judges felt that the fact that he was a Kerryman militated against him being picked for Cork in the Munster Hurling Championship. There is no doubt in my mind but that this great Ballyduff man, whom I interviewed on many occasions, fully deserves to be ranked with Kerry's greatest ever dual players. Indeed, perhaps amongst Ireland's greatest.

JOSEPH WHITE, *Kerry's forgotten world-record-breaking cyclist*

Castlecove native Patrick Joseph White left his beloved Kerry at seventeen years of age to travel to Dublin in 1948. While serving his apprenticeship in the Air Corps, he took up racing and became a friend of Dublin cycling legend, Shay Elliot. White admitted to me, 'He had a huge influence on my career, as Elliott's gruelling mountain training helped me build up tremendous strength and stamina that pushed me to become one of Ireland's top time triallists.' Joseph White's achievements on the road included All-Ireland Road Racing titles in 1953 and 1954, the Army Road and Track Championships in 1953, and many other wins from 1952 to 1954.

In 1954 White won Stage 4 of the Rás, from Tralee to Ennis; unfortunately, a bad crash brought a premature end to what could have been an even more successful career. During a recent interview in Killarney the Kerryman told me, 'I was certain I would have won that Rás only for that heavy fall.' He went on, 'I had ambitions of becoming a professional but I never really recovered fully following that crash.' That Rás in 1954 was won by Joe O'Brien. Joseph White's greatest sporting achievement came when he became the first man in the world to ride 100 miles in under four hours at Monasterevin, County Kildare; he achieved this in 3 hours, 58 minutes and 16 seconds. It was a magnificent achievement by the Kerry native, although it never received the acclaim it so richly deserved. Indeed, if not for Joseph's great friend in Castlecove, the landlord of the Black Shop, Brendan Galvin, it might still remain unknown. Brendan celebrated this world-record-breaking ride by erecting a stone plaque bearing an inscription near his pub, and it was because of this that I first became interested in this forgotten world-record-holder. I later befriended Joseph, did a series of interviews with him and was privileged to have the opportunity of bringing to light the truth of that 1954 record-breaking cycle ride in Kildare, after all these years.

Lorna Hannon, *a badminton legend*

The Hannon name has long been synonymous with the sport of badminton in Kerry and Munster. Sheila Hannon was a very successful player, having won many Kerry and Munster titles.

For many years she was closely involved in her club and county boards and eventually she was elected President of the Munster Branch of the Badminton Union of Ireland. All of Sheila's daughters, Janet, Carol, Jill, Lorna and Susan, played badminton at various levels for their club and county. However, it was Lorna who excelled on the badminton courts of Ireland.

Lorna's Senior career lasted from 1982 (when she was sixteen) to 2003. Between 1987 and 2003 she won both the Singles and Doubles titles for thirteen years in a row, only relinquishing her title during the three years that she was unable to take part. In the Munster Championships between 1991 and 2003 she played in seven Singles finals (winning six), four Doubles finals (winning all four), and was runner-up in two Mixed finals. In 1991 she reached the Singles, Doubles and Mixed finals, which often involved starting play at 10 a.m. and not finishing the last match until 10 p.m., after playing up to ten championship games in the same day. Lorna's interprovincial career began when she was fifteen years old and she went on to play for Munster every year up to the age of thirty-eight. Her first Munster title was the Munster Junior Championship when she was sixteen years old.

Lorna is best remembered for her brilliance and tenacity on the court and her humility off court, always gracious in victory and defeat. The Castleisland lady experienced her own personal best on the national stage when she was narrowly beaten in the third set in the final of the Irish Junior Championship, having lost the first set in a tiebreak. On her way to the final she had been in magnificent form, defeating the second and third seeds.

Her greatest and most consistent displays were when playing with the Kerry Team in the Butterfield Cup, a Munster competition that was usually played over two days on a Saturday and Sunday. She played for Kerry from the age of sixteen in this competition, which involved playing ten games over the weekend. During all the years that she played, she never failed to win all ten of her own games and the team manager's tactics were often built around the fact that Lorna's games were guaranteed wins. Kerry eventually had a historic victory in this competition under the guidance of the manager, Joe Crowley, from Killorglin, whose son Peter went on to play in the Kerry Senior football team.

Lorna helped her club in Castleisland to win many county titles, the All-Ireland Senior Club title in 1998 and the All-Ireland County Class 3 title in 1998. In both of the All-Ireland competitions she won all her own games to achieve the team wins. Her partnerships with Mary Lawlor (Brosnan) and Helen O'Donoghue (Twomey) gave many days of entertainment and excitement.

Lorna's achievements in sport were recognised in the county when she was nominated as the overall winner of the Kerry Sports Star of the Year Award in 1995. She had returned from surgery for a ruptured Achilles tendon in February that year and had subsequently won all her ten games to help Kerry gain the Butterfield Cup nine months later in November. (The tendon had been ruptured in the last set of the Singles final in the County Championships the year before and Lorna had played on to win the match.)

As Sheila handed the love of badminton to her daughters, Lorna has done likewise; as we watch her sons, Jonathan and Kevin, battle their way on those same courts today, once again we can recognise her familiar style, courage and graciousness.

Mary Geaney, *star of many sports*

Castleisland born Mary Geaney is arguably Kerry's greatest ever all-around sportswoman. Mary's father, Con, won an All-Ireland Senior football medal with Kerry in 1932 and her brother, Dave, also won a Senior medal with Kerry in 1959. Mary has had a magnificent career. In camogie she captained Cork to All-Ireland victory in 1982 and won four All-Ireland camogie medals with that county. In hockey she played for

Ireland in goal sixty-five times, winning her first cap against England in 1975. She starred as Ireland won the Intercontinental Cup in Kuala Lumpur in 1983 and helped Ireland defeat England when they were world champions in 1976 and again in 1977. Her collection in hockey also includes a Triple Crown medal.

In Gaelic football she helped Kerry to win two Senior All-Irelands, scoring 3-2 in the 1976 final, and was the first Kerry captain to lead her county to an All-Ireland win. Her vast collection of wins includes football medals in county championships, a national league medal, and All-Ireland club medals with Castleisland Desmonds Ladies. Mary has played squash and badminton for Munster, Senior golf for Killarney, and interprovincial golf for Munster. This amazing multi-talented Kerry woman was named Jury's Munster Sports Star for camogie in 1980 and for hockey in 1983.

MICK GALWEY, *a living legend*

Mick Galwey is one of those Kerry greats who can easily be described as a living legend. He was born in the village of Currow not far from the town of Castleisland, a spot that has produced three other rugby stars: Moss Keane and the Doyle brothers, Mick and Tom. As the holder of an All-Ireland Senior football medal, won with Kerry in 1986 when he was nineteen, Mick Galwey could easily have gone on and starred with his county in Gaelic football, but the tradition and lure of the oval ball proved too strong. Nevertheless, he still lent a hand when St Kieran's divisional team won the Kerry County Championship in 1988 and continued to play with his own club, Currow, for many years whenever his rugby career allowed.

Mick's career can probably be described as colourful and complex. Over an eleven-year period he was capped forty-one times but, for reasons that satisfy very few, was dropped an incredible fifteen times. He gained his first international experience when touring with the Irish Senior squad to France in 1988, but no caps were awarded. The following year he was capped at B level (subsequently changed to A), and in 1990 he played twice for the Irish Under-25 side. The following year he made his Senior debut against France on a day that saw six new caps line out for Ireland, including Simon Geoghean, captain Rob Saunders and Brian Rigney (who would later partner Mick in the second row for Shannon).

The Currow man consistently remained in the side between 1991 and 1995, and in 1993 he was picked on the British and Irish Lions tour to New Zealand. His appearances for Ireland between 1995 and 1999 were curtailed to just four, two as a replacement (to the amazement of the rugby public). The year 2000 marked the resurgence of his international career, with his outstanding performances and leadership displays for Shannon and Munster and a further seventeen caps, before he announced his retirement from the international stage in 2002. He 'officially' captained Ireland once in 2001 against Romania; in the course of his international career he scored two tries against England, the most memorable of these being in 1993 when Ireland beat England by 17 points to 3 in Lansdowne Road. Mick Galwey, a true Kerry legend. His rugby record includes:

- 41 caps for Ireland, four times as captain, scorer of three tries;
- team member on 1993 Lions tour to New Zealand;
- 130 caps for Munster, 85 as captain, 1 Celtic League;
- 10 Munster Senior cups and 6 All-Ireland Leagues with Shannon RFC;
- 113 games for Shannon in the AIL, scoring 28 tries; and
- coaching Shannon to 2 AIL victories and 2 Munster Senior Cups.

PAUL GRIFFIN, SEAN CASEY AND CATHAL MOYNIHAN, *Kerry's Olympic oarsmen*

Paul Griffin holds a unique place in the annals of Kerry sport. He is the only Kerryman to have participated in two Olympic Games and the first Kerryman to row in the Olympics; magnificent achievements in any man's language. Born in the townland of Barleymount, Fossa, just a few miles from Killarney town, Paul represented his country in the games of 2004 in Athens and 2008 in Beijing. In Athens Paul and his Irish lightweight four made it to the finals and finished a superb sixth. In Beijing they just failed to make it to the finals, finishing fourth behind Denmark. Another Killarney man, Cathal Moynihan, was a teammate that day in Beijing. A truly remarkable feat to have two men from the one town representing their country. But what was even more remarkable was the fact that a third Killarney man, Sean Casey, was also rowing in those 2008 Beijing games. Sean rowed with the Irish heavyweight four that qualified for the B final.

Paul Griffin rowed into Irish sporting history as a member of the Irish lightweight four that won the country's first ever gold medal at the World Cup Rowing Regatta in Lucerne, Switzerland, in 2005. Griffin, rowing in his customary stroke position, was inspirational as Ireland destroyed the field, which included the very best oarsmen in the world. That same year he collected silver in the world championships in Japan and completed the collection with a bronze medal in Munich, Germany.

Paul Griffin, Sean Casey and Cathal Moynihan, three exemplary Kerrymen, will forever be recalled as Kerry's Olympic oarsmen and I consider myself privileged to have sat down with these three great sportsmen to record their life and times before their departure to Beijing. Three men rowing out from the Muckross Rowing Club, Killarney, taking on the best in the world; three of my great sporting heroes who learned their rowing on the Lakes of Killarney.

Pa Fitzgerald, *king of the 'longtails'*

Pa Fitzgerald is a very remarkable Tralee man. As a brilliant Austin Stacks footballer, he was part of the Kerry team that won the 1955 All-Ireland final against Dublin. Professionally he was to become a very famous greyhound trainer, winning a plethora of classic events on track and field. Today Fitzgerald is still at the top of the training game, which is truly remarkable all these years later. He brought that brilliant track star, Ballymac Under (Ballymac Maeve by Ballymac Lark), to Tralee Track on 15 May 2010 and, despite a lack of competitive action since mid-November 2009, Ballymac Under treated a big crowd to a flawless exhibition of tracking on his way to a smashing victory over 525 yards in 28.62. In 2012 Pa Fitzgerald was in his eightieth year. I was privileged to meet one of Kerry's greatest ever greyhound trainers and his story stands shoulder to shoulder with any of the others in the galaxy of stars included here.

Born at 29 Rock Street, Tralee, he was reared in an area where greyhounds and football went hand in hand. He recalls the many men and families deeply involved in the greyhounds: Martin 'Bracker' Regan, Rory O'Connell, Dan Lynch, the Curtin family, Jim Brosnan and the Barretts, Kerr Boyle, Purty Landers and Den Lynch (father to one of Kerry's renowned greyhound men, my good friend Patsy Lynch of Tralee). In 1948, at just sixteen years of age, Pa went to Dingle where he trained his first major winner, Philandros, to win the Kingdom Cup and the Dr Griffin Memorial Cup.

He took the boat to England in 1951 and, while he came home occasionally, he remained in England where his success was unbelievable. He worked at the Burhill kennels of Jerry Hannifin in Surrey under Tralee trainer Paddy O'Driscoll, then later for Duagh native Patsy Byrnes, and he was involved in some magnificent successes. The Welsh, English and Scottish Derbies were captured, with the Peterborough Derby later joining the growing list of triumphs. Four Dundalk

International Invitation Cups were added (the three best dogs from Ireland and England battle for this Cup), as well as the Grand Prix victory at Walthamstow. He was also involved with the Royal Family when he trained one of their greyhounds. Prince Edward was given a half share in the dog, which ran in the English Derby. He won his five heats, qualified for the final and was narrowly beaten into second place. All monies raised went to the Prince's favourite charities. These are only a few of the many successes the Tralee man gathered before returning to his beloved Tralee in the 1970s.

His expertise continued in Ireland, with six magnificent Irish Cup victories. Ballyard Yank began the run in 1980, followed by Ballyduff Bobby in 1983, Black Rock in 1986, Castle Pines in 2005, Castlemartyre in 2008, and in 2009 Sandy Sea brought an unbelievable sixth victory for the Kerry trainer. Pa Fitzgerald is still going as strong as ever in 2012 and continues to be involved in victories the length and breadth of Ireland; his enthusiasm, passion and deep knowledge of the greyhound industry is second to none.

In his youth he was a superb footballer, winning a Minor All-Ireland medal with Kerry in 1950. He also played Junior with Kerry and was a member of the panel of the legendary Kerry team that shocked the so-called 'unbeatable' Dublin machine in 1955. During his time in England he lined out at full forward against Meath in the 1952 All-Ireland Junior final, however, defeat was their lot. Pa Fitzgerald is one of Ireland's greatest trainers and his record speaks for itself. A quiet, unassuming man, he values the defeats just as much as the long string of successes because, as he told me, 'The beauty of my work is meeting all those great greyhound people all over the country; that for me is more important than anything else.'

PADDY DOWNEY, *the star of Kerry handball's golden era*

The golden era for Kerry handball was unquestionably between the years 1951 and 1973. A wealth of honours came to the county, most notably twenty-three All-Ireland Senior titles, of which Paddy Downey (Tralee) has an astonishing seventeen to his name.

What makes Downey's All-Ireland sweep unique is the fact that he was playing at the same time as some of the all-time greats of the game, such as John Ryan (Wexford), Joey Maher (Louth), Fintan Confey (Louth), and the Rowe brothers (Dublin), all of whom are still regarded as some of the biggest names in handball history. Paddy is the only Kerryman to win the 60 x 30 Senior Singles title (which he won in 1958 and 1961) and the Hardball Senior Singles (which he won from 1958 to 1960, and again in 1962). He was also the first player from outside Leinster to win the Hardball Singles Championship.

He amassed eleven All-Ireland Senior Doubles titles in his glittering career: seven 60 x 30 Doubles with Jimmy O'Brien in 1955, 1956 and 1960 to 1964 inclusive; three Senior Hardball Doubles with O'Brien on three occasions in 1959, 1960 and 1963; and one Senior Hardball Doubles with Jimmy Hassett (a Tipperary man, who had won six Senior titles with his native county in the 1930s) in 1953. O'Brien and Hassett brought the first Senior titles to Kerry in 1951 when they won the 60 x 30 and Hardball Doubles, adding the 60 x 30 again in 1952.

Indeed, O'Brien's record of eleven All-Ireland Senior Doubles titles in the big court was only surpassed in 2010 when Tom Sheridan of Meath overtook the Tralee man's place in the record books. This was doubtless a golden era for Kerry handball, since twelve Junior and five Minor titles also came the Kingdom's way during that time, not to mention the prestigious Gael Linn title, won by Roundy McEllistrim in 1967. Paddy Downey's success was no doubt an inspiration to the McEllistrims, Roundy and Murty of Ballymacgelligott, who brought the 60 x 30 Senior Doubles title back to Kerry in

1968 and 1971; Murty partnered Nicholas Kerins to the last Senior title that came to the Kingdom in 1973.

I have interviewed Paddy on a number of occasions for Radio Kerry. A shy, courteous man, he is very reluctant to talk about his great career. Paddy Downey, a true gentleman, must rank as one of the Kingdom's all-time legends. It was a privilege to have met him.

PAUL GRIFFIN, *cycling star*

In February 1973 Mary and Billy Griffin had their fourth and youngest son, Paul. Influenced by his older brothers, Paul was involved in various sports, including being a member of Kerins O'Rahillys GAA, the Tralee Dynamos Soccer Club and St John's Athletic Club. But it was a chance meeting in 1987 that saw Paul find the sport that he would come to love above all others. Liam, Paul's older brother, took the then thirteen-year-old Paul into Tralee to see the start of the Nissan Classic. And it was there they met the then current World Cycling Champion and winner of that year's Tour de France, Stephen Roche. The cycling bug bit Paul hard: his father had been a competitive track cyclist and now Paul, fired up by Stephen, was inspired to follow in his father's footsteps. A magnificent new Kerry star was born.

By 1994 Paul was strong enough to be picked for the Kerry team to compete in the FBD Milk Rás and only four years later he won a stage in the Rás when it finished in Mallow, County Cork. On the sixteen occasions that Paul has raced in the Rás, he has been placed in the top three in numerous stage finishes and in the top fifteen overall. As a young rider Paul continued to show promising talent. In 1997 he was selected to race for a French club, ACBB of Paris, which at the time was sponsored by the man that started it all for Paul, Stephen Roche. The highlight of that year was finishing second in the prestigious French classic, the Paris–Chalette.

He was a natural for selection to represent Ireland in 2001 and, donning the green jersey, Paul won a stage, the mountains jersey and was placed third overall in the professional Tour of Hokkaido, Japan. He continued on his winning streak, gathering results such as a win at the Surrey 5-Day Race and the mountains jersey in the 2004 Tour of Greece. Naturally gifted in conquering the mountains with speed, Paul has won the Irish National Hill Climb Championships five times. Such results have led him to represent Ireland well over one hundred times in his 25-year career.

Paul turned full-time professional for Giant Asia in 2005, where he continued to dominate in the mountains for the next five years, winning mountain jerseys in the Tours of East Java and Indonesia, stages in the Tour of Azerbaijan, and finishing in the top ten in many difficult international races. This amazing Kerry sports star can still be found out on his bike around the roads of Kerry early on a Sunday morning wearing the colours of Tralee Bicycle Club.

Brendan Hennessy, *hurling star*

When Brendan Hennessy was awarded the Munster Hall of Fame for hurling in 2003, it was a truly amazing achievement. Here was a Kerryman being recognised by his peers for a game that is a long second to football in Kerry. And to have one of our own accepted as a legend, standing tall with all the great Munster hurlers down through the decades, is just a remarkable achievement. Brendan had proved his greatness on many occasions, both in Ireland and America, but one of his greatest ever displays was in the 1958 St Brendan's Cup final in Croke Park against National League champions Wexford.

This was a special competition, in which New York would play the reigning National League champions home and away on alternate years. Wexford had household names in their side, such as Ned Wheeler, Willie Rackard, Martin Codd, Podge Keogh and Nick O'Donnell. But it was Brendan

Hennessy who was the shining star at midfield on that memorable afternoon. And, to copper-fasten a never-to-be-forgotten New York victory, Brendan and his brother Michael (who also played midfield) were honoured as the *Irish Independent*'s Sports Stars of the Week. Such a national tribute as this had never occurred before – nor has it since.

He went to school in the famous St Flannan's College in Ennis, where he was regarded as one of the best players to have played with the college, along with the likes of Anthony Daly, Len Gaynor, Jamie O'Connor and Tony Reddan, to name just a few. He won the Dr Harty Cup and the Dr Croke Cup medals with the school during his time there. Brendan Hennessy was a dual player. He played football and hurling with New York, and hurling and Minor football with Kerry, as well as his local Ballyduff club. Before 1955 Brendan's club, Ballyduff, had won only one Kerry Senior Hurling Championship in 1891; but in 1955, with Brendan's brother Michael as captain, Ballyduff won the championship for the first time in more than sixty years. In 1957 Brendan himself captained Ballyduff to a championship win.

He spent most of his playing days in New York, where he played in a number of National Hurling League finals in the 1950s through until the 1970s. He also played in a number of National Football League finals, winning one in 1964 when New York beat Dublin. While in New York Brendan played hurling with the Kilkenny club; he never won a New York Senior Hurling Championship, but played in back-to-back finals in 1962 and 1963. He played football with the Kerry club and won New York Senior Football Championship medals in 1959, 1960, 1962, 1963, 1966, and 1967. He is regarded as one of the best players ever to have played in New York. He was a massive loss to Kerry hurling when he left for America.

In 2003 when he was awarded the Munster Hall of Fame, it surely confirmed the theory that Brendan Hennessy was probably Kerry's greatest ever hurler. Both he and his family have been the cornerstone of Kerry hurling for many decades.

TADGH KENNELLY, *a place in football history*

Tadgh Kennelly, born in Listowel in 1981, is the first Irish-born player to have won an Australian Premiership medallion, a magnificent and historic achievement. As a Minor with Kerry, he won two Munster Minor championships in 1997 and 1998, as well as an Under-21 Munster championship. Listowel Emmets is his club in Kerry, but in 1999 he signed a rookie contract with the Australian club, Sydney Swans. He made his debut in 2001 and became a regular fixture as a dashing re-bound defender. Tadgh was a high-profile member of the Swans outfit, well known for his exciting play, his nationality and his 'Talking with Tadgh' articles on the Swans' website. He became the first Irishman to win an AFL Premiership medal in 2005, after playing all twenty-six games for the Sydney Swans that year.

He was reportedly earning $750,000 (€350,000) while playing for Sydney. Kennelly also appeared in the 2006 Grand Final, but the Swans lost 85–84 to the West Coast Eagles. In 2007 and 2008, after several seasons when he had missed only a handful of games, Kennelly suffered a series of serious leg and shoulder injuries that became major setbacks to his AFL career. In one game his knee buckled from a heavy tackle, causing an anterior cruciate ligament tear; he was to miss several matches due to complications. In 2008 he again injured his knee, dislocating his kneecap and injuring his shoulder. He was selected in the Dream Team for the AFL Hall of Fame Tribute Match, but later withdrew due to injury. He was quick to recover, however, and made an appearance for the Swans the following week, though again succumbing to the injury curse. During the rest of 2008 Kennelly's shoulder continually dislocated during games and his unorthodox method of popping it back in with a little twist of his shoulder was the subject of much media interest.

In January 2009 Tadgh returned to Ireland to play with Kerry. He played his first competitive game for the Kerry Senior team on 8 March 2009, when he came on as a substitute in the game against Derry. He played in Kerry's first two games of the Championship in June. He picked up an injury during the qualifier series but his form continued to improve and, after an impressive appearance as a substitute in the All-Ireland quarter-final against Dublin, he broke into the starting team for the semi-final, in which Kerry beat Meath. On 20 September 2009 he played the first fifty minutes of the All-Ireland final, scoring 2 points and becoming the first person to win an AFL Premiership and an All-Ireland Senior football medal. He also won a National League medal and represented Ireland three times in the International Rules Series.

In November 2009 Kennelly informed the Kerry County Board of his intention to return to Australia in 2010. He had followed in the footsteps of his late father, Tim, and brother, Noel, in winning the coveted All-Ireland medal. On 12 November 2009 Kennelly signed a two-year deal with the Sydney Swans, marking his return to the AFL. In addition to his playing role, he took up a coaching role at the club. He was very consistent throughout the year, playing in his customary role of half back. He was chosen to be in the Irish squad for the International Series a number of times. Kennelly played his final AFL game in Sydney's semi-final defeat to Hawthorn in September 2011. As he bowed out of the game, he had played a total 197 AFL matches.

TOM O'RIORDAN, *from Ardfert to Tokyo 1964*

Tom O'Riordan, from the townland of Turbrid near the little village of Ardfert in north Kerry, is one of Kerry's, and indeed Ireland's, greatest athletes. He achieved the highest honour when he represented Ireland in the 5000 m at the 1964 Tokyo Olympics. He went on to become a noted sports journalist with the *Irish Independent* and when he was presented with the Kerry Hall of Fame Award in 2002 I sat down with him and listened in great admiration as he retraced his wonderful career.

Tom played a lot of football when a student in Tralee CBS but, after he took part in the Ballymacelligott sports day in 1954 and finished second in the 880 m handicap (taking home a silver dish and six spoons), running became his first love. At schools level he won Munster and All-Ireland titles, and in 1956 he was seven seconds inside the old record as he won the Irish one mile championship, the first Kerryman to win that title.

In 1957 Tom O'Riordan was offered an athletic scholarship to Idaho State University, USA. Here he was to develop into a world-class athlete, winning both the National Inter-Collegiate Cross Country Championship and the 3,000 m steeplechase title. He dominated many events on the white-hot competitive field of America, winning nine Conference Championships in the mile and two-mile distances. He returned to Ireland in 1962, after spending two years under the tutelage of the great Hungarian coach Michel Igloi. He blazed a trail of victories, winning twelve Irish National Cross Country Club Championships. He ran for Ireland on many occasions and just failed to win the British AAA title by a whisker, as he was beaten by the great Bruce Tulloch.

He has wonderful memories of those Tokyo Olympics and recalled for me his race in the qualifying round:

> After four or five laps I began to move up through the field and I took the lead. Imagine me, from Ardfert in north Kerry, taking the lead in the 5000 m in the Olympics and feeling great, and I held the lead for about five laps. Then I remember being clipped in

> the heels a number of times and being very annoyed. With two laps to go, I felt the field coming around me . . . and then this feeling of struggling, falling back, trying so hard . . . but I did not make the final. I was devastated, but I did set a new Irish record.

Tom later became coach to the Irish cross-country teams as they won silver medals in the world championships of 1979. When John Treacy won his second gold, Tom O'Riordan proved that not only was he a world-class runner, he was also a world-class coach. He ran his last race in 1977 and has covered all the Olympic Games, World and European championships since then as a journalist.

Tom O'Riordan must rank with the greatest of Irish athletes, up there with Ronnie Delany, Eamon Coughlan, John Treacy and others. His son Ian has followed in his father's footsteps and is the renowned athletics correspondent for *The Irish Times*.

AND A LAST STANDING OVATION FOR THE 'SAVAGE ROAD MEN' OF KERRY

There is something special about the bike men of Kerry and, while Gene Mangan is recognised as the greatest Kerry has ever produced and I fully concur with this, I have decided to extend my admiration and praise to all those wonderful Kerrymen whom I have been so fortunate to befriend and interview since becoming involved in Radio Kerry. They are a breed apart – and they need to be, to participate in this gruelling, dangerous, stamina-sapping activity whose major circuits criss-cross the highways and byways of Ireland. Hail, rain, or snow, these battle-hardened warriors chase each other up hill and down dale in the pursuit of victory. Cycle racing is a so-called 'minority' sport in this county, and yet for generations the tradition of honour in this sporting arena has persisted in the face of the highest profile always afforded the Gaelic games.

I have always been fascinated; in the 1950s and 1960s the Rás Tailteann was a powerful event that forced its way into my youthful consciousness and left an indelible imprint. The atmosphere surrounding the Rás was special; it was a flavour of something almost epic. In many ways it shaped my thinking, deepened my love for sport, and ingrained in my mind a deep and lasting admiration for these 'savage road men'. Part of the secret must be that the 1950s were also the glory days of cycling in this county, a decade when Kerrymen more or less dominated the then named Rás Tailteann. It was a magical time. Thousands of spectators lined the streets of Tralee, Killorglin and Killarney awaiting the arrival of the Rás. Onlookers would begin to take up the best vantage points hours before its arrival. The High Street in Killarney would be crowded and the riders were our heroes, men of steel, unaware of any danger as they careered around the streets of our home town displaying their amazing skills.

There was Gene Mangan, the greatest of them all: an overall winner in 1955 and winner of eleven stages during his career. And Paudie Fitzgerald, the man from Lispole who won in 1956. Then we have the amazing, unbelievable Mick Murphy from the townland of Sugrena just outside Cahersiveen, dubbed 'the Iron Man' for his exploits on the road. He came home first in 1958 and, if his story was portrayed in a Hollywood film, you would say 'sure, that's pure fiction'. It is almost forgotten that in the following year, 1959, Mick also won the third stage and then stole the limelight winning the final stage into O'Connell Street, Dublin. The year 1960 saw 'the Iron Man' take third place.

And then we have the great Ballymac man, Dan Ahern, considered by many to have been one of the best Rás riders never to have won the big event. He was second twice and also came third and fifth, winning six stages in all. His battle with the Pole Zbigniew Glowaty, the eventual winner in 1963 on the ascent and decent of the Wicklow Gap, is still spoken

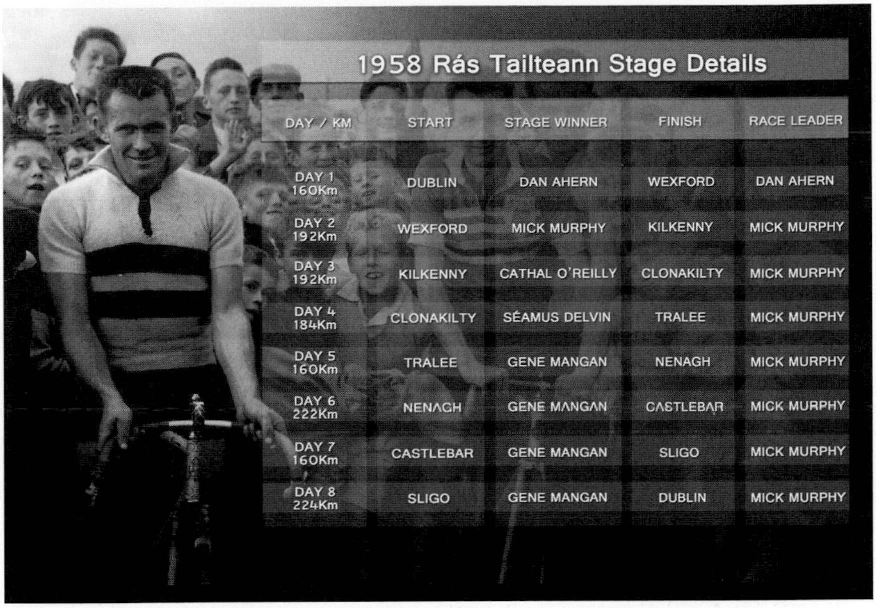

1958 Rás Tailteann Stage Details

DAY / KM	START	STAGE WINNER	FINISH	RACE LEADER
DAY 1 160Km	DUBLIN	DAN AHERN	WEXFORD	DAN AHERN
DAY 2 192Km	WEXFORD	MICK MURPHY	KILKENNY	MICK MURPHY
DAY 3 192Km	KILKENNY	CATHAL O'REILLY	CLONAKILTY	MICK MURPHY
DAY 4 184Km	CLONAKILTY	SÉAMUS DELVIN	TRALEE	MICK MURPHY
DAY 5 160Km	TRALEE	GENE MANGAN	NENAGH	MICK MURPHY
DAY 6 222Km	NENAGH	GENE MANGAN	CASTLEBAR	MICK MURPHY
DAY 7 160Km	CASTLEBAR	GENE MANGAN	SLIGO	MICK MURPHY
DAY 8 224Km	SLIGO	GENE MANGAN	DUBLIN	MICK MURPHY

A Kerry great and now a great friend, 'Iron Man' Mick Murphy, from Cahersiveen after winning the 1958 Rás Tailteann – he won seven of the eight stages in that year's Rás. His life story is the stuff of legend.

about to this day. Any decent support from others, it was said, and the Rás would have been his. Dan later went to America and became one of the top riders in that country. Some years ago I spent a fascinating afternoon at his home: we played snooker, talked about his career and Dan played some tunes on the box. A very unassuming, reserved person, Dan Ahern is, in my opinion, one of Kerry's greatest unsung heroes.

But how could you separate one of these great men out from the others? There are so many names engraved on my memory from those golden days of Kerry cycling: Johnny Switzer, Paddy O'Callaghan, Jackie O'Connor, Paddy Moriarty, Pat Healy, and Batty Flynn. Thanks for the memories lads, and Killorglin legend John Hangan. How fortunate I was to spend time in your company.

Index

Note: *Italics* refer to a photo caption.